Welfare's Forgotten Past

A Socio-Legal History of the Poor Law

Lorie Charlesworth

Routledge
Taylor & Francis Group

a GlassHouse book

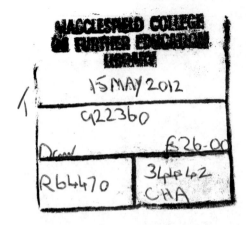
First published 2010 by Routledge
2 Park Square, Milton Park, Abingdon, Oxon OX14 4RN

Simultaneously published in the USA and Canada
by Routledge
711 Third Avenue, New York, NY 10017

A GlassHouse book
Routledge is an imprint of the Taylor & Francis Group, an informa business

First issued in paperback 2011

© 2010 Lorie Charlesworth

Typeset in Garamond by Taylor & Francis Books

British Library Cataloguing in Publication Data
A catalogue record for this book is available from the British Library

Library of Congress Cataloging in Publication Data
Welfare's forgotten past : a socio-legal history of the poor law / Lorie
Charlesworth.
p. cm.
"A GlassHouse book."
Includes bibliographical references.
1. Poor laws–England–History. 2. Public welfare–Law and legislation–England–
History. 3. England and Wales. Poor Relief Act (1601). I. Title.
KD3299.C48 2010
344.4203'25–dc22
2009023687

ISBN10: 0-415-47738-7 (hbk)
ISBN10: 0-415-68578-8 (pbk)
ISBN10: 0-203-86367-4 (ebk)

ISBN13: 978-0-415-47738-3 (hbk)
ISBN13: 978-0-415-68578-8 (pbk)
ISBN13: 978-0-203-86367-1 (ebk)

For my mother

Contents

Acknowledgements

I owe a debt of gratitude to many people who have supported and encouraged me during my research and the writing of this book; first, my supervisor Mike Rose at the University of Manchester, who shared his knowledge and expertise throughout my PhD. The generosity of my colleagues at the Law School, Liverpool John Moore's University made it possible for me write this book: Andy Baker, Simon Brooman, Anna Carline, David Lowe, Jamie Murray and Earl Selkridge, in particular. In pursuing the historico-socio-legal project, I have been fortunate in the encouragement I have received from the wider academic community, especially Peter Bartlett, Paul Brand, Mike Brogden, Ray Cocks, Josh Getzler, Cynthia Hogue, David Ibbotson, Michael Kandiah, Christine Kinealey, Debbie Legge, Andrew Lewis, Michael Lobban, Frank MacDonough, Les Moran, David Nash, Peter Linebaugh, Kim Stevenson, David Sugarman and my fellow directors at SOLON. I wish to thank Di Chappelle, John Cooke, Tony Harvey, George Mair and Judith Rowbotham for their friendship and support; my editor Colin Perrin at Routledge and finally, my family who are the centre of everything: Inge Cocard, Monique, Anthony, Siobhan, Oriel and Will.

Chapter 1

Introduction: a history of forgetting

[T]he law so positively commands, that the poor of every parish, shall be maintained in and by every such parish. However, all law of this sort, all salutary and humane law, really seems to be drawing towards an end in this now miserable country.[1]

It may seem rather obvious to state that: 'Poor law was law'; nevertheless, this basic legal truth has slipped from the consciousness of those researching and publishing nationally and internationally on the history of welfare in England and Wales; internationally as English poor law is 'understood' as the historical foundation of North American relief systems. As a result of this slippage, the legal underpinnings of that system of relieving poverty have been marginalised, misunderstood and forgotten. Although most current welfare textbooks make reference to welfare's poor law past, few acknowledge that England and Wales (Scotland and Ireland have a different welfare history) possess the oldest continuous surviving legal system of welfare relief in Europe; a 400-year-old common law (later administrative law) locally funded and administered system of relieving poverty. This positive cultural norm deserves celebrating. In addition, the weight of such a socio-legal history ensures that many echoes of that past resonate in modern welfare law. In particular, these comprise some elements of localism and an acceptance, albeit sometimes grudgingly by both governments and citizens, that the poor will be relieved of their poverty. These aspects predate the modern welfare state by hundreds of years.

One consequence of this neglect, the 'forgotten' of the title, is that many scholars are unaware of the extent of those legal foundations that ensured poor law was not simply local custom, able to mutate over time in response to changing circumstances as other unofficially negotiated 'social rules'. Rather, it constituted a slowly evolving fixed legal point of reference, which sometimes failed to adapt to significant social shifts. Indeed, once in place that law in turn fixed or hardened existing duties, roles and responsibilities that in the day-to-day negotiations of ordinary life normally modify and mutate over time. In this fashion, those legal aspects of poor law discussed in this book became entrenched within society creating long-term, if often unrecognised, legal norms. The most significant of these, discussed more fully in later chapters, is the largely forgotten, often denied and hence underestimated legal right to relief. Such denial extends to legal scholars of welfare law (see below) who might, at the very least be expected to return to contemporary legal textbooks and precedents for clarification, but prefer instead to rely upon the expertise of social and other historians for their legal knowledge. Such is the level of 'forgetting' that this book's fundamental assertion, that poor law encompasses a legal right to relief, remains controversial as counter to current orthodoxy amongst historians and in consequence a denial of this right has been followed in academic legal texts.[2] Nonetheless, this work will set out legal 'proofs', supported by archival and other research, to reveal those legal obligations, rights and duties that account for and underpin all poor law activities. Those primary archival primary sources consulted by the author are from the North West of England but, as will become clear later, a broader survey is not required as legal answers provide an explanation for local and regional differences.

On one level, this work constitutes a legal opinion that the law of settlement and removal is at the heart of the poor law, that its doctrines encompass rights, duties and obligations by all citizens of England and Wales and that the settled poor possessed a legal right to relief. This conclusion emerges from research conducted in two dimensions. The first is concerned with small stories, micro-histories of ordinary people and how they experienced law. The second dimension reconstructs law's pervasiveness, its theoretical and doctrinal nature, development and influences. This produces meta-narratives of an overarching legal framework and the legal opinion with proofs, that the law of settlement and removal is the legal basis of poor law. Such an approach, involving often contradictory methodologies, destabilises an orthodox approach to legal history, hence the title of this work is a socio-legal rather than a social or legal history. The second level of the work constitutes a revisionist reconstruction of current orthodox interpretations of poor law's history in order to [re] place that legal right correctly within its historical framework. In addition, Chapters 2 and 3 trace those contemporary juristic and contingent elements that have contributed to poor law historians adopting their incorrect legal stance. Chapters 5–9 reconstruct poor law's legal past from a number of perspectives: that of reformers, protestors, the excluded, those who administer relief and those who receive it.

In adopting a socio-legal analysis, this work demonstrates that poor law histories and empirical research, viewed through the lens of law, fully substantiate the existence of a right to relief. This remains so even where historians themselves, as we shall see in Chapter 4, believe that they are revealing cultural or political patterns of social negotiation and not a legal framework. Finally, it is important to underline that despite much resonance and some survivals, poor law is not the same as modern welfare law. That consists of public administrative law operating within a central bureaucratic framework funded by a system of national taxation and directed by whichever government is currently in power. On the contrary, poor law, until 1865 and in some aspects beyond, constitutes an overarching common law legal 'system' that encompasses local autonomy, local financial obligations, duties and responsibilities with *ad hoc* relief patterns. Within this 'system' the localities manifest individual characteristics according to specific and contingent financial, social and property-owning circumstances. Nevertheless, all local parishes share two common elements. The first, that the Justices at Sessions annually ratify and supervise their poor law activities. The second, that all relief decisions are made in the context of a legal framework comprising the common law of settlement and removal, the right to relief, other legal 'rules' and established legal processes. This is not that model of exclusion, control and 'undeserving' that is increasingly popular as an academic reading of poor law; rather it reveals a complex, nuanced and sophisticated system based upon rights.

In summary, this work maps one topographical layer of the long history of the relief of poverty in England and Wales. It reconstructs poor law to 1865, by which time the centralised bureaucratic elements of modern welfare are established and poor law bears a markedly public-law character. This is, of course, not the final word; in challenging conventional non-legal assumptions about poor law the writer wishes to reopen a closed discussion. It is timely to refocus both lawyers and historians' intellectual attention upon those rights-based elements that socio-legal research reveals as a fundamental element of welfare's past. For their part, historians have concentrated on discovering the nature, operation and changing social impact of the poor law from the archives rather than undertaking legal reconstructions. As we shall see in Chapter 4, they list statutes and name cases, but generally not according to appropriate legal methodologies, language and techniques. To take one example from 2000, Steven King includes a chapter on the 'Legal Framework' of poor law in his reconstruction.[3] Here he asserts that: 'Case law supported, modified or invalidated [sic] statute law'.[4] A lawyer reading this would look for the word 'interpret'. More esoterically but equally to the point, one of the most fascinating aspects of judicial interpretation until the twentieth century, and equally true of poor law, is its formalism; a topic that will be discussed in Chapter 2. In consequence, there is no legal basis for King's suggestion that case law over-ruled poor law statutes, that is declared them 'invalid'. This is possible today, for example under the legal authority of the terms of the Human Rights Act 1998, but is a modern development. Thus King's 'legal framework' opens with a legal solecism. His law chapter is largely constructed around a narrative account of statutes sourced from the work of other historians, not legal texts. The overall effect explains why the legal history of poor law often repels historians; but it is considerably more than: 'one damn statute after another'.

In spite of the above comments, this absence of legal knowledge does not represent academic failure. It is rather a manifestation of a lack of 'law mindedness'; no different from that 'history blindness' afflicting many legal academics. This lack, however, does partially explain why so many historians deny the existence of a legal right to relief. Of course, this writer acknowledges that historians produce detailed and scholarly analyses. These are derived from reconstructions undertaken within that abundance of surviving poor law archival materials. These records are held in the National Archives at Kew; in all local record offices; in many church vestries and in numerous other archives and private collections throughout England and Wales. Paradoxically, the explanation for the continued survival of these records is found in their legal nature, that they record poor law legal duties, rights and responsibilities. In consequence, both the existence and survival of these archives are evidence of the power and significance of that overarching framework of substantive legal rules surrounding the relief of poverty.

More specifically, at base all these records owe their origins to three legal imperatives contained within poor law. First, that every parish and vestry in England and Wales had a legal duty to raise a rate to maintain its poor under the authority of an Act for the Better Relief of the Poor 1601.[5] Second, a common law presumption underpinning that Act and so understood and expressed in all subsequent case law, that every person born in England and Wales possessed a settlement somewhere and in that place a settled person was legally entitled to relief if destitute. That precise geographical place could only be established via legal interpretation of the 'rules' and precedents contained within the law of settlement and removal. The settlement entitlement was codified and first expressed in statute in 1662, whose formal title is An Act for the Better Relief of the Poor.[6] For some reason, historians persistently cite this as the 'Settlement Act', one of a number of solecisms that will be noted and not followed throughout this work.[7] The third imperative was that a poor person could only be removed to their settlement parish by operation of law if they appeared likely to, before 1795 (see Chapter 3), or actually sought poor relief. Thus, it was not social altruism and custom that motivated the provision of poor relief, rather long-standing legal 'rules'. In short, underpinning all poor law documents recording the activities of officials administering the system, setting and collecting a poor rate, recording details of those relieved, indeed the very system of poor law itself, is the legal right of the settled poor to relief when destitute. From a lawyer's perspective it appears perverse that this legal 'truth', constantly attested to in case law and stated within contemporary legal texts and Justices' manuals, is rejected by historians and thus lost to legal and other academics who follow their lead. This book aims to undermine this incorrect yet persistent stance. One explanation for that law-blindness (more will be explored in Chapter 3) may be found in assumptions concerning the legal nature of the reforms implemented via the terms of the Poor Law Amendment Act 1834. This initiated the new poor law, a baby born of Benthamite positivism and Whiggish reformist theories of political economy. The birth of this baby heralded the arrival of the hated new poor law with its national system of prison-like workhouses. Although settlement law remained after 1834 as did the right to relief, the manner of that relief became bureau-cratised and the poor a problem to be contained, controlled and stigmatised out of their state of poverty. This direction cast the die for English welfare, pathologising poverty, and may have served to further influence historians' continuing rejection of the existence of legal rights possessed by the poor.

What is more, so influential and pervasive were the negative social effects of those reforms that a cultural stigma surrounding poverty persists today despite the establishment of the Welfare State in 1948. This work reconstructs how elements of that new poor law mind-set developed and continue as negative assumptions and presumptions concerning the poor today. Such persistent deformation, dichotomising welfare values, represents a problem that continues to profoundly affect the modern application of welfare law, thus forming part of the inspiration for this book. For this reason, the work is not intended as a study of an historical curiosity but rather an exploration of when, how and why such negativity arose and how it continues to hold sway despite the 'abolition' of the last of those hated poor law remnants by the Beveridge reforms. In consequence of that past, the horrors of the post-1834 poor law system are well known, although not those positive rights-based aspects whose origins lie much earlier.

There are other factors that may have contributed to current mis-understanding of welfare's legal past. The first is the persistence of a negative ideology prevalent within Sidney and Beatrice Webb's poor law histories, prompted by their political agenda that saw little good in the poor law.[8] Their works remain influential and although they have been subject to criticism they remain part of the poor law canon, for many scholars both in Britain and North America; they provide a wealth of detail unsurpassed in quantity and coverage. The second problematic is that the 'abolition' of poor law in 1948, swept away by the new broom of Beveridge, left a message that nothing in welfare's past had value for society and the poor. The third is a result of that legal abolition; namely that poor law as a legal subject has utterly disappeared from legal practice and legal memory. Although the right to relief was diluted oper-ationally by those many administrative and bureaucratic reforms from 1834 yet until abolition in 1948 all contemporary lawyers understood that the right existed and was so stated in all legal texts and sources. The fourth element derives from that last point; such legal knowledge was by the time of abolition a technical esoteric doctrinal matter and not an immediate matter of concern to poor law administration. It appears likely that all these factors helped to obscure the right to relief.

That forgotten right is the focus of this study. In 'forgetting', hence dis-missing, the legal, personally enforceable right to relief located within the possession of a legal settlement, historians have underestimated its role and significance within the lived experience of the poor. As a result, a 'history of poverty' has developed which denies the power and legal formality of that right or, at best, seriously underestimates its significance for the poor, local ratepayers and those who administered the system. This book aims to redress that

Still today.

imbalance to provide an historical reconstruction of a 'legal' history of welfare placed within a wider traditional historical context. As a result, it is one reply to that rhetorical question posed by Richard Evans: 'What has law to say to history?' This writer suggests that for poor law studies at least, an inter-disciplinary historico-socio-legal approach viewing welfare's past through the lens of law opens other windows to that past to disclose an alternative land-scape. Examining its topography reveals that poor law was law, that a legal framework informs all poor law activity and that there was a common law right to relief. Such rights, enforceable by the poor themselves are rare indeed and deserve to be remembered and celebrated. That is the purpose and function of this book.

This aspect of welfare's past will require further analysis once the legal nature of poor law is acknowledged and returned to its rightful place within legal and other scholarship. Indeed, as Peter Bartlett suggests, the socio-legal project itself must recognise the fundamental challenge that history poses to academic law. Chief amongst these is an acceptance by doctrinal legal scho-lars that:

> The message from history, however is that the rights of Englishmen ... [and others] ... are in fact not transcendent at all, but contingent, flowing from political and social factors in the past. In part this re-enforces an important lesson for lawyers, socio-legal and otherwise: the rights we have, such as they are, were won through political struggle and they are therefore always at risk. Complacency is not an option.[9]

Finally, the expectation that law evolves in a linear purposive way, from an imperfect to an improved state through a rational process of law reform is deeply entrenched within the discipline of law. It is one that is commonly found in the introduction of standard law textbooks used to initiate first-year law students into an understanding of the allegedly progressive nature of law and legal process, including legal developments and the reform of law.[10] Empirical support for this assumption is non-existent and this book treats such a position as one to be questioned rather than a self-evident starting point. To that end, it rejects any suggestion of teleology or that a linear 'improved' model of the development of welfare can be supported by an examination of legal and historical evidence. In short, this work suggests it is important to revisit that alternative, positive, rights-based past as a model rather than considering welfare provision from the perspective of current theories based upon incorrect legal reconstructions of that past. This is per-tinent, as those negative aspects of settlement discussed later, of not belonging and worse of exclusion, remain 'understood' within much modern welfare provision. Contrarily, how might a welfare system look if based on personal, legal and humanitarian rights? This is one question raised by the research project and posed by this book.

Notes

1 William Cobbett, *Rural Rides*, 1830, George Woodcock (ed.), London: Penguin Books, 1967, p. 341.
2 See for example: Nick Wikely, *Child Support Law and Policy*, Oxford: Hart Publishing, 2006; Amir Paz-Fuchs, *Welfare to Work: Conditional Rights in Social Policy*, Oxford: Oxford University Press, 2008.
3 Steven King, *Poverty and Welfare in England 1700–1850*, Manchester: Manchester University Press, 2000, pp. 18–47.
4 Ibid., p. 18.
5 So expressed in all precedents until 1948: 43 Eliz. I *c*. 2 (1601).
6 13 & 14 Car. II *c*. 12 (1662).
7 Aschrott seems to be the instigator of this. He titles a section of his book: 'The Act of Settlement of 1662' [sic]: P.F. Aschrott, *The English Poor Law System Past and Present*, 2nd edn, London: Knight & Co., 1902, p. 9.
8 S. Webb and B. Webb, *English Local Government Vol. 2, The Manor and the Borough*, Part. 1, 1908, reprint London: Frank Cass and Co., 1963;— *English Local Government Vol. 3, The Manor and the Borough*, Part. 2, reprint, London: Frank Cass and Co., 1963;— *English Poor Law History, Part I, The Old Poor Law*, 1929, reprint, London: Frank Cass and Co., 1963;— *The English Poor Law History. Part II, The Last Hundred Years*, 1929, reprint, London: Frank Cass and Co., 1963.
9 Peter Bartlett, 'On Historical Contextualisation: A Lawyer Responds', *Crimes and Misdemeanours*, 1, 2, 2007, 102–6, at 105.
10 M. Doupe and M. Salter, 'The Cheshire World View', *King's College Law Journal*, 11, 1, 2000, 49–77.

Chapter 2

Rights of the poor: towards a negative modernity

As this text is written from within the discipline of law, a conventional beginning would take an overview of current and likely future welfare provision. However, the dramatic collapse of global markets from 2008 followed by international financial disaster have ensured that whatever developments were planned in Britain, the United States or elsewhere, all bets are off. The future is uncertain, current trends are no longer current, the poor are more vulnerable than ever, their numbers are increasing daily and no one can predict how and when the crisis will end. Today, schemes for the unemployed in Britain that concern forms of 'workfare' operated in partnership with private companies are failing as those companies withdraw their support. In all these contexts, it is likely that governments themselves are unsure what will be needed or what funds available to relieve poverty in the short term, never mind long-term trends. Worse, it is unclear what ideological, political, juristic or cultural norms will inform those choices. This book has no solutions and 'history' offers no lessons, save that we have continuously relieved poverty in England and Wales for hundreds of years through many economic and political crises, originally as a common law obligation. In reconstructing that legal past this work aims to demonstrate that welfare is not simply the brave new world of Beveridge, but a fundamental cultural and legal norm long embedded within our society. As Britain faces major financial problems it is timely to consider how in the past themes of negativity, bureaucracy and control became embedded within welfare provision and the role jurists played in those changes. It is important to note, therefore, that welfare scholarship in law and history has implications beyond academic careers and may influence changes that resonate unpleasantly upon the immediate personal experience of the most vulnerable in our society, the unemployed, the young, the sick, the disabled and the elderly amongst others. This is the reason for a consideration below of a recent publication on workfare, which illustrates, amongst other matters, how current theories concerning conditional welfare 'rights' draw largely upon the negativity of juristic and operative elements that were fundamental within the new poor law.

In short, although long abolished poor law remains of concern today for many of its later positivist assumptions and presumptions remain embedded within the current welfare system. As we shall see in Chapter 3, the 'modern' Welfare State action of paying benefits is itself of ancient lineage. Equally, it also contains a specific negativity that may be traced back to 'improvements' introduced by the welfare reforms of 1834. To that end, this work explores the complex origins of a legal dichotomy that surrounds the relief of poverty, as mistrust of the poor crystallises into the dominant social convention; most notably at its tipping point in 1834. Some of that negativity remains entrenched within modern welfare provision. In that context, Pat Thane has written persuasively of those continuities in the cultural and institutional legacies left by the old and, more especially, new poor law.[1] In particular, such echoes of the past can be seen in loans from the Department of Work and Pensions to the unemployed from a capped local fund; the right (or otherwise) to be rehoused when homeless; the [mis]treatment of refugees; the continuation of the 'means test' by other names and aspects of the current Benefit Appeals system. Although this study is written from a twenty-first century perspective, similar new poor law 'values' may be observed within many aspects of the Welfare State at any point since the abolition of the poor law in 1948.

In order to reconstruct that journey from past to present, it is necessary to recognise the jurisprudence of poor law as an integral part of its legal history. An overview of that jurisprudence serves in part to explain why poor relief as a legal right has been disregarded and why historians have denied that legal right in their poor law reconstructions. Poor law has become a victim of its juristic past. To that end, what follows considers those legal theories which are relevant to an analysis of poor law. These include work by twentieth century jurists, as much of our current understanding of concepts introduced by Jeremy Bentham and John Austin has derived from the work of modern theorists. In consequence, it would be intellectually indefensible not to refer to them. The discussion that follows will concentrate upon the jurisprudential shift in poor law which occurred from 1834 that first engendered, then accompanied a transformation from common law personal rights towards administrative procedures. That legal transformation was achieved through implementation of the terms of the Poor Law Amendment Act 1834 to create what is now known as the 'new poor law'. Its main administrative features were that parishes in England and Wales were joined together into poor law unions, often based upon the ancient County sub-divisions of Hundreds. Each union was instructed to build a workhouse to house the able-bodied poor and relief was only to be given in the workhouse; there, families were divided and a prison-like regime, diet and discipline bound all from babies to the elderly. As we shall see, the new poor law constituted a centralised bureaucratic system controlled, supervised and enforced from London; its creation marks the birth of English administrative law. However, it also represents the physical manifestation of elements of utilitarianism and positivist jurisprudence.

This may seem an odd assertion, for jurisprudence is not generally 'seen' and is more usually understood through its purposes, including the evaluation of law as a discipline. This is a reflection of how law in practice has been accompanied from the earliest times by a struggle to give intellectual form to concepts such as 'justice' and to define law's fundamental nature. It is traditionally accepted that Coke was the most influential English common lawyer and jurist of the early modern period. Appointed Chief Justice of the Common Pleas in 1606, his opinions dominated legal thought until the emergence of positivist theories of law and state. In his readings of legal history, Coke 'discovered' a lineage tracing back to ancient constitutions from the Anglo Saxon age. His methodology revealed to him that judge-made law is custom and therefore represents the wisdom of generations of predecessors; more, that law-wisdom was of unchanging authority from time immemorial.[2] His view became universal among common lawyers and led Theodore Plucknett to declare that Coke's view of the supremacy of common law: 'represented public feelings based upon centuries of medieval thought which had always looked to law rather than the state'.[3] This assumption, of unchanging authority, lay at the heart of common lawyers' attitude towards and interpretations of history; an intensely superior intellectual position. Consequently, legal judgements were deemed to provide historical evidence of law's immemorial nature.[4] Coke and the common lawyers constantly reiterated the consensual fiction that law was 'discovered' and not made. As a result, common lawyers learnt about history from the study of law alone and thus English lawyers came to regard their law as a: 'self enclosed, natural process which could only be comprehended in its own terms and according to its own logic'.[5] Unsurprisingly, as this is a powerful elitist position, Coke is venerated by many common lawyers today, but as we shall see, those claims of historical right and tradition became perceived by reformers and other as an outmoded jurisprudence during the nineteenth century.

Later William Blackstone, who wrote *Commentaries on the Laws of England* between 1765–69, expressed a desire to harmonise the practising lawyer's vision of the medieval writ system as a gift from the Crown, with the view that legal rights derived from an original social contract.[6] He reiterated Coke's position; that the cornerstone of English law was the common law derived from immemorial custom, from time to time declared in the decisions of the courts of justice. Blackstone's larger purpose was a harmonisation of traditional law with the recognition of the reality of parliamentary supremacy.[7] Both these scholars considered 'history', as they understood the term, to be a fundamental element of the common law method. In order to read the present into the past Coke researched the records for precedents and today a version of this technique accompanies English common law interpretation.[8] In a perceptive account F.W. Maitland characterises this as:

> That process which old principles and old phrases are charged with a
> new content is from the lawyer's point of view an evolution of the true

meaning and intent of old law; from the historical point of view it is almost of necessity a process of perversion and misunderstanding.[9]

Grant Gilmore's reading of *Hadley v Baxendale* reveals one example of this process.[10] In addition, the doctrine of precedent as historical 'perversion' has produced a significant effect. Its particular juridical form rendered Coke and Blackstone's positions vulnerable to intellectual challenges by positivist theories of law as appeals to 'history' and historical legal traditions were destabilised by changes in society.

That instability resulted from a shift within aspects of the social order that rejected traditional structures of deference and paternalism. As a result, one major feature in the triumph of positivism is that it belongs within a philosophical tradition that proposes it is possible to create an objective intellectual position from which legal structures can be critically and impartially evaluated. Traditionally, versions of natural law theory provided conceptual methodologies by which to consider legal doctrines, running parallel to and congruent with, theories of English common law. Thus natural law formed a significant component of intellectual cultural life in the eighteenth century, although it has at differing times been used to support almost any ideology. Natural law is understood as containing two fundamental precepts: that there is a universal order governing all men and that individuals possess inalienable rights. It has a long history which began with the Greeks and continues today, providing intellectual justification for such extreme positions as absolute power (Hobbes) and absolute democracy (Rousseau). In taking that 'universal order' position, theorists culturally allied themselves with traditionalists. Philosophically, the greatest intellectual attack upon natural law doctrine came from Hume who rejected their proposition that normative statements may be deduced empirically.[11] Nevertheless this claim, although still supported by many positivists does not necessarily invalidate the natural law position as a technique of legal analysis and the debate continues today. What remains fascinating is that, in spite of numerous attempts, no successful Hegelian-type synthesis or hybridisation acceptable to both camps has emerged between the two doctrines.

However, one fundamental point remains, during the period prior to poor law reform, a moral perspective was held to be irrelevant to the positivist analysis of law's validity. To perhaps oversimplify, it is a feature of 'modernism' in historicist analyses that jurisprudence traditionally has two provinces, the analytical and the normative.[12] The analytical approach, adopted within positivist theorising, requires the examination of central legal theories, action, intervention, responsibility, black letter law and the legal system. This method denies any moral basis and, crudely put, stands opposed to natural law's normative approach. In summary, a positivist approach uses analytical systems of thought in the examination of legal theories. H.L.A. Hart, the most influential modern positivist, identifies five possible tenets of positivism in *The Concept of Law* (1961): (1) that laws are commands of human beings; (2) that there is no necessary connection between law and morals or law as it is and law as it ought to be; (3) that analysis of legal concepts is worth pursuing and distinct from historical enquiries into origins of law and sociological inquiry; (4) that a legal system is a closed logical system and that correct legal decisions can be deduced by logical means without reference to social aims, policies and moral standards;[13] (5) the statement that moral judgements cannot be established or defended as a statement of fact, is not so. They can be by rational argument, evidence or proof.[14]

Although these definitions date from the mid-twentieth century and have not stood unchallenged, they summarise much that was implicit in the positivist mind-set from its genesis; noting that points (4) and (5) would have been anathema to early nineteenth century English society. In adopting a positivist position, poor law reformers' debates concerning the juristic nature of poor law were diverted away from historical traditional rights towards technical legal analysis. This, in turn, rejected the validity of moral concepts as analytical tools. In consequence, neither Austin nor Bentham (who specifically reviewed law surrounding the relief of poverty) privileged any reference to Christian origins, historical traditions or common law rights.[15] Moreover, in considering Hart's position, Morton Horwitz notes that as with his predecessors, Hart wished to define the province of jurisprudence in order to reinforce boundaries:

> especially the boundaries between law and morals, law and custom, and, most important of all, law and politics. [Hart] followed Austin in allying jurisprudence with science by means of sharp categorical distinctions between jurisprudence and those of other realms.[16]

The apotheosis of this approach is Hans Kelsen's definition from 1967:

> It is called a pure theory of law because it only describes the law and attempts to eliminate from the object of this description everything that is not strictly law. Its aim is to free the science of law from alien elements.[17]

Alternatively, Ronald Dworkin in 1977 suggests that in spite of the distinction it is possible to argue that a theory of law must still have analytical and normative elements.[18] His modern critique may explain why a purely utilitarian approach to poor law reform was not accepted (see below). Without normative elements, contemporaries could not have accepted a system of relieving poverty utterly, clinically, divorced from traditional cultural and religious considerations.

Although few poor law reformers agreed completely with the new positivist ideas, nevertheless many found their clarity and order seductive. Of those theorists who developed this new approach Austin was the most influential, particularly in reconceptualising law as distinct from the laws of God, from moral imperatives and from any natural law philosophy.[19] He originated a technique of presenting a legal system as a structure of laws properly so called, considered without regard to their goodness or evil. Such a perspective has relevance to, and connections with, techniques of legal practice. However, it militates against the recognition of custom which would rarely qualify as law under this definition.[20] In consequence of the reception of these novel ways of thinking about law, the publication of Austin's *The Province of Jurisprudence Determined* in 1832 marks the establishment of analytical jurisprudence as the dominant theory of law.[21] It is evident that Austin's timing was highly politicised as the lectures which formed the foundation of his book were given during the period of popular agitation which produced the Reform Bill 1832. However, in *Province*, Austin claimed to 'depoliticise' utilitarianism and produce 'certainty' in the law, thereby creating a science of unambiguous and static definitions, scientific because the method produced the 'right answers'. In short, the ultimate purpose of this new jurisprudential methodology was to 'protect' law from the perceived destabilising threat of changing contexts or changing meanings.[22] Ironically, that search for certainty produced some of the greatest changes in English law.

In order to consider the effect of these positivist theories upon poor law reform it is necessary to examine the influence of Bentham and his *Fragments on Government*, written in 1776.[23] Although much of Bentham's work was not published until 1970 and some more recently,[24] there is evidence that his writings were circulated widely among the most influential circles of society.[25] *Fragments* was in circulation and influential at a point in time, the late eighteenth century, when poor law costs escalated and contemporaries imperfectly understood the reasons for that increase. Reforming poor law to reduce those costs became a priority and, as contemporaries sought for explanations and solutions, Bentham and Austin's intellectual clarity, expressed through the originality and 'scientific' nature of their jurisprudence must have seemed a way through the difficulties of reforming a traditional, entrenched, common law relief system. Other theorists, too, added their perspective to this heady intellectual mix. Thus, in 1798 Thomas Malthus suggested that money distributed as poor relief could not stimulate productivity. His solution lay, amongst other considerations, in prudence born out of fear, holding that men need misery or at least insecurity to prod them into virtue.[26] Malthusian theories became an essential part of the classical doctrine on wages as part of theories of political economy. According to his theory of wages, poor relief actually tended to increase misery:

> Finally, the system as a whole, the harshness of cruel overseers, and the law of settlement in particular formed a collection of grating and tyrannical laws, totally inconsistent with the genuine spirit of the constitution.[27]

As we shall see in Chapter 9, this negative perception of settlement was common amongst reformers of the period. Malthus' remedy in 1798 was to abolish parish laws, all poor relief and especially settlement, in order to benefit the poor by allowing them to obtain higher wages in a free labour market. He supported a national scheme of county workhouses for cases of extreme distress. Nonetheless, the case for describing the 1834 reforms as Malthusian is weak, his views were largely abolitionist and the Poor Law Commission in 1834 rejected his position taking a positivist route to reform.

From that reform perspective, Bentham was a compulsive proposer of systematic legislation.[28] Alan Harding notes that the sheer volume of Bentham's theories ensured that few of the reforms that were carried out after his death were not hinted at in his work, but that rather begs the issue.[29] Significantly, although Bentham was concerned with reforming poor law he acknowledged the right to relief as he defined settlement:

> [T]he law giving each man a right to be maintained in case of indigence, in and at the expense of some particular Parish or Parish-like District in which he is said to have his settlement.[30]

In fact, Bentham viewed that local rating as inefficient and proposed a national system to pay for the poor and a central board to manage his scheme. He also proposed a national scheme of no fewer than 250, preferably 500, houses of industry for the poor, designed upon the Panopticon principle; imposing a high degree of regimentation upon those poor held within these massive model workhouse-prisons.[31] However, he concludes that in applying principles of utility (see below) to the problem of poor relief there was a conclusive argument against abolition, as repeal would allow beggars to 'thrive'.[32] Instead, Bentham sought to establish an objective difference between paupers in condition and status, between deserving and undeserving, whilst at the same time taking steps to prevent 'labourers' being forced into pauperism. This was to be achieved by the principle of 'less eligibility'; that conditions in the workhouse should be less favourable than that available to the labouring classes by their own efforts. Finally, Bentham concluded that the only reasonable ground for settlement was birth.

When implementation of the terms of the Poor Law Amendment Act 1834 is viewed against these positivist proposals, it appears that in its administrative innovations reformers achieved their jurisprudential objectives. Thus, although some legal historians do not support the view that positivism was a major juristic influence in the nineteenth century, the argument for its influence in poor law reform remains valid; it is the extension of the argument to other areas of law reform which are doubted.[33] As an example of jurisprudence linked to law in action, the consequences of introducing a regimented bureaucratised scheme exemplifies all the juristic weaknesses of rule-based systems. This is most apparent as we shall see in the marginalisation of settled paupers' personal legal right to poor relief on the basis of need, replaced by the workhouse test and relief administered upon the principle of 'less eligibility' to benefit the majority, the ratepayers of a parish. Thus, in satisfying this 'majority' it is apparent that Bentham did influence a jurisprudential model for poor law reform, one linked to principles of utility.

This connection may be traced through an examination of the broader aspects of utilitarianism; a goal-based theory which evaluates actions in terms of their propensity to maximise goodness (however defined).[34] There are three components in utilitarian theory: the evaluative (ranking states of affairs so that one may judge which is the better); the consequentialist (the rightness or wrongness of an action depends upon the consequences it produces); and a claim about who is to be considered when estimating what the likely consequences of an action are. Bentham's theory of utility, which he applied to the 'problem' of the poor, achieves its evaluations in calculating happiness (the felicific calculus) by ranking pleasure. The consequences of an action determine its rightness, thus a lie is acceptable if it produces good consequences. Utility has attractive aspects: in its secular approach, in valuing happiness as a goal and that individualist approach which considers the well-being of each person in its calculations. These same aspects are open to criticism. Pleasure is subjective, consequences are notoriously difficult to predict and the doctrine allows the happiness of the many to be secured at the expense of the few; here one might point to an intention that the poor will only be relieved in the workhouse.[35]

Although looking back the route to the union workhouse is clear enough, from a twenty first century humanitarian perspective it appears a cruel and cynical choice of destination. It might be argued that aspects of these reforms are conceptually so new that their proposers may have lacked the imagination to understand the inherent 'cruelty' of their proposals; or how harshly future popular opinion would judge them. Unfortunately, it is more likely that the nature of positivist jurisprudence, one of its many and continuing attractions for some, permits theorists to abdicate personal and ethical responsibility for its consequences. In summary, it is evident that the new poor law's administrative structures may be placed within that juristic framework discussed above. In this manner, utilitarian principles are expressed through positivist legal structures to marginalise historical common law traditions. Nonetheless, although influential in law-making, positivism provides only narrow answers to the questions: What kind of law was poor law? How may we understand the nature of that law today? A positivist reply might be that after 1834 poor law was a set of rules and delegated Orders, administered by a local bureaucracy under the immediate control of a central administrative body, carried out under the legal authority of the 1601 Act. This narrow description reflects the doctrinal characteristics of positivist analysis. A further element, both a function and consequence of that search for certainty demonstrated in both Bentham and Austin's approach, is that 'law' is understood as the same everywhere and therefore divorced from time and place within which that law functioned. This inherently denies the validity of historical context and custom as law and divorces juristic analysis from its contingent elements.

Yet it is evident as we shall see throughout this work, that those elements of utilitarianism and positivism contained within the new poor law were also very much of their time. In reconstructing positivism historically albeit briefly as here, this writer is drawing upon another juristic approach to understanding the nature of law; that proposed and developed by Sir Henry Maine in *Ancient Law*, published in 1861.[36] Although his work appeared after many of the poor law reforms were implemented, there is resonance in Maine's conceptual creation for those opponents of poor law reform who adopted an historicist position. Maine's contribution and hence value to our legal understanding, indeed his contribution to socio-legal historical reconstructions, stands somewhere between a juristic theory and a methodology. In summary, Maine reconceptualises and therefore positions 'law' as a product of its environment, to be viewed and reconstructed within its context. For Maine, law may be understood in terms of social development as he concludes that social conditions change law rather than vice versa.[37] Unquestionably, Maine's early work emphasises the importance of knowledge of legal history; a position reiterated for modern legal scholars by A.W.B. Simpson, Raymond Cocks, Patrick Atiyah and David Sugarman.[38] Moreover, as Maine argued that a contemporary version of a law cannot be understood outside its historical context, his position was both in opposition and constituted a later challenge to the positivist approach. In this context, Austin's separation of law and custom was a particular target for Maine's attack, as he argued that the failure of Austin (and Bentham) to follow the historical method led to generalisations on the basis of law in the modern nation state. Consequently, it is evident that Maine was attempting to use history and custom as conservative checks upon what he perceived as unrestrained Benthamite radicalism.[39]

Although what follows is *ex post facto*, the juristic techniques provided by Maine permit another perspective from which to understand those legal reforms of the poor law whose form was influenced by novel contemporary theories of the nature of law. If we understand law in its historical context as Maine suggests, then this reinforces a perception that positivism too was of its time. In summary, adopting his approach aids our comprehension of the power of these new juristic developments and the powerlessness of those whose lives it changed. Additionally, his methodology permits clarification of the relationship between law and society and the pervasiveness of law in history. Thus in *Ancient Law*, Maine reconstructed Roman, Greek and Sanskrit law amongst others in a method that became characterised as 'historical jurisprudence'. His work represents an attempt at synthesis, covering a great breadth of material concerned with the concept of progress in a general sense rather than the precise nature of that progress.[40] His most famous conclusion, a massive over-simplification but of powerful, immediate and continuing impact, is that the movement of progressive societies has hitherto been from 'Status to Contract', an expression now understood in many quarters as the emergence of modernism.[41] Not a doctrinal text, *Ancient Law* was unconcerned with black letter reconstructions, but rather with establishing general principles of development in early law. As the first (and last) of its kind, the work has many technical weaknesses and historical inaccuracies which led, after an initial public success, to it being attacked and subsequently ignored.[42] Maine's failure to produce a synthesis of law, history and philosophy, a challenge that still eludes us today, produced a lasting negative and narrowing effect upon legal historical reconstructions within the legal establishment.[43]

Fortunately, recent legal scholarship has reassessed that position. Both Cocks and Neil MacCormack suggest that Maine's strength lies in his assertions that law and legal institutions are related to specific social conditions and that this social development may be viewed as a 'progression'; linear and temporal although not teleological as Maine asserts. Their reappraisal of Maine's scholarship has validated two specific methodologies.[44] The first is grounded in the question: What is the relationship between certain kinds of society and certain kinds of law? The socio-legal project in all but name. The second is to reconstruct narrow legal subjects, such as the history of contract or poor law, by placing these legal subjects within their specific historical and social contexts. Although Maine's view of a series of fixed stages is largely discredited, the English lawyer's chronological common law methodology lends itself to this latter type of historical analysis. In spite of this, those leading modern legal philosophers Dworkin and Hart have shown no interest in Maine's work. Cocks has posited that: 'for a modern jurist to take an interest in Maine, a strong belief in the importance of historical explanation is almost a pre-requisite'.[45] Consequently, although Maine was concerned more with the relationship between things than the things themselves, a modern socio-legal jurist or critical legal scholar could usefully analyse or reconstruct law in its historical context following his precepts.

A further modern value of Maine's work lies in his critique of any jurisprudence (including that of Bentham and Austin) which at least by implication claim to be of universal application but which can only be related to the circumstances of a few societies.[46] For example, adopting Maine's juristic methodology has permitted this writer elsewhere to deconstruct current legal scholarship founded upon the Nazi Carl Schmitt's theories concerning the constitutional 'state of exception'.[47] That research challenges such legitimisation by reconceptualising the 'state of exception' into its historical juristic and political context, a methodology that permits alternative readings. This was achieved following Maine's proposal that jurists might begin legal analysis by examining social arrangements for preserving harmony in order to locate explanations for the existence and nature of law. In short, Maine presents historical reconstructions as a vehicle for his deductions in a firm belief that jurists should ask historical questions.[48] Seen in these terms, Maine's theories are a vital model for reconstructing legal history in order to place the study of law firmly in context, with the caveat that Maine viewed legal change as a teleological progression. As a final point, it is now well understood that as law operates in context and develops over time in responses to changes in that context, original purposes tend to vanish into antiquity and their influence fades. However, this is not obliteration and leaves traces within current law, either in the legal application of precedent to new situations, or in cultural understandings of the role of law itself in society. It is this aspect of legal development to which Maine instinctively reaches.

Relating these concepts back to poor law, reform was fiercely contested and the 'new' jurisprudence was far from universally popular. Nonetheless, juristic opposition was not grounded in natural law theories but instead based upon appeals to ancient custom and historicism, defined by Horwitz in a legal context as:

> [A] conception of history that assumes that change and flux are permanent, and insist that the meaning of an idea or concept – right, liberty, sovereignty, positivism – may change depending upon its historical context ... It is where our ideas about frames of reference, paradigms, conceptual systems come from.[49]

This historicism constituted a challenge to Bentham and Austin's closed system of law. In substance, critics cited the traditional authority of common law and the weight of ancient Saxon constitutions, largely on behalf of parish legal autonomy and not the rights of the poor.[50] Once defeated in 1834, that position became largely discredited in poor law and other reforms only re-emerging in the 1850s in the work of Maine and Joshua Toulmin Smith (see Chapter 9). No effective alternative legal doctrine was raised against the poor law reforms but, albeit counterfactually, a reinterpretation of Maine may be raised today. As we will see in the next chapter, the common law right to poor relief by the settled poor was a personal legal right of historical authority. However well understood at the time, this was not debated; jurisprudential rights theories are in fact a twentieth century preoccupation. Moreover, supporting the rights of the poor became stigmatised as emotional and anti-reformist at a time when economic pressures and political mood called for poor law reform. This doomed opponents to failure.

It is apparent that Bentham influenced this separation of historical legal tradition from jurisprudential argument. Although continuing after 1834, appeals to the authority of history in legal debate became characterised as reactionary, paternalistic and simply outmoded, a view some support today.[51] As noted above, in addition to this exclusion of historical authority, positivists maintained a further separation between law and politics; extending in turn to a division between law, custom and morality. It is, therefore, apparent that poor law reform was a battleground not just within the political sphere but between competing jurisprudential theories. It is within this intellectual context that we may appreciate why Bentham's attack on Blackstone's jurisprudence was aimed to demystify the common law judges and: 'deligitimise the common law'.[52] Consequentially, parliamentary sovereignty and legal positivism would become a favoured doctrine of the triumphal middle classes. From this perspective, further legislative codification of the common law, combined with new administrative processes may be understood as the political expression of positivist jurisprudence. A vast gulf emerged between the new analytical and the traditional historicist legal methodologies which served to further weaken those arguments based upon custom, tradition or right. Horwitz concludes that Bentham's *Fragments on Government* and Austin's *Province of Jurisprudence*, both published in 1832, demonstrate that an historical approach to legal theory was considered by contemporaries to be conservative, outmoded; the new analytical approach was both reformist and radical.[53] This further confirms a perception that those who wrote on law and jurisprudence during the period of major poor law reform, and who most influenced the law and its reformers, were unsympathetic to those arguments which appealed to traditional or historical rights. In future, appeals to the past would be outdated in theories of jurisprudence.

Some critics of the 1834 poor law reforms raised humanitarian objections which the Poor Law Commission recognised and which should have given opponents of reform an enormous rhetorical advantage.[54] Unfortunately, linking an humanitarian appeal to a political position which idealised historical institutions weakened that position. Today their criticisms may perhaps be read as political paranoia, with heated and exaggerated condemnation of government growth and state intervention as a 'conspiracy' against political and social values which developed over time.[55] As a result the historicist opponents lost ground against the ostensibly 'reasoned' approach of poor law reformers who shared no such ideals and who, some consider, followed an incremental model of political reform.[56] For example, William Lubenow suggests the reformers proceeded towards modest goals using pragmatic methods and engaged in cautious modifications aimed at reducing perceived local corruption, whilst retaining those values and benefits the localised system was seen as containing. However, a teleological view of centralisation initiated by the Webbs' writings on the poor law and local government (see Chapter 4),[57] supported in the writings of Lubenow and Oliver MacDonagh, oversimplifies the complex interdependent relationship between central and local government during the eighteenth century.[58] David Eastwood, by way of contrast, considers that the reforms in local government were not purposive, rather that they were a particular consequence of the specific history of local government, including poor law administration.[59] It is evident that all these observations require nuancing in order to take into account the effect of those developments in legal theory discussed above, in order to explain that unique creation of bureaucratic modernity, the new poor law.

In spite of all the discussion above, the reforms of 1834 were not entirely positivist. The Poor Law Amendment Act 1834 was not collectivist; it was limited both in function and form although, it was also passed with an express aim to actively transform the idle and improvident into industrious members of the labouring classes. It is therefore a mistake to regard the terms of the 1834 Act as entirely purposive, such an interpretation grants more credit to the utilitarian perspective than the terms of the Act contain or achieved as we shall see in Chapter 3. However, there was sufficient that was innovative to demonstrate that it was not a creature of the old poor law and it is against this newness that many reacted. Those same eighteenth and nineteenth century positivist juridical theories retain their influence today within academic debate upon the nature of law, whilst consistently failing to provide any inherent protection for humanitarian social and cultural values. Groups within nineteenth century society that were marginalised by those changes appealed to traditional rights; these were understood as sentimental appeals to an irrelevant historical past. This largely remains the juristic position today as an absence of jurisprudential recognition of traditional legal positions in any form except common law precedent has left many sections of society subject to law-making whims; with the justification that a democratically elected Parliament can only be expressing the will of the people.

Hart's belief that positive law can protect rights has proved less than accurate for numerous citizens and others currently living in Britain, in spite of the implementation of the Human Rights Act 1998 backed by the jurisprudence of the European Court of Human Rights. One is thinking here of increasing and punitive criminal justice legislation, Public Order Offences, detention without charge for 27 days, increasing police powers and aspects of government surveillance ... the reader may fill in the rest. By the time this work appears in print there will no doubt be more. This political reality affected those who opposed the reforms of 1834. For then, as today, any appeal to England's past, all claims of lost historical rights, led to charges of an emotional idealisation dismissed as mythology.[60] One consequence of this rejection was that to opponents of reform all state intervention became, by definition, despotic and corruptly unconstitutional. Critics expressed a longing for a return to those forms of local government they believed enshrined within tradition. However, many contemporaries, and not just poor law reformers, loathed some elements of that 'tradition' such as paternalism, social subordination and deference, thus further reducing opponents' chances of success. In consequence, elements of legal 'truth' contained within reformist arguments became overlaid and subsumed within those constituent elements and perceptions of paternalist patronage. Furthermore, the emotional as opposed to that [quasi] rational argument adopted by positivists ensured that the historical argument failed at a parliamentary level.

As we shall see in the doctrinal reconstruction, after 1834 poor relief began a fundamental juristic shift from common law to administrative (public) law. This change is reflected within the works of A.V. Dicey, the most influential jurist writing on the nature and development of public law in the nineteenth century. Although produced 50 years later (1885), his *Law of the Constitution* was concerned with earlier legal changes including those within poor law. In consequence of this and his continuing academic stature, Dicey's views have value for this reconstruction as they continue to influence modern under- standing of that legal past. This is not entirely helpful, for Dicey was hostile to the 'historical' perspective. Although he rejected a teleological view of an unwritten evolving constitution,[61] this was a reflection of his dislike of any consideration of the manner in which institutions evolved; believing this deterred and prevented students from paying sufficient attention to the law of the constitution: 'as it actually was'.[62] In short, he was concerned that the analysis of institutions could influence people's perceptions of those institu- tions and that this was undesirable. At base, Dicey believed that concerns about origins could lead to controversy about the present and fear of such a challenge contributed to Dicey's attempts to distinguish law from politics; reflecting positivist aims of legal certainty and stability. In turn, Dicey's theories influenced Hart in his insistence upon the separation of law and politics, law and history.[63] Finally, 'legal' for Dicey meant law in the strictest sense; law controlled by lawyers and judges to ensure that legal change was slow-paced and conservative.[64] This perspective, the separation of the legal from the political with both divorced from their history, became characteristic of academic debate amongst public lawyers in the nineteenth century. That separation also characterises the drift away from personal legal rights in poor relief, influencing the administrative form taken by public law in this period.

Expressing that separation juristically, Dicey emphasised the authority of parliamentary sovereignty, which under his readings of the English Con- stitution has the right to make any law whatsoever. He concluded that no person or body is recognised by the laws of England as having the right to override or set aside the legislation of Parliament.[65] Dicey supposed, in a position that has been much debated, that this was achieved within his conception of Parliament, with an extended franchise thus expressing the will of the people, as a self-correcting majoritarian democracy.[66] Moreover, Dicey disliked written constitutional rights preferring the 'rule of law', for him the decisions of the common law in the ordinary courts, as providing better protection for the people. The fallacy of this reading of the rule of law, and indeed of 'people' is demonstrated in the loss of legal rights experienced by the poor in the nineteenth century, although Dicey might have argued that they were not lost, merely 'rationalised'.

That 'rationalisation' of law took the form of a considerable expansion of functions performed by central government between 1830 and 1850. These changes were initiated in poor law administration, followed by legislation which attempted to centralise control of other aspects of society; attempts which met with varying degrees of success for regulating factories, railways and securing public health improvements, including the draconian Vaccination Acts.[67]

Although advocates of reform had differing objectives, their significance for law is that in total these reforms gave a legal form to centralised administrative control and initiated those debates upon the uses and purposes of public institutions which remain current today. However, these reforms were more proto-modernist than modern although reflecting the new positivist jurisprudence. They succeeded politically through claims that such reforms would reduce escalating costs. In addition, much poor law reform was achieved by building upon contemporary local and central administrative structures in an evolving model. Thus the administrative structure of the Poor Law Commission in London introduced after 1834 was based upon pre-existing government boards; the most usual form of central administration during the eighteenth and nine-teenth century. Those boards constituted an integral and established part of the machinery of government, whose membership formed a useful source of patronage.[68] In addition, boards possessed varying degrees of independence from direct parliamentary control and all, including in the Poor Law Commission, later Board, were sufficiently competent to cope with the reforms initiated in 1830–50. However, development of a centralised bureaucracy was achieved with some difficulty: one problem was that a government implementing a reform was not always the government which passed it. The modern development of Ministries with a direct responsibility to Parliament, which grew out of these boards, was not an obvious one. Eventually such boards declined as the franchise was extended and Parliament itself wished to control their operation. This trend is currently operating in reverse with a proliferation of quangos ('non-departmental public bodies') some 790 in 2008, at a cost of £43 billion, of which £34.5 billion is supplied by the taxpayer.[69]

As is the case with contemporary quangos, the Poor Law Commission had no member entitled to sit in Parliament and thus no one who could be called to answer or to defend its actions in the House. In 1847 the Commission became a Board with one member entitled to sit in Parliament.[70] This reform did not resolve other problems and the Board was reconstituted in 1871 as the Local Government Board and then the Ministry of Health in 1918 when it acquired a Minister responsible for its activities directly answerable to Parliament. These Boards and their successor Ministries held administrative discretion in their activities separately from Parliament, even when accountable for their actions. The Poor Law Board also exercised a judicial function, described to a Royal Commission in 1867:

> [T]hey [the Board] do not give judicial decisions, but they have got the cases all before them ... they give advice, and armed with that advice ... the parties are then prepared if necessary, to appeal to the law.[71]

In a traditional common law response, the courts developed a process of challenging bureaucratic assumption of legal authority by questioning their exercise of discretion. However, this process of judicial review was and is very different from procedures available to individuals to protect their personal rights at common law.

According to P.P. Craig, the eventual collapse of the Board system was due in large part to the Commons' desire to monopolise ('control') their exercise of public power.[72] The outcome of this process was that a system of non-constitutional review developed to ensure that those to whom power had been granted did not transgress the 'sovereign will' of Parliament. If authority were granted to a Minister to perform a task, the courts' function in the event of a challenge to the Minister was to check that only those tasks were performed, however, this action was only available when the conditions for such a challenge were present. In the case of poor law, this was a great change in the operation of law. The origins of the review process are obscure, but in the nineteenth century its rationale was slowly transformed.[73] As the procedure developed, the judiciary justified the exercise of their powers from two perspectives. First, they acted (ostensibly) as a check to ensure that the authority in question had not extended the area over which the legislation gave it jurisdiction. The second arose as judges became more aware of the limits to their power. In reaction to what was perceived as a loss of judicial authority, the courts began to exercise juristic control over administrative discretion, legitimised by a link with legislative intent. Much of this was achieved through case law in the twentieth century but the origins of modern judicial review lay in nineteenth century developments.[74]

The shift from poor law as common law to a public-law subject fundamentally altered juristic approaches to poor law matters; it ensured that concern about rights moved from the individual pauper's immediate financial needs in his or her place of settlement to a preoccupation with the government's exercise of power. Other common law rights, but not the right to relief, remained a feature of the law in this area but only as a qualification to enter the review system. In this context, a citizen required a right in contract, tort or property in order to take legal action. The gateways to administrative law, natural justice, standing or the right to apply for relief in the case of a pauper were barred to those who did not possess those other qualifying rights listed above. Without detailing the complexities of the review action it can be said that this was a very different undertaking at law from anything under the old poor law. In practice, in the nineteenth century the courts were not so nice in their distinctions, case law demonstrates their willingness to hear an action without inquiring too closely if an applicant had a right (e.g. in tort). Alternatively, the courts concentrated upon their other function, that of policing the over-enthusiastic exercise of an authority's power.[75] From a poor law perspective, this change in emphasis left a gap in the legal rights of the poor. The courts appear to demonstrate an awareness of this change in a flexible approach adopted during the nineteenth century, but the focus of legal actions moved from the rights of the individual (common law), to the correct exercise of power by authorities (public law). To sum up, such changes were triggered under statutory authority that both necessitated and created a centralised administrative state authorised, governed and occasionally checked by Dicey's preferred form of the rule of law (the exercise of ordinary law in ordinary courts), all operating within the growing doctrinal influence of positivist theories.[76]

In light of the above, it appears that the growth of administrative law in England was a consequence of the extension of the activities of central government into poor law and other areas rather than a deliberate constitutional creation. That growth required the progressive erosion of the rights of individuals in order to maximise the benefits to all (a utilitarian model). Choices were made about how to operate the new poor law upon the basis of costs and alleged efficiency. Individual rights, barely protected under the new public law, became stigmatised. This position was firmly established by 1928 when one commentator on administrative law wrote disparagingly:

> The intense legalism of the English system of law is one of its most notable features, and one which results in a tendency to sacrifice the public welfare to private interests where the latter case can lay claim to private rights ... it is concerned less with social righteousness than with individuals. It has questions of the highest social import as mere private controversies ... and it is so zealous to secure fair play to the individual that it often secures very little fair play to the public.[77]

This 1920s legal orthodoxy reflects a transformation of poor law from common law to public law; not one accompanied by discussions concerning the legal rights of the poor. However, it must be acknowledged that the influence of legal theories upon this expansion of government bodies remains the subject of debate. MacDonagh views the growth as functional via incremental stages, whereas others emphasise uncertainty as to how widespread was knowledge of those theories of utility.[78] Craig concludes that the development and extension of government bodies in this period was a function of a combination of organic change and contemporary ideologies, with that of Bentham as the most prominent. Whatever the rights or wrongs of these assertions, it is evident that something new emerged juristically in the nineteenth century and much that was traditional was lost, the good with the bad.

Historians may consider that in reconstructing poor law and the reforms of 1834 jurisprudentially this work is adopting an over lawyerly approach; yet poor law is a legal subject and legal theory is one established element of a socio-legal analysis. Another is to reconstruct that law's 'functions' within contemporary society. For poor law, these included: providing security for the localities (parishes) in helping to prevent unrest;[79] tempering criminal poverty as the settled poor possessed a personal legal right to relief; enforcing and permitting local autonomy and community obligations; providing an overarching legal framework; perpetuating Christian values of an earlier age within a developing industrial state; ensuring that the poor did not starve and so on. In terms of 'pure' legal analysis, a positivist critique actively rejects such considerations Natural law theories entertain some of these matters and may offer the potential for an alternative juristic critique. The rights lawyers, whose work is modern and complex, have concerned them-selves primarily with contemporary issues (although see below for discussion of a recent rights-based reconstruction). Alternatively, Maine provides one broad model for an historico-socio-legal reconstruction; his methodology supports the use of many sources when analysing law and emphasises the value of examining law in context. The weakness of his approach is that it excludes the black letter approach and thus permits the possibility of legal errors. In summary, there is no authoritative comprehensive juristic frame-work available for reconstructing the legal past.

Formalism in legal history

This perspective explains why much jurisprudential analysis of legal history falls within a narrow area. Most legal studies of developments during the eighteenth and nineteenth centuries take their reference point as above, the much debated effects of utilitarianism, rather than concentrating upon social, political and economic forces. Sugarman proposes that this approach by jur-ists has tended to produce a passive, conservative interpretation of the role of law in history.[80] One consequence of such interpretations is that they sup-port an emphasis upon continuity which effectively neutralises any critical view of law as coercive or oppressive. Sugarman believes that this perspective reduces the critique by lawyers of the institutions of the law, and of lawyers' relationship with the rest of society, to the level of a statement of technical legal developments. In such circumstances, the overall impression is one of conservatism both within English law and by its practitioners. This reflects a reality, that much practice of law in England both was and remains innately conservative; indeed one of its defining characteristics is a tendency towards legal formalism. This formalism may be understood as a reaction to that other innate feature of the common law, the application of the doctrine of precedent on an almost daily basis to amend, alter and reinterpret legal 'rules' in an organic, emergent, constantly mutating yet 'seamless web' of common law in operation. Traditionally this process amends law on a con-tinuous basis in concert with the non-stop creation of legislation that is also subject to legal interpretation. All this occurs within a conceptual framework of 'unchanging' legal authority. As a result, the continuity or change debate of the historians requires nuancing in legal history; for modern lawyers understand law's continuity as embedded within this permanent state of flux operating within a legal framework of technique, authority and jurisdiction. However, this is not how lawyers have always understood legal process.

Horwitz's analysis of the American common law courts 1780–1860 demonstrates that during this period there was a shift in contemporary understanding.[81] He deduces that there was a movement from belief in law as a static set of principles based upon customary and natural law as noted above, to a more instrumentalist view of law. In particular, that after 1790 judges began to view the common law purposively as equal with legislation for governing society and promoting socially desirable conduct.[82] Horwitz concludes that this purposive approach to the interpretation of precedent has subsequently been rendered opaque by judiciary who both spoke and speak of the common law as a 'seamless web' and claim to declare the law and not to make it. Similarly, Horwitz has argued that, in England, the role of the judiciary was vital both in the development of modern common law from 1770–1870 and, perhaps, as a reaction to their rule-making function, in the emergence of formalism. That formalism is characterised by a tendency to literalism in the interpretation of statutes and precedents and the legal construction of rights in absolute terms. In formalism, rules are perceived not as an expression of government but rather as purely legal. Another aspect is the emphasis upon the importance of rules as rules regardless of the reasons underlying them. Great stress was and is laid upon the proprieties of the surface.[83] As the traditional style of English judges is understood as having changed little over time, it might be argued that this formalist technique for deciding cases is the English legal tradition at work. Nonetheless, formalism was and is more than this; it consists of an inherent denial of the law-making function of judges and a claim for a higher authority, a knowable, attainable, perfect solution to law. It is considered to personify the common law mindset exemplified by Coke and Blackstone and, over time, has rendered decisions more opaque, particularly through a denial of the existence of policy considerations as the basis of legal decisions.

In its modern context, Atiyah defines formalism as:

> [T]he attitude of a judge who believes that all law is based upon legal doctrine and principles which can be deduced from precedents; that there is only one 'correct' way to decide a case; that it is not the function of the judge to invoke policy considerations, or even arguments about the relative justice of the parties' claims; that the reasons behind principles and rules are irrelevant; that the role of the judge is purely passive and interpretive; the law is the science of principles, and so on.[84]

It may be that formalism was partially engendered by and reinforced as judicial 'resistance' to the new positivism, in an attempt to re-establish the primacy of the common law. Interestingly, a formalist method of legal interpretation mirrors positivist certainties. In thus parodying new principles

of political economy and positivism, formalism fosters the illusion of inex-
orable deductions within the common law techniques drawn from 'neutral
principles'.

In spite of this 'new' direction, there is evidence that in some aspects of
commercial life in the nineteenth century custom prevailed over formalism
and that doctrinal forms were sometimes marginalised in the honouring of
commercial agreements which were not enforceable *per se*; however these are
exceptions, survivals.[85] Atiyah's opinion is that until the mid-nineteenth
century both English law and lawyers were significantly influenced by the
theories of utilitarianism and political economy but that by the 1850s
formalism was an increasing feature of legal decisions.[86] This occurs parallel
to the emergence of discretion as a factor in legal decision-making as governments introduce legislation designed to achieve general social purposes.
However, although poor law reform is one such social policy example, within
its case law formalism emerges as a significant element of judicial interpretation. In one example drawn from a decision in 1856, Shee J.J. states:

> It is important that points arising on settlement law when once deter-
> mined, should not again be disturbed, except on most cogent grounds;
> and we should not feel justified in over-ruling the three cases already
> decided on this subject, although we may doubt the correctness of the
> original decision.[87]

Later in 1889, Lord Esher M.R. in deciding a settlement case states of an
earlier House of Lords' decision: 'I do not ask myself whether I agree with
their reasons or not, as that is immaterial. I am most clear that they decided
the point which is before us.'[88] Nevertheless as Ferguson points out, formalism in judicial discourse did not prevent changes in the law or exclude
judicial decision-making which contains expressions of moral indignation.[89]
However such developments accompanied formalism as fundamental components of legal culture during this period and beyond.

The inherent tenets of legal formalism have tended to reinforce a doctrinal
approach to reconstructing England's legal past. Where this is the case, and
this is Sugarman's point, it may be construed as a legacy of formalism that
some doctrinal legal history places emphasis upon an historical truth that can
only be found in the cases; Sugarman provides one such example. He notes
that Horwitz's analysis concerning the historical relationship between law
and economy is weakened by his lack of data on economy and the narrowness
of the definition of what constitutes law.[90] However, in his turn, Horwitz
reconstructed those ideological presumptions found in lawyer's legal history.[91] Two of these reflect the common law method: the emphasis upon
continuity and the search for origins. Horwitz points out certain faults that
are often associated with these including: adulation of the common law;
hostility to codification; measuring legal achievement and sophistication in

terms of narrow categories; remaining within the received legal tradition and separating law from politics and economic change.

However, this work is not a damning account of the common law, much that follows in subsequent chapters constitutes praise of common law rights, specifically those once possessed by the poor. Nevertheless this should not be read as undiluted admiration for there is a negative side to common law, especially during this period. It is with this understanding that Harding subtitles his discussion of law in the nineteenth century: 'Stagnant law in a changing society'.[92] He notes that through the nineteenth century society the common law [courts] became increasingly inappropriate and inadequate to deal with the demands being made upon it. R.W. Kostal takes a similar view about the effects of the common law, analysing its largely negative impact upon the rise and development of the steam railway industry.[93] This is a perspective shared by the conservative historian Himmelfarb.[94] Nevertheless, as we shall see, poor law contained personal legal rights and, in this area at least, the common law once had social effectiveness. Finally, as a partial answer to Horwitz's criticism concerning the legal autonomy of much legal history, this reconstruction places poor law within its jurisprudential and historical context; *pace* Sugarman, it will not attempt an economic or political analysis.

From a different perspective, it is noticeable that British and American legal theorists, particularly Hart and Dworkin, have virtually ignored the role of history in modern jurisprudence. This is all the odder for it is evident that one stimulus for the natural law-positivist debate is the shock and horror engendered by those atrocities perpetrated in the Third Reich. In this context, a modern reading of those theories of legal development suggested within Maine's *Ancient Law* offers the possibility of alternative methodologies to be used in reconstructing law in history.[95] It is from this perspective that Cocks suggests modern lawyers are not in communication with their past, instead they adopt ahistorical reconstructions:

> Law students and practitioners and judges use libraries which are full of primary sources of legal history, in the form of law reports and statutes, but very few of them are taught the techniques of historical interpretation. Instead they develop the techniques of relating the words in these sources to what are acceptable modern arguments.[96]

Cocks asks the pertinent question, how much of the past may be taken out of modern legal reasoning without the latter being totally transformed? Equally, Maine's work serves as a model for the hypothesis that theories about the past become a fundamental part of legal thinking which are at the same time at variance with that historical past. The corollary to that, found both in Maine and in the work of Gilmore, is that any broader historical reconstruction of that legal past may result in a change in our understanding of contemporary law, as we begin to appreciate the variance between research evidence concerning how law operated in the past and our modern assumptions and legal traditions concerning that past.[97] The sub-text to that discussion is that such reconstructions may have power to influence current legal perceptions.

The role of poor law reconstructions in theories of welfare

One such work, *Welfare to Work: Conditional Rights in Social Policy* by Amir Paz-Fuchs published in 2008, encapsulates both the current status and relevance of poor law to contemporary welfare theory and reveals a major problematic: that reconstructions of welfare's legal past by legal scholars are based predominantly upon historians' accounts.[98] Although questions raised by the largely non-law-minded and hence legally misleading historiography of those works will be discussed fully in Chapter 4, nevertheless at this point it is useful to examine their role within legal and jurisprudential theories of welfare today. To that end, this section will briefly consider Paz-Fuchs' writing on modern welfare, noting that he writes from the discipline of law. The first point is that, in common with a developing orthodoxy in wider socio-legal and legal scholarship, Paz-Fuchs grounds his account within a framework of historians' reconstructions of welfare's past.[99] Unfortunately, although a lawyer, he draws upon non-legal accounts resulting in a chaotic 'legal' narrative. In his account, 400 years of law run into a nebulous whole where very different eras are conflated into one amorphous 'poor law'.

There is a further issue as this work will demonstrate: poor law historical reconstructions are generally legally incorrect, raising the problem of the destabilising effect of reliance upon such works. In Paz-Fuchs' account, this is compounded by his over-reliance upon two historians from amongst an extensive poor law scholarship produced from within the discipline of history. In short, Paz-Fuchs draws upon the politically motivated writings of the Webbs produced a century ago and his understanding of poor law theoretically and conceptually draws extensively upon Himmelfarb's work. Although an established poor law historian, her innate conservatism colours her analysis. In short, she and the Webbs are informed by agendas that are not necessarily articulated within their texts but are well known to historians; moreover, none of these works includes doctrinal legal analysis. Thus Paz-Fuchs' 'legal' narrative of poor law is unstable, leading to his assertion that poor law may be situated within contractual models of welfare, not merely social contract but also that of traditional common law contract. This incorrect deduction is set against discussions of 'alternative' rights-based models that Paz-Fuchs suggests are not found in welfare's legal past. This is not so, for as we shall see that legal past provides some of those elements of a welfare system he regards as desirable. These include reciprocity or citizenship (read settlement), mutuality, legal rights duties and obligations combined with responsibilities.

Although Paz-Fuchs emphasises the importance of legal rights and deplores the moral stigma often attached to welfare claimants, he remains unaware of the full breadth of a legal past that contains those elements listed above.[100] However, in critiquing the 'conditionality' of modern welfare in the United States and its development in Britain under a 'workfare' blanket, he grounds his discussions in a comprehensive analysis of modern rights theory. In these theoretical discussions, contextualised within a legally incorrect and largely historicist poor law reconstruction, the line becomes blurred between descriptors of the nature of welfare past and present and explanations of its authenticity, existence or conceptual nature.

This raises a further difficulty as it is not clear from Paz-Fuchs' work if welfare's legal past is one or many, of what precisely it consisted or even when these (opaque) 'legal' events occurred. If one adds to that mix the actual existence of a juristic rights-based welfare system with a right to relief, then Paz-Fuchs missed a trick. The legal existence of a right to relief substantiates aspects of his arguments and strengthens parts of his thesis. He acknowledges that this would be so were the right to have existed, a suggestion he subsequently rejects to follow historians' negative orthodoxy. Indeed, he does not appear to have consulted legal texts and misquotes relevant legal historical reconstructions.[101] In this context, Paz-Fuchs repeatedly mis-states law in remaining convinced that poor relief was linked with a 'labour test'. This is a legal matter that confuses historians and represents a modern pre-occupation. Put simply, in order to obtain relief the first hurdle faced by a poor person is to demonstrate destitution. If this was due to 'bad' behaviour, such as refusal to work and so on, then that person became subject to a different legal system, that of the criminal law, to be punished as a vagrant. As we shall see, the vagrancy provisions punished those who refused to work or neglected their families, lived a dissipated life and so on. That decision, vagrant or pauper, was highly subjective (see Chapter 8) but legally separates poor law from the treatment of those who 'refused' to work. Paz-Fuchs is reading a modern welfare requirement of 'actively seeking work' into poor law in an inappropriate manner. He subsequently abandons legal techniques to 'read' s. 1 of the 1601 Act, without its 350 years of legal interpretation acknowledging it as the legal foundations of the right to relief of the settled poor. Instead, Paz-Fuchs offers us, s. 1: 'phrased as a duty and not as a right bestowed upon the beneficiaries'.[102]

This example, drawn from the discipline of law, underlines the importance of technical doctrinal law as a fundamental component of historical reconstructions of legal subjects. Although poor law has been repealed, it is not impossible to read it as a legal subject. Undeniably and unfortunately, Paz-Fuchs has grounded his valuable scholarly conceptual and juristic writings within legally inaccurate reconstructions of the legal subject he is discussing. He is not alone in this: such misunderstandings are increasingly distorting modern theoretical conceptions of the current role of welfare in society. At this juncture it is worth noting that, had Paz-Fuchs not included poor law 'history' within his text, that lack would have diminished the scholastic validation increasingly conferred by such reconstructions. However, leaving aside the unfortunate legal account [mis]constructing poor law, the remainder of Paz-Fuchs' study constitutes a subtle, complex theoretical analysis. In summary, and admittedly over-simplifying his account, Paz-Fuchs considers the concepts of social inclusion and the requirements for a normative basis of equality within welfare provision. He theorises that such a project would take into account inter-reactions between the individual and the state and between individuals, a form of social inclusion that represents society as a network.[103] He rejects punitive and negative models (poor law in his interpretation) and argues in terms of responsibilities and reciprocal obligations. In every sense, his starting point is conditioned by that legacy of negative cultural norms inherited from poor law reform and the new poor law. Had Paz-Fuchs understood the legal nature of poor law before and after reform, he might have recognised that elements of his 'theoretical' model have a long legal pedigree. It is to that pedigree we now turn.

Notes

1 For a comprehensive discussion of this, see: Pat Thane, 'Histories of the Welfare State', in William Lamont (ed.) *Historical Controversies and Historians*, London: UCL Press, 1998, p. 58.

2 C.P. Rodgers, 'Humanism, History and the Common Law,' *The Journal of Legal History*, 6, 1985, 129–56, at 137.

3 Theodore Plucknett, *A Concise History of the Common Law*, 5th edn, London: Butterworths, 1956, p. 244.

4 Rodgers, 'Humanism,' p. 138.

5 D.R. Kelly, 'A Rejoinder', *Past and Present*, 72, 1976, p. 143: cited in Rodgers, 'Humanism,' p. 139.

6 Morton J. Horwitz, 'Why is Anglo-American Jurisprudence Unhistorical?' *Oxford Journal of Legal Studies*, 17, 4, 1997, 551–86, at 555.

7 Ibid.

8 Rodgers, 'Humanism,' p. 145.

9 Cited in: Ibid.

10 Grant Gilmore, *The Death of Contract*, Columbia, OH: Ohio State University Press, 1974.

11 For a positivist critique of natural law: H.L.A. Hart, *The Concept of Law*, Oxford: Oxford University Press, 1961.

12 Austin defined the normative issues (concerned with positive morality) as those concerned with questions such as what rights should be recognised within the legal system and should conventional morality be enforced: John Austin *The Province of Jurisprudence Determined*, 1832, reprint, London: Prometheus Books, 2000, p. 11.

13 Austin held the views expressed in (1)–(4): Howard Davies and David Holcroft, *Jurisprudence: Texts and Commentary*, London: Butterworths, 1991, p. 5.

14 A view refuted by Alf Ross, *On Law and Justice*, Berkeley, CA: University of California Press, 1959, pp. 274–80.

15 Jeremy Bentham, *Writings on the Poor Laws*, vol. I, Michael Quinn (ed.), Oxford: Clarendon Press, 2001.

16 Horwitz, 'Anglo-American', p. 582.

17 H. Kelsen, *The Pure Theory of Law*, Berkeley, CA: California University Press, 1967, p. 1.

18   R. Dworkin, *Taking Rights Seriously*, Cambridge, MA: Harvard University Press, 1977.
19   Austin, *Province* and *The Uses of the Study of Jurisprudence* (1832); *The Lectures on Jurisprudence or the Philosophy of Positive Law,* 1863, reprint, London: John Murray, 1920.
20   Kelsen, *Pure Theory.*
21   Horwitz, 'Anglo-American', p. 554.
22   Ibid., p. 561.
23   P.S. Atiyah, *The Rise and Fall of Freedom of Contract*, Oxford: Clarendon Press, 1979, p. 151.
24   H.L.A. Hart (ed.), *Bentham, Of Laws in General,* London: Croom Helm, 1970; Bentham, *Writings on the Poor Laws.*
25   S.E. Finer, 'The Transmission of Benthamite Ideas, 1820–50', cited in A. Brundage, *England's 'Prussian Minister'. Edwin Chadwick and the Politics of Government Growth 1832–1854,* Pittsburg, PA: Pennsylvania State University Press, 1988, pp. 14–15.
26   Thomas Robert Malthus, *An Essay on the Principle of Population and a Summary View of the Principles of Population* 1798, Anthony Flew (ed.), London: Routledge and Sons, 1970, pp. 67–68.
27   J.R. Poynter, *Society and Pauperism. English Ideas on Poor Relief 1795–1834,* London: Routledge and Kegan Paul, 1969, pp. 150–53.
28   Ibid., p. xxi.
29   Alan Harding, *A Social History of English Law*, London: Penguin Books, 1966, pp. 6, 336.
30   Bentham, *Writings on the Poor Laws,* pp. 4, 25.
31   Poynter, *Society and Pauperism*, p. 101.
32   Ibid., p. 124.
33   Michael Lobban, 'Was there a Nineteenth Century "English School of Jurisprudence"?', *Journal of Legal History*, 16, 1995, 34–62.
34   For a full discussion of Bentham's theories: Philip Schofield, 'Jeremy Bentham and Nineteenth Century English Jurisprudence', *Journal of Legal History*, 12, 1, 1991, 58–88.
35   The American welfare system has elements of utility, where the needs of the weak for aid do not outweigh the needs of the rest to be wealthy.
36   Sir Henry Sumner Maine, *Ancient Law*, 10th edn, London: John Murray, 1905.
37   R.C.J. Cocks, *Sir Henry Maine, A Study in Victorian Jurisprudence*, Cambridge: Cambridge University Press, 1988, p.5.
38   See: Ibid.; A.W.B. Simpson, *Leading Cases in the Common Law*, Oxford: Clarendon Press, 1995; on the value of law examined in its historical context: Atiyah, *Rise and Fall*, p. 388; D. Sugarman, 'Writing "Law and Society" Histories', *Modern Law Review*, 55, 1992, 292–308.
39   Horwitz, 'Anglo-American', pp. 567–68.
40   Cocks, *Maine*, p. 59.
41   Maine, *Ancient Law*, p. 151.
42   F.W. Maitland, *Bracton and Azo*, vol. VIII, London: Selden Society, 1884, p. xiv. This was not so of Vinogradoff who believed that Maine's method was valid, provided that generalisations were preceded by a careful study of individual cases: Peter Stein, *Legal Evolution, The Story of an Idea*, Cambridge: Cambridge University Press, 1980, p. 116.
43   Cocks, *Maine*, p. 146.
44   Prof. N. MacCormack, paper presented at the W.G. Hart Legal Workshop, London, July 1984, cited in: Ibid., p. 153.
45   Ibid., p. 192.
46   Ibid., pp. 210–12.
47   Lorie Charlesworth, 'Theory's betrayal of legality, is there no law after Auschwitz? An historical reconstruction that explores how far juristic posturing colludes with negative

political agendas', paper presented at From Human Rights to the Primacy of the Political Conference, University of Lancaster, November 2008.

48 Stein, *Legal Evolution*, p. 89.

49 Horwitz, 'Anglo-American', pp. 552–53.

50 First used as legal authority by Coke in his *Reports*: Rodgers, 'Humanism', p. 139.

51 Gertrude Himmelfarb, *The Idea of Poverty. England in the Early Industrial Age*, London, Faber & Faber, 1984.

52 Horwitz, 'Anglo-American', p. 556.

53 Ibid.

54 PP, 1840, XVI, p. 192: William, C. Lubenow, *The Politics of Government Growth*, Newton Abbott: David & Charles, 1971, p. 66.

55 Richard Hofstadter, *The Paranoid Style in American Politics and Other Essays*, New York: Knopf, 1965, pp. 3–40.

56 Lubenow, *Politics*, p. 67.

57 Paz-Fuchs sources: S. Webb and B. Webb, *English Poor Law History Part I The Old Poor Law*, 1929, reprint, London: Frank Cass and Co., 1963;— *The English Poor Law History Part II The Last Hundred Years*, 1929, reprint, London: Frank Cass and Co., 1963;— *The Public Organisation of the Labour Market: Being Part Two of the Minority Report of the Poor Law Commission*, London: Green and Co.,1909— *English Poor Law Policy*, London: Cass, 1963. Noting this last is a reprint.

58 Oliver MacDonagh, *Early Victorian Government 1830–1870*, London: Weidenfeld & Nicolson, 1977.

59 David Eastwood, *Governing Rural England. Tradition and Transformation in Local Government 1780–1840*, Oxford: Oxford University Press, 1994, pp. 3–4.

60 Lubenow, *Politics*, p. 183.

61 A.V. Dicey, *A Study of the Law of the Constitution*, London: Macmillan and Co. Ltd, 1885, p. 3.

62 Horwitz, 'Anglo-American', p. 571.

63 Ibid., pp. 578–81.

64 David Sugarman, 'The Legal Boundaries of Liberty: Dicey, Liberalism and Legal Science, Review', *Modern Law Review*, 46, 1983, 102–6, at 110.

65 P.P. Craig, 'Dicey: Unitary Self-Correcting Democracy and Public Law', *Law Quarterly Review*, 106, 1990, 105–43, at 106.

66 Ibid., p. 108.

67 Judith Rowbotham, 'Legislating for Your Own Good – Criminalising Moral Choice. The Modern Echoes of the Victorian Vaccination Acts', *Liverpool Law Review* 30, 1, 2009, 13–33.

68 P.P. Craig, *Administrative Law*, 3rd edn, Oxford: Sweet & Maxwell, 1994, pp. 46–47.

69 Source Cabinet Office: *The Independent*, 19 March 2009.

70 D. Roberts, *Victorian Origins of the British Welfare State*, New Haven and London: Yale University Press, 1961, p. 133.

71 *Royal Commission on the Railways*, Minutes of Evidence, (1867): A.H. Manchester, *A Modern Legal History of England and Wales 1750–1950*, London: Butterworths, 1980, p. 153.

72 Craig, 'Dicey,' p. 112.

73 Ibid., p. 114.

74 See *Associated Picture Houses Ltd. v Wednesbury Corporation* (1948) 1KB 223.

75 Craig, 'Dicey', p. 119.

76 Dicey disliked the idea of administrative courts: Ibid., p. 118.

77 Robson, *Justice and Administrative Law*, 1928, cited in: Craig, *Administrative Law*, p. 139.

78 Craig, *Administrative Law*, p. 52.

79 As revealed in comparative studies with Europe: Robert Jutte, *Poverty and Deviance in Early Modern Europe*, Cambridge: Cambridge University Press, 1994.

80 David Sugarman, 'Theory and Practice in Law and History: a Prologue to the Study of the Relationship between Law and Economy', in B. Fryer, A. Hunt, D. McBarnet and B. Moorhouse (eds) *Law, State and Society*, London: Croom Helm, 1981, p. 71. Sugarman echoes the argument of Morton J. Horwitz, 'The Conservative Tradition in the Writing of American Legal History', *American Journal of Legal History*, 7, 1973, 275–94.
81 Morton J. Horwitz, *The Transformation of American Law, 1780–1860*, Cambridge, MA: Harvard University Press, 1977.
82 Ibid., p. 30.
83 P.S. Atiyah, *Law and Modern Society*, 2nd edn, Oxford: Oxford University Press, 1995, pp. 59–60.
84 Atiyah, *Rise and Fall*, p. 388.
85 See, for example, a discussion of the dealing in 'cotton on the spot' in the Liverpool and Bradford wool trades: R.B. Ferguson, 'Commercial Expectation and the Guarantees of the Law, Sale Transactions in the mid Nineteenth Century', in D. Sugarman and G.R. Rubin (eds) *Law, Economy and Society*, London: Butterworths, 1984.
86 Atiyah. *Rise and Fall*, p. 660.
87 *The Guardians of the Hastings Union v The Guardians of Saint James, Clerkenwell* (1865) LR 1QB 38 at 43.
88 *The Guardians of the Poor of the West Derby Union v The Guardians of the Poor of the Atcham Union* (1889) 24 QBD 117 at 121.
89 R.B. Ferguson, 'The Horwitz Thesis and Common Law Discourse in England', *Oxford Journal of Legal Studies*, 3, 1983, 34–57.
90 Sugarman, 'Theory', p. 78.
91 Horwitz, 'Conservative Tradition'.
92 Harding, *Social History*.
93 R.W. Kostal, *Law and English Railway Capitalism 1825–1875*, Oxford: Clarendon Press, 1998.
94 Himmelfarb, *Idea of Poverty*.
95 Cocks, *Maine*, p. 215.
96 Ibid., p. 213.
97 Gilmore, *Death of Contract*.
98 Amir Paz-Fuchs, *Welfare to Work: Conditional Rights in Social Policy*, Oxford: Oxford University Press, 2008.
99 For a full discussion of this development, see: Lorie Charlesworth, 'On Historical Contextualisation: Some Critical Socio-Legal Reflections', *Crimes and Misdemeanors: Exploring Law and Deviance in Historical Perspective*, 1, 1, 2007, 1–40.
100 Paz-Fuchs, *Welfare to Work*, noting that the author refers to the 'Christian Organisation Society' throughout although the title is 'Charity Organisation Society'.
101 Paz-Fuchs incorrectly references this writer's work as 'ambiguous' concerning the legal right to relief: Ibid., pp. 67 nn. 8, 71 and 75.
102 Ibid., p. 67. There are other such legal solecisms; this example may stand for the remainder.
103 Ibid., pp. 172 and 3.

Chapter 3

Socio-legal juristic narratives: poor law's legal foundations

Settlement law: 'has (perhaps) been more profitable to the profession of the Law than any other point in English jurisprudence'.[1]

This chapter reconstructs the legal foundations of poor law taking a long-itudinal perspective in order to recover its 'forgotten' history. For legal scholars who write in and of the present, law is experienced by and familiar to their readers. However, as poor law is an abolished legal subject, this chapter pro-vides a route through the legal sources, statutes, cases and textbooks following the lawyers' technique of tracing the relevant legal authorities chronologically. Unlike current law subjects, there is no introductory text to which the reader can be directed, moreover this reconstruction requires consideration of poor law's common law establishment from the sixteenth century. However, these events did not occur in legal isolation; therefore the following analysis also includes a survey of some earlier ecclesiastical and manorial sources of welfare. In addition, as poor law retains many of those early legal presumptions and 'rules' expressed in statutory form and case law until abolition in 1948, this has required discussion of developments over a broad sweep of time. In con-sequence, this work will focus upon the basic legal principles of poor law, the foundational elements of the Law of Settlement and Removal, and not the vast complexity of the legal doctrines found within that law. Finally, as this work is within the liberal paradigm it constitutes a celebration of the value of a right to relief from poverty for the labouring classes of England and Wales.

In one sense, that long legal history bears witness to welfare's importance structurally in the development of cultural norms in English society. How-ever, the right to relief is more than a liberal ideal, it constitutes a doctrinal black letter right. Consequentially, 'forgetting' denies this foundational legal value in our society. In summary, this chapter suggests that when the early history of the relief of poverty is reconstructed through the lens of law, it reveals the existence of a 'legal economy' of entitlements, duties and obliga-tions hitherto disregarded, marginalised or mis-stated in poor law recon-structions. The chief of these entitlements lies in the legal right of settled poor to be relieved when destitute at the cost of their settlement parish. The corollary to that right lies in the obligation of each parish, township or place that maintains its poor, to raise a poor rate on a demand-led basis in order to fulfil that legal obligation to relieve.

Relief of poverty to the Reformation: state, church and manor

It is evident that relieving the poor in England and Wales has a long history predating the Reformation; a complex system of aid and support provided by a mix of manorial custom and ecclesiastical duty with strictures against those who 'wander about'. Accordingly, one feature of the many poor law legal texts is that they include a statutory account of poor law that begins with legal developments in the fourteenth century. Modern research reveals the relevance of this position; as the Black Death decimated the population of England and Wales during this period, so too law and legal structures underwent upheaval and structural changes.[2] Although the problem of dispossessed, landless vagrants was of primary concern it was also the voluntary movement of the poor away from their homes that concerned the 'state'. A 'system' developed, utilising pre-existing local courts and the offices of the Justices of the Peace, who from 1389 (13 Rich. II St 1 *c.* 7) had the role of regulating wages and fixing prices.[3] Under the terms of an earlier statute (12 Rich. II *c.* 7, 1388), the poor who needed aid were ordered to return to the place where they were born. Thus we see the earliest common law recognition of poor people 'belonging' to a specific, geographic hence ascertainable place. In addition, rather optimistically, one term stipulated that labourers should not leave their residence without permission. Further, by the terms of a 1494 Act (11 Hen. VII *c.* 2) such poor were ordered to repair to the place where they last dwelled, by that of 1503 (19 Hen. VII *c.* 12) to where they were born or had resided for seven years. This narrative, albeit somewhat historicist, underlines that at the time of the Reformation local officials, Justices of the Peace and local courts took an active interest in overseeing the movements of the poor; a matter discussed more fully below. This, however, was simply one of the legal jurisdictions that concerned the poor; discussion of those others briefly follows.

The precise nature of that ecclesiastical aid to the poor is still shrouded in uncertainty. Gratian, in the *Decretum*, set out the canon law authorities for charity and poor relief in about 1140 based upon moral, Christian and charitable principles.[4] The difficulty today is translating those principles into the practicalities of poor relief before the Reformation as Gratian drew on legal sources written between the fourth to the sixth centuries. This anomaly has led to a presumption that no system of apportioning ecclesiastical relief for the poor existed.[5] However, relief for the poor may still be viewed as an essential aspect of ecclesiastical life; evidence for which exists, for example, in a plethora of records concerning local charities.[6] More problematic is the extent of aid for the poor by religious foundations. By way of contrast, in considering the legal history of poor law, especially the marked increase in statutory activity in the sixteenth century, such doubts appear counter-intuitive; particularly as there is considerable contemporary literature concerning the harsh effects of the Reformation upon the poor. Finally, if customary manorial rights alone relieved the poor (see Chapter 4), why did the state intervene so prominently after the Reformation? Fortunately recent research has provided a partial answer. Tierney, in 1958, questioned the accuracy of research into the monastic financial returns in Henry VIII's *Valor Ecclesiasticus*, 1535, which had suggested low expenditure upon aid for the poor.[7] Subsequently, Rushton re-examined the *Valor* returns and other contemporary sources. He concludes that the pre-Reformation ecclesiastical establishments were providing substantial and thus genuinely beneficial poor relief.[8] That reassessment supports a view of poor relief as ancient, complex and multi-jurisdictional representing a pattern of relief embedded within English society.

Furthermore, ecclesiastical participation may supply one explanation for that pervasive and long-lasting normative cultural acceptance that the poor will be relieved. Supporting such an assertion is evidence of early inter-connected legal, spiritual and financial relationships between monastic foundations, churches and manors. To take one such example from Birkenhead on the Wirral; in 1333 the Priory of Birkenhead held, amongst others, the right to operate a ferry across the Mersey, the right to hold a Court for the Manor of Claughton and the living of the parish church of Bidston. There the Priory possessed a granary to receive church and monastic tithes and a house for the monks (both buildings are still in existence).[9] In addition, the Priory ruins still retain the window through which daily doles of food were handed to the local poor. The church at Bidston, as was usual, held charitable gifts of land and money from which to relieve the poverty of local poor. Additionally, such charities were strengthened legally in 1601 and their numbers continued to increase, in a parallel development to the Elizabethan poor law.

These and other characteristics of poor relief, often financially and socially differentiated by historians, constitute part of that great mystery which continues to baffle the modern observer, that of legal jurisdiction. Thus the common law courts dealt with aspects of poverty, as did the ecclesiastical system under monastic rules and religious principles. In addition, Chancery held jurisdiction over matters involving charities. The final legal jurisdiction to be considered here, also retaining welfare responsibilities up to the Reformation and beyond was that of the manor. Manorial courts (Leet and Baron) provided a semi-autonomous local jurisdiction, whose amercements (fines) could be transferred to the Justices and hence the common law system for enforcement. Such matters appear more complex in towns and boroughs, where guilds, parish churches, cathedrals, port moots, borough courts and others held complementary but jurisdictionally differentiated legal responsibilities for, amongst other matters, aid for the destitute. This melange of legal responsibility appears chaotic today and resists any comprehensive description or analysis. However, we must accept that for contemporaries no such problem existed and it was clear where to go for aid, where obligations, rights and duties lay and who was so entitled.

Recent research by J.M. Neeson has emphasised a complex social and economic relationship between post-Reformation poor relief, customary law and manorial tenure.[10] It is therefore not unreasonable to deduce that before and during the Reformation much aid for the poor was received via their local entitlement to customary rights. It is noticeable that much manorial responsibility for supporting and regulating those 'belonging' to the manor later became absorbed into the operation of poor relief. This was as much a result of early manorial enclosure as the imposition of a top-down common law structure. However, where manors remained intact their responsibilities to the poor complemented civil vestries' relief activities. Continuing manorial customary responsibility provides another strand in the explanation why poor law is a last resort, as a 'top up' for many of the destitute. Hence the bafflement that sometimes permeates historians' attempts to define poor law as if it can be detached from this broader legal context. This was law, for manorial law is customary law and customary law is law.[11] In brief, although common law is often described as the custom of the King's Courts, custom also comprises a more localised set of rules.[12] These include the regulations and customs of manorial tenure, customs of individual counties and the customs of cities and towns. In consequence, the local customs of England and Wales regulated much of the daily lives of the population.

It is important to note that local customary courts of manor, fair and borough, upholding local custom and imposing sanctions where necessary, represent a discrete and authoritative legal jurisdiction available to all who reside in, or hold legal rights in those jurisdictions. Loux defines custom as:

> The doctrine by which ancient customs practised by a definite community in a distinct geographical location are recognised by royal judges to constitute local common law for the law and people of the region.[13]

The significance of custom as law lies in that recognition by the Royal Courts and for those who could afford to bring an action, there was also the possibility of common law remedies. However, not all customs could be successfully protected under the common law. Some customary rights were attached to property, others to 'belonging' to a manor, settlement in fact if not in name. Many of those rights were part of the feudal manorial structure of unenclosed land such as gleaning after the harvest, collecting furze, berries and acorns, grazing cattle, cutting turf and so on. Unfortunately, after enclosure many of these rights were forfeit and therefore not transferred to the jurisdiction of the common law courts and thus they were lost to the poor. Otherwise, the common law protected (and protects) custom under a complex process of rules, legal fictions and local evidence. To be enforceable a custom must be ancient, continuous, certain and reasonable. However, disputes over customary property rights would only reach the King's Courts if the right were of sufficient value to be worth litigating and if the litigant were of sufficient substance to bring the action. From a legal perspective, customary aid although forming part of the subsistence regime of the poor, did not include relief payments *per se* and thus technically may not be considered a part of poor law. However, there is evidence that in the eighteenth century manorial courts were still occupying themselves with matters connected to settlement (see p. 106).[14] In consequence despite manorial courts belonging to a different legal jurisdiction from the poor law, customary rights also provided subsistence for the poor that had legal protection.

The Reformation produced many unforeseen political social, economic and legal consequences in England and Wales. Equally, the dissolution of the religious houses ended whatever role they previously played in poor relief. Moreover, having severed connections with Rome, Henry VIII necessarily took a more immediate interest in parish activities which already extended beyond religious duties to include, for example, control of vagrants, maintenance of roads, bridges etc. As a result, those legal measures taken to facilitate the King's new role as Head of the Church in England permitted, necessitated, legitimised and thus created the secular, administrative parish that forms the origins of English local government. In consequence, from a poor law perspective there is much of interest in an examination of the legal history of welfare from c. 1530 to 1601. Reconstructing that past reveals reactive, contingent statutory efforts to deal with the broader problems of poverty as England (and Wales) moved into a post-dissolution world of collapsed ecclesiastical social duties. Incremental change, shifting jurisdictions and establishing reliable sources of revenue characterise the emergence of common law jurisdiction over poor relief. Through such changes, parochial financial responsibility for relief is crystallised into a funding mechanism whose administration is supervised and enforced by the long-established system of local Justices. In tracking these developments below it becomes evident that the Act for the Better Relief of the Poor 1601, and thus the great Elizabethan poor law, emerges from a legal fog of contradictory statutory responses. That Act contains innovative elements, but is also a quasi-codification of 'best practices' intended to solve perceived contemporary failures, anomalies and uncertainties in dealing with poverty.

In short, poor law's legal route to 1601 reveals many facets that remain of interest, not least those questions surrounding enforcement, income and jurisdiction. Remembering too that law is part of each individual's life, the daily experience of those who lived through this turbulent period is equally important. For the reader who wishes to travel that journey, Eamonn Duffy's work provides an illuminating and thorough account of how the inhabitants of one parish experienced some of those changes and interventions 1520–74.[15] However, what follows here is a doctrinal legal narrative which necessarily glosses those social, religious, political and economic changes that influenced and necessitated legal developments. These legal changes began, according to

Richard Burn writing in 1764, with the first 'poor law' statute, the 1531 Act (22 H. 8. *c.* 12).[16] From a legal perspective, the terms of the 1531 Act represent the first link in a causal chain leading to the establishment of poor law as common law in 1601. Its terms authorise Justices to enquire concerning all: 'aged, poor, and impotent persons, which live, or of necessity be compelled to live by alms of charity of the people'. Some of these individuals are to be allowed to beg, some not, but those who are permitted may do so in specified places only. The punishment for breach is imprisonment in the stocks for two days and nights with bread and water and then to be returned to the place where they are authorised to beg.[17]

These themes, of place and permission represent in part a continuation of earlier statutory exhortations concerning vagrants (see Chapter 8). More significantly, one term of that 1531 Act requires that those poor listed above should return to the place they were born or resided for three previous years. This constitutes legal recognition of local responsibility for the poor. It can be argued that it is at this point the relief of poverty has its statutory common law origins, as the terms of the Act set out what are implicitly poor law foundational principles of place, obligation and hence entitlement. (Noting that common law settlement by birth probably has much older origins.) Five years later in 1536 the terms of a further Act (27 H. 8. *c.* 25) attempts to establish how localities are to pay for those returnees and others. This Act is generally, perhaps incorrectly, deemed by historians to be the first occasion on which poor law 'principles' emerge in statutory form. The funding mechanisms set out are weak, enforcement is non-existent, but it is clear (as earlier) that each place must maintain its poor. The terms state that: 'governors and ministers of every such place, shall succour, find and keep every of the same poor people, by way of voluntary and charitable alms', in order to prevent begging: '[O]n pain that every parish in default shall forfeit 20s a month'. The 'mechanism' for ensuring such money is collected is that parochial giving on Sundays, holidays and festival days is to be 'encouraged'.

Duffy's work illuminates the extent to which local priests organise and encourage giving by parishioners, initially for decorating and renewing altars, statues and for other religious giving. Thus the 1536 Act represents a pragmatic solution as it draws upon pre-existing parish culture as its terms instruct clergy to: 'exhort, move, stir' parishioners to give for the relief of the: 'said poor, impotent, decrepit, indigent and needy people'. Further terms of the 1536 Act order that personal giving to the poor is not permitted and that no bread and other sustenance shall be distributed to poor people by the authorities, rather the money is to be put in poor boxes. This indicates an attempt to systemise and control both donors and recipients and end *ad hoc* charitable giving. That theme of increased supervision and control of parishes is also evident in Duffy's account. To that end, collectors of charitable giving must make account of that money to churchwardens, or: 'four of their honest neighbours', some expenses are available from the collection and collectors need serve no more than one year. Excess money is to be used to aid other parishes, but if insufficient funds are collected, officials and others will not be penalised. Finally, books are to be kept in every parish recording how much was collected and to whom it was given. An ecclesiastical continuity at the end states that the terms of the Act shall not be prejudicial to any form of charitable giving or maintenance by monastic and other religious foundations.

It is 11 years before further legislation is passed, in 1547 (1 Ed. 6. *c.* 3). This Act returns to a much earlier theme, the perception of social mobility as a problem. Its terms include that 'mayor, constable, or other head officers' must convey such poor persons to where they were born or resided for three years. This repetition suggests that the terms of those earlier Acts are not being followed or successfully enforced. It does, however, underline the legal presumption of a local duty to support the poor. Two subsequent statutes concern themselves with the children of beggars (3 & 4 Ed. 6. *c.* 16, 1550); with listing the names of all inhabitants including the poor, annually appointing two collectors of 'charitable alms', distributing the same weekly and accounting quarterly (5 & 6 Ed. 6. *c.* 2, 1553). In what now appears a survival from the past yet reflects the contemporary *status quo* of the power of the Church in local parish life, the terms of this latter Act state that those who do not give to the poor will be reported to the bishop. He is directed to send for them and exhort them to mend their ways. As the efficacy of any legislation depends both upon enforcement and financial resources, this last provision indicates a system under strain. However, the bishop represents the likeliest local authority figure with sufficient status to influence parishioners to pay in a still quasi-voluntary relief system. In 1555 the terms of an Act (1 & 2 P. & M. *c.* 5) instruct that collectors are to be appointed after Christmas and that refusal to serve incurs a 'forfeit' of 40s. Further financial strain is apparent as, in a measure to relieve their poor, parishes may now license (and badge) beggars when finances are inadequate.

By the reign of Elizabeth, enforcement is increasingly an issue. The terms of a 1563 Act (5 El. *c.* 3) emphasise the responsibility of collectors to produce accounts; the penalty is that the bishop shall: 'commit them to ward'. In consequence, refusal to give to the poor collection still results in being 'sent' to the bishop. However, and rather more effectively, the bishop is instructed to bind the recalcitrant non-donor in the sum of 10l (pounds) to the Sessions. There, the Justices will assess what sum the individual is able to pay weekly. In addition, should that individual refuse, Justices are granted authority to send them to prison until they pay. It is at this point we see the emergence of the poor rate; not so described but enforceable in the common law courts with a sanction of imprisonment, on the same terms that remain in force today for its modern British descendant the Local Council Tax. However, it appears that bishops are not particularly effective within this system, thus in the terms of a 1573 Act (14. El. *c.* 5) bishops are no longer mentioned and Justices are instructed to administer the system. Now Justices are responsible for listing the poor, for finding a place to 'settle' them if the parish: 'within which they shall be found cannot provide for them'. They are to set a weekly charge for the poor costs, set a weekly tax for inhabitants and appoint collectors and an overseer of the poor for a year. In addition, clearly foreshadowing the later removal procedure, local officials must send those poor not born in their division, not 'conversant' there for three years, back to the place which so qualified, conveyed by cart or horseback from constable to constable. Collectors of rates are to account half yearly, non-payers are to be brought before two Justices and committed to gaol until they pay. Justices are authorised and hence required to appoint officials annually, to raise money from neighbouring parishes where funds are insufficient and hear complaints from aggrieved citizens that the charges were too high. The most notable feature of this Act is a term instructing local Justices to personally perform the administration of poor relief, placing an increased and novel burden upon those officials. It was probably not widely adopted and its failure provides one plausible explanation for the transfer of those duties back to parish officials in 1597, restoring Justices to their original supervisory roles.

It is important to remember that personal charitable giving, as illustrated by Duffy, continued during this period. One example will serve to stand for all; it consists of a bread dole established at Walton on the Hill, Liverpool in 1586. Thomas Berri, a local man who made his money in London, sought to benefit the poor of his birth parish by providing 12-penny loaves every Sunday for the needy. He died in 1601 and left more money in his will to the charity. This charity continues today administered by the Rector and is used to supplement harvest gifts and provide Pot Noodles for the homeless.[18] Numerous such charities were established elsewhere and continued to provide aid to the poor, their operation and legal existence enforced in Chancery, later following equitable rules set out in the preamble and terms of the Charities Act 1601. This charitable dimension continues today under amended legislation and developing case law; it thus constitutes a relief 'quasi-system' co-existing with, but legally differentiated from poor law.

The full emergence of poor law as common law may be technically dated from 1597 via the terms of an Act (39 El. *c.* 3, re-enacted in 1601). It is that later restatement which constitutes the legal authority of all poor relief and welfare in England and Wales until abolition and as noted earlier is so stated in all case law. The terms of the 1597 Act authorise, perhaps instruct is a better description for a version of this was followed for hundreds of years, that the churchwardens of every parish and four: 'substantial householders there ... under the hand of the justices, whereof one to be of the Quorum, dwelling in or near the said parish' shall be called overseers of the poor. Their statutory duties ('with the consent of the justices') comprise: setting children and those with no means to maintain themselves to work; raising a weekly tax from all inhabitants and occupiers of lands in the parish; obtaining a stock of materials to set the poor on work; putting out poor children as apprentices; meeting once a month and preparing annual accounts for the

Justices (default 20s). Furthermore, where a parish could not relieve the poor by its own resources, Justices are authorised to tax other parishes in the Hundred or from the County at Quarter Sessions if necessary. This latter provision has great significance as it authorises a poor law system that is demand led, uncapped financially and hence, both in theory and in law, bound to relieve all who qualify and are in need. In order to achieve these ends, two Justices could issue a warrant for distress for failure to pay the rate and if distress fails then the defaulter is to be sent to prison without bail until payment is made. The same fate awaited churchwardens and overseers who refused to account to the Justices. The young are to be apprenticed, poorhouses to be built and land for the latter to be obtained from and with the consent of the Lord of the Manor, housing at least two poor families in each cottage. In this the statute connects manorial concerns with poor relief. Those who wish to appeal their tax (poor rate) assessment may still do so.

Section 6 of the Act sets out a further point, always implicit but expressed in this form for the first time; that parents and children of the poor: 'being of sufficient ability', have a duty to maintain the same at a rate assessed by the Quarter Sessions at pain to forfeit 20s for every month that they fail to do so. Michael Nolan explains: '[T]he law compelling the maintenance of relations as it is to be administered by justices of the peace depends entirely upon the statue of Elizabeth.'[19] Nolan lists what relations are chargeable, what Orders may be issued and the punishments for disobeying such Orders. In short, this duty to maintain constitutes a fundamental aspect of poor relief. Families retain legal responsibility for the maintenance of other family members and this remains the legal position beyond 1948. Nick Wikely usefully provides a full reconstruction of this legal responsibility and the complexities of its development over time.[20] Thus the family is the first port of call for the destitute and family poverty forms one of the proofs of destitution. In this context, parish officials had a duty to enquire into family circumstances and, as responsible for minimising parish rates, a duty to recover poor relief costs from families if possible. They were not obliged to seize the property of equally poor family members thus forcing them upon the poor rate. Equally, parish officials had a legal duty to seize and sell the property of paupers to defray their relief costs.

This statute may be read partially as innovative but as also combining those successful elements of the previous 50 years, noting that it is the civil rather than ecclesiastical components that endure. There are three points of legal interest. The first is that the obligation by each parish to relieve is 'understood' as in earlier statutes but as a legal presumption and not articulated; it is the financial and administrative issues that are detailed. The second, that who is to be relieved is also 'understood' from the earlier statutes; that is a person born in the parish, or who has resided there for three years, this constitutes recognition of the settlement entitlement that will be more explicitly set out in Chapter 6. It is important to note at this point that the legal authority of those earlier statutes was not cumulative. In the period under discussion, statutes lapsed unless regularly restated. Nevertheless, birth as a qualification for settlement remains both understood, predating all poor law acts as a common law entitlement (see Appendix) and is so understood within the case law until abolition in 1948; residence for three years however was superseded by 1633 (see below). Finally, in its terms this Act clones the ecclesiastical parish as a civil parish as it appoints parish officials to administer the poor law. Thus two discrete legal bodies, each with their own specific functions and responsibilities, co-exist in one parish, comprising the same individuals in the same geographical place.

The terms of the 1601 Act restate all the above but add a number of detailed clarifications that emphasise the civil administrative elements of poor law. However, it is still understood that the parish poor are, must and will be relieved; the terms of this later Act concern administrative practicalities surrounding that relief. Thus the churchwarden and four, three or two others will be annually appointed as overseers of the poor; the rate will be made upon all occupiers, including on tithes, coal mines or saleable woods; the poor who refuse to work will be sent to the house of correction, not the 'common gaol'; poor children are to be apprenticed; cottages built under the terms of the 1597 Act are solely for the poor and impotent of the parish and liable relatives are extended to include grandparents and grandchildren. There is one further matter in line with a legal opinion that vagrancy and poor relief are separate in law (see Chapter 8), the clauses against wandering and begging in the 1597 Act are omitted.[21] In summary, under the terms of the 1601 Act, each (now) secular administrative parish is responsible for raising a poor rate from each resident householder (it is eventually established that this will be based upon the value of the property they occupy) according to local financial need. This rate is set annually taking into account any money in hand and any parish debt outstanding from the previous year's expenses. Parish lands, charities and any other parish income are factored into this total, which is to be presented to and ratified by the Justices at Sessions. To sum up, each person resident in a parish or township has a legal obligation to contribute to the poor rate and failure to pay leads to the distrait of goods and imprisonment until the payments are made in full. Finally, this structure of poor relief administered by local vestries composed of ratepayers, funded by a local demand-led rate and supervised by Justices at Sessions now constitutes the poor law system operating under the common law. Admittedly this 'system' is not yet fully operational, neither does it in any way resemble modern, centrally supervised, welfare bureaucracies. Nevertheless, it contains all the necessary legal and administrative elements that will underpin and provide technical legal authority for the relief of the poor in England and Wales for the next 350 years.

One clarification is required here: what constitutes a parish whose ratepayers must maintain their poor? The term 'parish' itself has legal status within the Law of Settlement and Removal and hence within poor law as its meaning develops via statute and case law. Those definitions were codified in s. 109 of the Poor Law Amendment Act 1834:

> The word "parish" shall be construed to include any parish, city, bor-
> ough, town, township, liberty, precinct, vill, village, hamlet, tithing,
> chapelry, or any other place, or division or district of a place maintaining
> its own poor, whether parochial or extra-parochial.

This convention will be followed within this work. In addition, 'parish'
constitutes a precise geographical location whose boundaries were an ongoing matter of dispute, negotiation and agreement between neighbours.
Those boundaries in some cases may be traced back to Saxon times. Their
importance in settlement entitlement serves as a legal explanation for one
local custom prevalent in England and Wales; that of parishioners 'walking
the parish bounds' once a year to reinforce and affirm parish boundaries. This
custom still continues in some parishes today, generally organised by local
churches as part of Easter or harvest festival celebrations. It is long divorced
from any poor law connection. However, as a cultural survival it is testament
to the power of those social and financial duties and obligations shared by
the ratepayers under the poor law.

It is noticeable that the relief of poverty from 1601 is a legal entitlement
only for those who are settled in a particular geographical place, the parish.
In addition, those individuals and their families may not be sent away from
that place to allow the parish to escape liability. In 1618, the legal interpretation of the 1601 Act is held to be:

> [N]o man to be put out of the towne where he dwelleth ... being
> impotent to be there relieved ... [and] ... such as shall remove or put
> any out or their parish, ... this is against the statute concerning the
> relief of the poor and finable; And if any have been so sent, they may be
> sent back again.[22]

By 1630 it is also accepted that settlement provides personal rights:

> No man is to be put out of the town where he dwelleth, nor to be sent
> to his place of birth or last habitation, but a vagrant rogue. [Lamb,
> *Eirenarch*, 2 vols, London: 1630, Book 2, p. 209 and at the summer
> assize at Cambridge] So it was laid down by Sir Francis Harvey that
> Justices of the Peace, especially out of their session, were not to meddle
> with the removal or settling of any poor, but only of rogues.[23]

Nolan's expert opinion in 1805 concurs; that the origin of parish settlement
is to be referred to the reign of Elizabeth: 'if not to an earlier period'. He notes
that in *Margaret Brown's Case* (1631)[24] it was decided that a new settlement
replaced a settlement acquired by birth and *Suckley v Whitborn* (1649)[25]
established that a parish's obligation to relieve impotent and settled poor
continue not only while they remained in the parish, but also after leaving it

until they became vagrants. Nolan concludes that: 'these two cases go some way to show that before 1662 the poor were entitled to relief in their settlement parish'.[26]

As we will see in Chapter 8 'rogues' constitute those whom parish officials and Justices judge to be subject to the Criminal Law of Vagrancy, a different and still surviving legal process which placed convicted individuals outside the poor law system.[27] This legal process established that some poor people were criminals and not paupers and it always began with a subjective judgement by officials. The parallel criminal justice procedure to which paupers were vulnerable may have assisted and influenced poor law reformers' decision to include the concept of 'undeserving poor' within the new poor law provisions of 1834. In consequence of this legal position, historians who base their denial of the existence of the right to relief upon the recognition that those who 'refused to work' were subjectively excluded from the poor law have misunderstood the legal position. As, indeed, have those who assert that poor relief was 'conditional' upon willingness to work. Rather, it is an inability to work or the absence of any available work for a poor person that remains a fundamental aspect of the proofs of 'destitution'; the pre-requisite for receiving parish aid. As noted in the previous chapter, interpreting this as resembling some aspect of the modern requirement of 'actively seeking work' is an ahistorical solecism. For local officials and Justices who dealt with 'rogues', they were criminals to be sent to prison and not poor people entitled to parish aid. Harvey's Resolution in 1630 reveals that this is understood to be the legal position as he differentiates the legal treatment of settled poor from 'rogues'; those who beg, those who have no 'visible means of support', those who wander and give no good account of themselves.

Although discussions above reveal a prior legal existence, the basic legal authority of parish settlement is codified in the terms of an Act for the Better Relief of the Poor of this Kingdom 1662 (13 & 14 Car. II c. 12); noting that the 1601 Act remains the legal authority for the duty to relieve settled poor. The terms of the 1662 Act spell out the details, that the settled poor of any place are entitled to a share of the poor rate and how settlement is acquired by renting a tenement. The three years' qualification set out in the terms of post-Reformation statutes vanishes in a codification of current legal 'opinion'. Nolan, who wrote the definitive and still the best legal text on settlement law, considers that the first technical definition of lawful settlement entitlement was declared by a Resolution of the Judge of Assize in 1633, which states:

> [T]he law unsettleth none who are lawfully settled, nor permits it to be done by a practice or compulsion; and everyone who is settled as a native, householder, sojourner, an apprentice, or servant for a month at the least, without a just complaint made to remove him or her, shall be held to be settled.[28]

In their turn, the terms of the 1662 Act adopt aspects of that 1633 Resolution for the modes (heads) of gaining settlement but amends the residence
requirement from: 'a month at least', to: '40 days at the least'. The Preamble
to the 1662 Act adopts the tone of those earlier statutes concerned with social
stability, understandable in the Restoration period, to declare its purposes:

> [P]oor people are not restrained from going from one parish to another
> and therefore, do settle themselves in those parishes where there is the
> best stock, the largest commons or wastes to build commons and the
> most woods for them to burn and destroy and when they have consumed
> it then to another parish and at last become rogues and vagabonds to the
> great discouragement of parishes to provide stocks where it is liable to
> be devoured by strangers.

The Preamble explains:

> [B]y reason of some defects in the law concerning the settling of the
> poor, and for want of a due provision of the regulations of relief and
> employment in such parishes or places where they are legally settled ...
> together with the neglect of the faithful execution of such laws and sta-
> tutes as have formerly been made for the ... good of the poor.

In setting out additional and precise methods by which settlement may be
acquired, the terms of this Act once more recognise the legal status of possessing a settlement. It is in this manner that settlement is explicitly
acknowledged as a legal right that is possessed by an individual. Possessing
that right confers entitlement to relief when destitute, paid at the expense of
the ratepayers of that settlement parish. In legal terms, this is a clarification
of that right which is implicit within the terms of the 1601 Act. The chief
provision under s. 1 of the 1662 Act was that any person coming to settle in
a tenement valued at less than £10 per annum was vulnerable to be removed
to their last established place of settlement. These included any person
seeking poor relief and until 1795: 'any person or persons that are likely to
be chargeable to the parish' (see below).[29] This removal is achieved by the
order of any two Justices of the Peace upon a complaint made by the overseers of the poor or churchwardens of any parish, within 40 days of the
pauper arriving. There was a right of appeal to Quarter Sessions by: 'all such
persons who think themselves aggrieved by any such judgement' (s. 3). In
fact and in law, this largely means the other named parish, for although a
poor person could appeal they were unlikely to have the necessary funds. In
addition, there were other complex technical difficulties in bringing such an
action. However, under the authority and terms of the 1662 Act, a formal
legal process evolved for asking and answering the settlement questions. This
was based upon a fundamental legal presumption that every person born in

England and Wales possesses a settlement somewhere (*R v All Saints, Derby*).[30]

As noted earlier, in its earliest form settlement was acquired simply through birth or residence. However, gaining and proving a legal settlement became an increasingly technical matter. This law continued to evolve from those terms both introduced and 'understood' in the 1662 Act, via further amending statutes and case law, to become extremely complex and a major source of contemporary lawyers' incomes. The proportion and volume of income generated by settlement issues was equivalent to that earned from British criminal law practice until recently. In 1888, Montague wrote of the volume of legal material settlement law had produced:

> [T]he statutes relating to the subject are more than thirty in number and their number gives no measure of their difficulty ... new law is frequently grafted on the old without repealing the old, so that it becomes difficult even for a lawyer ... to know what the law really is. But the statutes are a trifle to the case law. The cases indexed under the heads of settlement and removal in the latest index of Fisher's Digest occupies one hundred columns. More than five hundred pages of Burn's Justices are filled with them.[31]

In order to arrive at this monolithic status, a multitude of legal 'rules' and principles attached to settlement, which as a legal subject became defined as the 'Law of Settlement and Removal'. Amongst the most important of these are that the term settlement meant:

> [A] permanent right to take the benefit of the poor laws in a particular parish or place which maintains its own poor. A settlement is not for-feitable, and may be communicated from person to person. It ceases and is destroyed in the parish or place where it once existed upon the acquisition of a settlement in any other parish or place.[32] [Therefore] a person cannot have two settlements' (*R v Knaresborough*).[33] ... Prima facie every English-born subject has a settlement, and that settlement is the place of birth ... (unless) displaced by any other settlement (*R v All Saints, Derby*).[34]

In summary, settlement conferred legal status and an individual could only be settled in one specific geographical place. The acquisition of settled status elsewhere automatically destroyed the previous settlement and the responsi-bility for maintaining that pauper then lay with that new settlement parish.[35] Any person could exchange their place of settlement for another via the qua-lifying rules for each head of settlement (see Appendix).[36] A married woman acquired her husband's settlement upon marriage and lost her previous set-tlement unless her husband possessed no settlement at all (unsettled) and then, subject to some technical caveats in a rare legal exception, should he die she may be deemed to have recovered her earlier settlement.[37] A family's settlement always followed the father's settlement and thus they were removed as a unit by one legal action, although it became a requirement that the name and age of each member so removed should appear upon the face of the Order.[38] Individuals who had qualifying status acquired a settlement wherever they resided. Anyone, including the 'better sort' could be removed by legal process if they became destitute and had not acquired a settlement in the removing parish.[39]

Common law developments

The two statutes of 1601 and 1662 remained the primary legal authority underpinning all poor law activity in England and Wales until 1948 and 1930 respectively. (In reality, the 1930 Act restated the provisions.) However, much subsequent legislation amended, added, clarified and enforced aspects of settlement law and the duties, responsibilities and liabilities of vestries, paupers, ratepayers and Justices in poor law matters. These and the developing case law are too numerous to cover in full. The interested reader might look at contemporary commentators and legal texts in the bibliography for a full overview of all aspects of poor law's doctrinal past. These clarify that the legal authority of the 1601 Act remained intact during the Civil War period (c. 1640–60). In consequence, even though for other matters this period was characterised by a collapse of central control, poor relief continued, supervised by local magistrates and administered according to local needs by parish authorities. Much of the following is drawn from research published by Joanna Innes.[40] She notes that High Court judges sitting in London heard cases from all over the kingdom and twice a year travelled the country as Circuit Judges on the Assize Circuit. As today, it is probable that lawyers, officials, local Justices and Circuit Judges socialised and thereby consolidated a congruence of legal processes. This relationship represented and still represents an institutional link between central government and the localities.[41] Innes has uncovered evidence from the seventeenth century that Circuit Judges brought pressure upon magistrates to ensure that they implemented legislation.[42] Although most of the examples she cites are drawn from criminal procedure and trials, this does not invalidate the application of her argument to settlement law. These same legal personalities would also hear settlement litigation and such an institutional link goes far to account for both the continued adherence to law and procedure during the seventeenth century and the development of what looks like a remarkably consistent national picture of settlement operation when the legal cases are reviewed.

However, that homogenous picture should not mask the reality (permitted under the legal umbrella) of much local variation in relief practices throughout the seventeenth and eighteenth century and beyond. Very differing circumstances led local officials to cope with local paupers on *an ad* hoc basis. These measures included variously wages, assistance for large families, provision of housing, apprenticeships for pauper children and extra payments as an allowance system to top up depressed wages. This payment of a wage supplement, 150 years later in 1795, achieved notoriety as the Speenhamland System in Berkshire, where the magistrates met to introduce a system of top up wage allowances paid on a sliding scale according to family size, varying with the price of bread.[43]

Yet all the while, despite contemporary and some modern allegations of the restrictions on movement 'imposed' by the Law of Settlement and Removal, the population of eighteenth and nineteenth century England and Wales was remarkable for its mobility. This constitutes empirical evidence that the right to remove was not always exercised by all parishes, or at all opportunities.[44] A manufacturing town might not remove non-settled poor during slumps to ensure that a labour supply would be available when trade picked up. The expense of litigation itself was discouraging; costs could escalate as parishes appealed removal decisions.[45] However, without detailing the shifts and changes in English society over the period 1601 to 1834 and beyond, it is apparent that much poor relief was needed and given throughout this period to support the old, infirm and indigent. In times of economic crisis, the poor law system processed a large proportion of the labouring population and this system consisted of the operation of poor law administration by each legally autonomous parish in England and Wales.

A poor person's legal right to relief

In order to access aid, a poor person would approach a parish official, usually but not exclusively the overseer, to request aid. The first legal requirement was to demonstrate that they were destitute. Satisfying this requirement lay within the judgement of individual officials; although relief could be given as an emergency measure. However, if the poor person possessed a settlement in the parish, no matter what the official decided, that parish had a legal obligation to relieve the poor person when destitute: 'The Parish Offices are under a legal obligation to relieve and support their poor ... without an Order obtained for this purpose' (*Hayes v Bryant*).[46] However if relief is refused then the Justices: 'may make an Order to compel them ... where the officers have improperly refused to relieve'.[47] Such an Order could be obtained by a poor person upon personal application to the Justices, thus allowing an individual a more formal opportunity to demonstrate their destitution.[48] This is not an appeals procedure, on the contrary it represents a long-standing personal right that was eventually given a procedural formality in the terms of an Act in 1714 (1 Geo. I ss. 1, 2). These clarified that the signed Order was to declare that x of parish y:

maketh oath that he is very poor and impotent, and not able to provide for himself and his family and that on – last he did apply to the parishioners of the said parish ... (or to two overseers of the poor): and was by them refused to be relieved.[49]

Parish officials are now bound to assist the pauper and obey the magistrate's Order, failure to do so is contempt of court and the overseer incurs a personal liability. Cranston cites three eighteenth century cases where local vestries appealed against these Orders to King's Bench, in the earlier two cases the Orders were quashed.[50] However, in 1780 *R v North Shields* established that poor law authorities could not appeal from a Justices' Order because: 'the poor person might starve while the cause was in suspense'.[51] For the most part, these applications for Orders to relieve were made to the Justices at Sessions and over time a 'system' of applications in writing developed, often carefully crafted using 'experts' to draft the letters. These developed into varying *ad hoc* local practices and many of these letters survive to be a valuable source for historians. Jonathan Healey has produced an illuminating case study of one pauper's ongoing attempts to obtain relief by application to Lancashire Quarter Sessions 1701–6. As has become the convention in such studies (see Chapter 4) the legal context is omitted and the procedures are reconstructed in terms of the 'politics of poor relief' and the 'politics of survival'.[52] However, Healey's work illustrates how such applications were experienced by paupers, how Justices oversaw local relief by parish officials and the high level of parochial (and legal) autonomy in the manner and amounts such relief was given. It is also worth mentioning that a poor person did not have to apply for relief at Sessions, or in writing. He or she could do so at the Justice's home or on the hunting field, although this may not have been sympathetically received.

The courts and Parliament refined procedures concerning the enforcement of the right to relief. The terms of an Act of 1714 (1 Geo. I ss. 1, 2) clarify that: '[T]he pauper must be relieved while in a state of destitution in the parish where he happens to be whether it is his parish of settlement or not.'[53] In 1803 it was established in *R v Eastbourne (Inhabitants)* that foreigners were entitled to relief wherever they became destitute. This case contains the following striking anti-positivist statement decision by Lord Ellenborough:

> As to there being no obligation for maintaining poor foreigners before the statutes ascertaining the different methods of acquiring settlements, the law of humanity, which is anterior to all positive laws, obliges us to afford them relief, to save them from starving.[54]

In addition, this legal obligation to maintain the settled poor forms the legal authority for sanctions to which parish officials were subject for breach and/or neglect of duty. Many of these concern the bureaucratic elements of poor law administration, the timing and regularity of parish meetings, preparing accounts and so on; others concern relief payments. In this context, s.2 of the 1601 Act states that officials who are negligent in office or fail to execute Orders made by or with the assent of Justices are liable to a 'forfeit' of 20s.[55] Section 5 of the 1662 Act set a penalty of £5 from the overseers to be levied for the use of the poor should they refuse to receive a person removed by Justices' warrant. Nolan discusses an extensive case law developed from the statutes to underline that relief is a legal obligation both to the poor and the ratepayers: 'If an overseer, therefore, does not provide for the poor; and if he shall relieve when there is no necessity for it, this is a misdemeanour' (*Tawney's Case*).[56] Equally, parish officers are to be protected in the discharge of their duties; from 1601 complaints against officials acting under the authority of the Act which are found for the official or non-suited will result in awards of treble damages and costs against the complainant.[57] However, apart from actions for the unlawful removal of pregnant unmarried women which have attracted some scholarly attention, this subject has not been researched in great detail by historians. Thus this is conjecture, but it may be that potential punitive damages for failed challenges discouraged actions against parish officials by fellow ratepayers.

In conclusion, whatever disadvantages and complexities emerged from the operation of settlement rules, the fundamental entitlement to poor relief in times of hardship remained and could not be denied. As we shall see below, this remains the legal position after 1834 even if the methods of relief drastically changed. The terms of the 1834 Act expressly prohibited Justices of the Peace from ordering relief to any person. The Justices continued to possess authority to order the relieving officers to provide medical relief or relief in kind in cases of illness or of sudden necessity even for non settled poor. If the relieving officer failed to do so he was personally liable to a fine not exceeding £5. If death resulted from the failure to give relief, the relieving officer could be indicted for manslaughter.[58] In the light of all these continuing legal rights, duties and obligations it is not surprising that the first question a responsible parish official was duty bound to ask was: Does this person possess a settlement here?

Legal rules and procedures of the Law of Settlement and Removal

As noted above, the terms of the 1662 Act restrict Justices' authority to remove non-settled poor people to a period within 40 days of an individual's arrival at a new parish. In consequence, anyone who remained undetected and thus not removed during that period acquired a settlement. This caused various difficulties and certainly favoured the poor. To resolve this situation, the terms of a 1685 Act (1 Jac. II *c*. 17) introduced a qualification to this term. From this date, the 40 days were to be calculated from the time notice was given to the parish officers of a poor person's place of abode and the

number of his or her family. From 1701 (3 Will. III *c.* 11) notice of residence was to be reckoned from the date of the publication of that notice in
the parish church. These terms reveal a legislative reluctance to extend poor
law rights to strangers and reinforce parochial consent as the basis for this
head of settlement.

Any pauper could forestall a Removal Order if he or she gave security in a
bond (often for substantial sums of money) that the Justices found sufficient
to discharge the new parish of any prospective liability. In addition, s. 3 of
the 1601 Act confirmed a scheme for certificates to be issued by minister,
churchwarden or overseer of the poor. Possession of this document permitted
individuals to work in other parishes without fear of removal. However, a
certificate could only be granted at the discretion of officials from the settlement parish. Originally, a certificate guaranteed to a named parish that a
named settlement parish accepted responsibility for an individual (and their
family) should they become destitute. This system, which allowed seasonal
movement of the poor under the authority of some form of documentation,
certainly predated the 1601 Act. However, the variety of practices that
emerged stimulated further legislation. Section 3 of the 1662 Act allowed
the seasonal movement of harvesters and this was supplemented by the terms
of an Act of 1697 (8 & 9 Will. III *c.* 30). These state that a certificate is to
be signed by the overseers of the poor or, if none and no churchwardens, it is
to be attested by two creditable witnesses. In addition, when issued and
supported by two Justices of the Peace any parish must accept such a certificate. The bearer of the certificate and his or her family may not be removed,
technically they are 'irremovable' until chargeable to (they request relief
from) this new parish.

Although this certificate protects the poor person from removal, coextensive
with that protection is that party's inability to acquire a settlement under
that certificate.[59] Ethel Hampson examined certification in detail and her
research reveals the legal difficulties faced by certificated paupers who were
effectively barred from obtaining a new settlement. Thus a widow, who had
spent 44 years in the parish of St. Bene't [sic], upon the death of her husband
in 1744, a 'certificate man', was removed to his and therefore her parish of
legal settlement.[60] The terms of an Act of 1691 (3 Will. & Mary *c.* 11 s. 5)
tempered this harshness by allowing a certificated person to acquire a settlement, but only through holding public office, paying taxes or completing an
apprenticeship to a master possessing a settlement in that parish. Early certificates seem to have been issued mainly to productive individuals and consist
of a statement by parish authorities that *x* possesses a settlement in their
parish. The legal significance of these certificates was to avert removal, as
prior to 1795 non-settled poor were subject to removal upon the grounds that
they were: 'likely to be chargeable'. This intensively subjective criterion was
initially a judgement call by overseers, who might then initiate the removal
process of inquiry, establishing the settlement parish and so on. This

subjectivity was noted by legal commentators; thus in 1742 Michael Dalton comments that the words 'likely to be chargeable' gave officials too great discretion to look into the livelihoods of those:

> who have done no wrong. A man without his offence is deprived of his natural liberty, upon a possibility remote enough, may be made a beggar and a prisoner, at the same time deprived of the company of friends, and relatives, choice of air and place of trade.[61]

The possession of a certificate protected the holder from this process. In addition, there is evidence that certification in Cambridgeshire may have been linked to the custom, established by the eighteenth century, of paying relief to paupers in alien parishes in order to forestall their removal and hence their return.[62]

The issuing and use of certificates resulted in extensive case law. Examples include: that a certificate was technically only valid under the statute when delivered (*Rex v Wensley*);[63] and that it did not need to be directed to any particular parish (*Rex v Lillington*).[64] However, any evidence of an attempt by a named pauper to obtain settlement in a third parish by moving to and residing there, or if they returned to the certificating parish for two years, determined (invalidated) the certificate (*Rex v Newington*).[65] These and other cases underline that the settlement parish is the central legal authority concerned in the certificate and not the pauper. A certificate was often issued for a specific place and it was not a ticket to travel, even where some parishes issued open certificates containing no destination.[66] Close readings of these certificates reveal their official legal status, many are both authorised and issued by two Justices of the Peace. In addition, all Justices retained discretionary powers either to refuse or to allow a certificate.[67] This reflects the legal reality that no authority existed under the statutes or at common law to oblige certificates to be issued (*Rex v St Ives*).[68] Furthermore, until 1795 a settlement parish bore the legal and other costs if their certificated labourers applied for relief and thus were removed from that other parish. In consequence, it was not financially prudent for a parish to issue certificates to the halt, the sick and the lame. However, no parish possessed legal authority to make their settled poor remain; all such authority in this matter concerns the removal of non-settled poor and the issuing of certificates to those settled. More to the point, should the 'dubious elements' amongst the labouring poor leave to find work without certificates there would be the possibility of their surviving elsewhere. In such cases at least, the risk of their upkeep would be temporarily removed. Thus, theoretically, a financially prudent parish might issue certificates to their 'respectable' poor whilst rigorously concentrating upon removing non-certificated non-settled individuals. This assumes a vestry 'of one mind', that is a 'close' parish, with a few landowners who are able to limit newcomers as tenants and lodgers in order to keep down poor law costs.

Finally, such a place would usually lack that developing commerce or industry which requires an increased labour force.

For these and other economic and social reasons, by 1795 the system of certificates was considered to be 'failing' and an Act was passed in that year, whose terms had great significance for parochial decision-making. The Preamble to that 1795 Act explains that the 1662 Act had defects:

> which prevented industrious poor people, chargeable to the parish ... merely from want of work there ... are for the most part compelled to live in their old parishes and are not permitted to inhabit elsewhere, under pretence that they are likely to become chargeable to the parish ... into which they go for the purpose of getting employment.

The Preamble adds that Acts of 1696–98 had proved ineffective in operation. Section 1, the most important term of the 1795 Act, rendered a non-settled individual irremovable until actually chargeable to a parish; that is, they asked for poor relief.[69] Previously, only a person residing outside his or her settlement parish under the authority of a certificate was irremovable at common law. He or she could only acquire a settlement under the statute of 1691 (see Appendix), but could not be removed unless they sought relief. Irremovable meant not settled, but not able to be removed: s. 1 placed all the poor into this position (*Great Bedwin v Wilcot*).[70] The terms of this Act state that the non-settled poor (except pregnant unmarried women) could no longer be removed to their parish of settlement on the grounds they were: 'likely to be chargeable', but only when they actually sought relief.[71] This removed one major cause of litigation between parishes and, in addition, the primary legal reason for certification. There is, however, considerable evidence in local studies that certificates continued to be issued by Justices after this date.[72] It may be that many parishes continue to demand these certificates and the fact of their continuation demonstrates both the strength of traditional practices and the administrative autonomy of local parishes.

There is much debate amongst historians as to how many certificates survive today. One indication that many have been lost is the widely attested mobility of the population in eighteenth and nineteenth century England; there really ought to be more certificates. However, parishes had discretion whether to require the production of certificates, whether to keep them in the parish chest or to leave them with the pauper. As a result, many still exist in their descendants' hands, a great treasure for family historians. For legal reasons some certificates were retained by families throughout the nineteenth century, valued as proof of derivative settlement (inherited down the generations) as methods of obtaining a new settlement became increasingly limited for the labouring classes. However, all the various uses to which certificates could be put were intimately connected with settlement and hence removal. In addition, the 1795 Act made one significant change to funding mechanisms; liability for paying the costs of transporting non-settled poor to their settlement parish was transferred onto the poor rate of the removing parish. This was an innovative departure, which ensured that removal attempts always entailed costs to the removing parish. In its way, this might be understood as a legislative attempt to encourage parishes to allow a little tolerance to the labouring classes permitting increased mobility.

In legal terms, however, a Removal Order from the Justices was not necessarily the end of the story for a parish. A term of the 1662 Act allowed the receiving parish to appeal against that Order. Soon after, in 1669, an appeal case (*R v Inhabitants of Rislip*) established a fundamental rule of settlement cases, that confirmation of an Order for removal was conclusive against the entire world that a pauper was settled in the parish to which he or she was ordered to be removed and that they were entitled to poor relief from that parish.[73] Thus the primary motive for establishing a poor person's settlement is to determine who is legally liable for their relief. In consequence, once clarified in statute after 1662 that each parish is bound to support its own poor, any non-settled poor person was vulnerable to be sent back to their settlement parish. Under the general legal authority of the 1662 Act a basic technique evolved for asking and answering settlement questions based upon that fundamental legal presumption noted above, that every person born in England and Wales possessed a settlement somewhere.

In that context the process of inquiry developed; churchwardens or overseers would enquire into the status of new arrivals to their parish or townships. Prior to 1795, they would ascertain those who were unlikely to qualify for settlement available by the various current means, those holding certificates guaranteeing a settlement in their parish of origin and the financially solid. The last two groups would remain unmolested and the parish had the discretion to grant members of the first group temporary residence if they were not settled, but still begin the formal settlement inquiry to check their status. This involved a settlement examination by warrant, under oath, before two Justices. Any poor person could at this stage produce or procure a certificate or indemnity from his or her settled parish to give security to the examining parish. Failure to produce or obtain a certificate could lead to the poor person once again being brought before two Justices under warrant at the Petty Sessions, examined under oath in a removal hearing and a Removal Order might be issued (or at yet another subsequent hearing) to a named parish where their settlement is established. If so, that poor person and family were liable to immediate removal (pre-1795) at the expense of the receiving parish. The receiving parish could appeal against this decision to the Quarter Sessions only upon the grounds that the poor person possessed no legal settlement in their parish, or that there was a procedural fault in the removal process. The legal issues thus raised could be litigated to the highest level. If a poor person became actually chargeable to the parish (now technically a pauper) the settlement inquiry and the removal process were available under the terms of the 1662 Act. If no settlement could be proved then it was deemed to be where the pauper was born. If that was outside England and Wales then he or she could only acquire settlement under the terms of the 1601 Act. If that place was not ascertainable then the default position was finally established in 1803, that a non-settled pauper (usually a foreigner) must be relieved where they were (*R v Eastbourne, Inhabitants*).[74] This case gave effect to what was widely accepted as the rule in an emergency, although some parishes had refused aid for fear of setting up a legal presumption such a pauper possessed a settlement (settlement by estoppel).

This chapter does not consider both local and other Acts passed during this period concerned largely with the technicalities of poor law administration, particularly those authorising the combination of parishes into single administrative units and the establishment of Select (i.e. elected) Vestries. Aspects of these will be considered in later chapters and do not concern the fundamental poor law doctrines discussed here. Those doctrines are evidenced by an emphasis upon settlement within the wording of the statutes founded upon legal presumptions underpinning that law; that is the legal obligation to relieve and its corollary, the personal common law right to relief of those who possess a settlement. This legal position continues as subsequent statutes refine and add to the heads of settlement (set out in the Appendix). An Act of 1696 (8 & 9 Will. III *c*. 30 s. 6) formalised where appeals could be heard; terms included in an Act of 1722 (9 Geo. I *c*. 7 s. 5) amended certain technical aspects of settlement.[75] These amendments were introduced because, although much of the legal argument in the cases centred around the power to remove, the greater number of appeal cases concerned technical procedural matters of removal; for example, the numbers of Justices needed to be present, what constituted admissible evidence and so on.[76] The terms of The Quarter Sessions Act 1731 represent an attempt to remove some of the problems caused by these technical errors especially in those judgements concerning Orders, which, upon appeal to the Quarter Sessions, had been quashed for that reason.[77] This Act permitted Justices of the Peace at General or Quarter Sessions to rectify and amend any defects of form. Local practice would not always have been technically precise and these Acts provide a solution to those tensions inherent in a poor law system where vagaries of local practice needed to be harmonised with the formalities of precedent and legal procedures.

The Law of Settlement and Removal from 1795

Nevertheless, prior to and after 1795 it remained a fundamental tenet of the rules of settlement that if an individual resides in a parish where they do not possess a settlement and subsequently applies for poor relief, they are liable to be removed to their place of settlement by operation of legal process. That formal removal process remained unaltered in 1795. The terms of the 1795 Act did not repeal earlier statutes concerning certificates or the case law; they added a requirement of 'chargeable' to the preconditions of the removal process. The Poor Settlement and Removal Act 1809 allowed the suspension of a Removal Order by reason of illness or injury. The terms of the Poor Relief Act 1814 contain a provision that any illegitimate child born in the poor house took the settlement of his or her mother, this introduces one legal exception to the rule that such a child took his or her settlement where they were born. These amendments somewhat liberalised the legal operation of settlement law, in summary placing all the poor except pregnant unmarried women in the position formerly occupied by those who held certificates.

Escalating costs ensured that poor law reform became an increasing priority for Parliament in the early nineteenth century. In 1817 a Select Committee met to consider the poor laws, taking a critical view of settlement.[78] By this point in time, the expenses of settlement litigation, especially appeals between 1776 and 1815, show a rate of increase greater than that increase in sums expended in poor relief during this period.[79] The Committee examined contemporary settlement entitlement and its possible effects but came to no conclusions. Its deliberations were followed by a series of bills to reform settlement law introduced into Parliament between 1819 and 1832. Some, like Thomas Wood's of 1822, aimed for total abolition. Despite the Royal Commission's inquiry and the resulting *Poor Law Report* of 1834, which recommended the simplification of settlement entitlement to birth alone, settlement was not repealed. The technical system of giving notice of removal and appealing removals was 'improved' and after 1834 poor law guardians could apply to make the union the district of settlement if they so consented.[80] In spite of this, pauper removals continued after the Act and it was estimated that in 1840, 11,000 Removal Orders were issued in England and Wales; in 1849, 13,867 Orders; in 1856, 6,000 Orders and in 1867, 4,600 Orders.[81]

This work is primarily concerned with the 'forgotten' aspects of welfare's past: settlement and the right to relief. As academic historians have produced many valuable and rich texts reconstructing the politics, implementation and social consequence of the terms of the Poor Law Amendment Act 1834, including the significance of political theorists within the 'modernising' Whig government, the author directs the reader to such texts in the bibliography. The following section concentrates rather upon those aspects of reform that directly impinged upon the legal rights of the poor. For the poor themselves, the terms of the 1834 Act had one major effect; that is the manner in which the relief to which they were entitled was to be provided for all. The draconian sections of the Act declare that the able-bodied poor may only be relieved in a workhouse in regimented, prison-like conditions. This was accompanied by the abolition of a pauper's right to seek an Order from a Justice ordering the payment of poor relief; in future Justices may only order relief in kind and medical aid and these solely in an emergency (s. 54). This section did not abolish the right to relief for the settled poor, as that constitutes the legal foundations of and explanation for poor relief provision. If relief must be given, as indeed it must, then this new poor law system was intended to control the manner of that relief, to move its control away from the localities and introduce 'discipline' and 'efficiency' by grafting elements of bureaucratic proto-modernism onto a quasi-medieval survival.

It is difficult to imagine how great a loss these reforms represented to the poor; however there is sufficient evidence of poor law protest and resistance to show that they were resented (see Chapter 9). It was perhaps not quite so intended, but settlement reforms over time relegated the role of settlement law to an economic cost-allocation mechanism. Moreover, those reforms ensured that destitution became a route into the new union workhouses for many. However, the legal position is more complex. Localism, both in its own right and as an expression of Tory objections to the Whig new poor law, added a potent element to the mix. That spirit of localism still dominated vestry poor law activity and therefore the new system sometimes struggled to assert itself fully across England and Wales.

Deconstructing the Poor Law Amendment Act 1834: text v reality

Reading the 1834 Act produces the impression of a firm, decisive, authoritative, almost modern Act of Parliament. Of course, the language has its archaic elements, nevertheless its 109 sections, including an interpretation section (s. 109), is of a type and form anticipating the detailed legislation of the modern bureaucratic state. Such proto-modernisms include: the setting up of a central quasi-government authority (the Poor Law Commissioners) who report to one of the Principal Secretaries of State (ss. 1–4 and s. 5); appointments of full-time salaried officials in London and the localities (s. 9); nine Assistant Commissioners to carry out the terms of the Act (s. 7) with the delegated powers and authority of the Commissioners (s. 12) and an extraordinarily broad authority over poor law matters. Section 12 also states that those Assistant Commissioners are empowered to summon and question upon oath, which they are authorised to administer: 'such Persons as they may think necessary ... upon any Question or Matter relating to the Poor or their Relief'.

As is well known, under the terms of the Act all parishes in England and Wales are 'instructed' to join together into Poor Law Unions, usually based upon the County sub-divisions of the Hundreds. Each union is further instructed to build a workhouse to house their able-bodied poor; each Union is to be run by a Board of Guardians with members elected from each of the Union parishes and so on. The Poor Law Commissioners in London (later the Poor Law Board in 1847 and the Local Government Board from 1871) via their staff of clerks and inspectors (Assistant Commissioners) are to supervise and authorise all these matters. The terms of the Act set out some of the details of that process. Under instructions from the Commission, pauper inmates are divided into eight classes, males physically separated from females, husbands from wives, children from parents and all are to live a regimented, prison-type regime with fixed dietary, clothing and discipline as 'less eligibility' in practice meant a regimented life. Every detail of work-house life is to be reported, confirmed, audited, authorised and recorded through the central bureaucracy in London, supervised locally by the Assis-tant Commissioners. Once in force, these procedures generated tons of official records; some held today in Local Record Offices, the central records are now at the National Archives, Kew, London where currently there is a project to make them available online. However, a literal reading of the statute as if it represents a true record of change is misleading. The point is not just that so many sections were only slowly put into effect, but rather that many were difficult to enforce and some of the terms were never fully achieved. This space between intention and result stands out clearly in archival reconstruc-tions of the development of the new poor law, revealing a long and complex history of resistance, negotiation, 'disobedience' and eventually compliance.

In spite of this, the juristic significance of this Act for legal historians is that it constitutes the first 'effective' technical administrative bureaucratic legislation in English law, for many of those grand purposes of centralisation and bureau-cratic control over poor law in England and Wales were eventually achieved. In turn, its successful innovations influenced the subsequent administrative direc-tion of English public law. One of the 1834 Act's modern qualities is in those terms of the Act that authorise the Commission to create delegated legislation (s. 15, ss. 42–3) with supervisory mechanisms and punishments for failing to obey those Orders. With this legal development, common law poor law begins its mutation into public law welfare and the personal common law rights of the poor practically and jurisprudentially are slowly submerged under bureaucratic decision-making processes. In this juristic shift, poor relief as a legal obligation between fellow parishioners eventually elides into the modern public law rela-tionship between individuals and the state. Similarly, unpaid poor law officials operating at a local level transform into salaried agents of the modern bureau-cratic state; but not quite yet. As we shall see in Chapters 5 and 9, the poor were well aware of their rights and their losses: they and political opponents resisted this 'new' poor law. In addition, local vestries especially in the North of England operated around the margins of the Act to exploit continuing ele-ments of their legal autonomy. However, centralising forces were powerful. The terms of the Act provided some 'national' funding mechanisms (money would be lent to build Union workhouses), inspections and controls. Its terms also state that the Commission has 'authority' over all poor law matters. However, in reality this could not be so; the basic funding for all poor relief remained as before. Each parish or vestry in England and Wales paid for its settled paupers whether in or out of the workhouse. In addition, each parish was still required to account to its own ratepayers for poor law expenditure and have those accounts annually verified by local Justices. Moreover, the Act explicitly recognises those personal legal connections of rights, duties and obligations between settled paupers and parish, for it states that neither Commissioners nor Assistant Commissioners: 'shall interfere in any individual Case for the Purpose of ordering Relief' (s. 15). Consequently, in the absence of actual fraud, parishes could still spend as much as they liked how they liked; their legal responsibility *de minimus* is to relieve their settled poor under the continuing authority of the 1601 Act. Nothing in the 1834 Act changes this fundamental legal 'rule'.

Contemporary legal texts demonstrate that lawyers understood the juridical nature of the relationship between settlement and the right to relief. However, the reformers of 1834 had no interest in emphasising the existence of legal rights when any reform must overcome the resistance of the localities. Crucially, poor relief ceased to be a 'right' in the worldview of political economists who believed that the marketplace recognised neither rights nor obligations. This, of course, is not true of the commercial contracts of the period, which contained many traditional rights and obligations.[82] It is noticeable that the *Poor Law Report* of 1834 refers to contracts in a world of capital, land and labour, where an individual's share of each was determined by supply and demand.[83] In spite of this, the new poor law places the poor outside that commercial world as outcasts (a different reading from Paz-Fuchs' assertion, see Chapter 2). From their perspective, in 1834 the able-bodied labouring poor were deprived of their rightful legal, cultural and social position in the world. If they now required aid that might only be available in the new Bastilles. This shift of status, from rights to control, was achieved through a process whereby economic pressures, combined with new theories of law, developed in a society where the poor possessed few democratic rights (many did not qualify for the voting franchise under the 1832 Act; no women could vote) and the common law was increasingly regarded as reactionary and outmoded. Poor law reform in 1834 can be perceived as a triumph of parliamentary sovereignty over traditional rights, a feature of emergent modernism.

Settlement reform in an administrative context

Nonetheless, in spite of reformers' intentions, the terms of the 1834 Act left settlement unrepealed. Sections 64–68 removed a number of the minor heads of settlement (see Appendix) and one of major importance to the poor: the abolition of settlement by hiring and service (ss. 64–65). This amendment drastically reduced the possibility of acquiring a new settlement for many of the labouring classes. As a settlement could be inherited and passed down through the generations from parent to child, the abolition of this head led to disastrous consequences. From this point onwards, successive generations of labouring poor were unable to acquire settlement in their own right. Thus they and their families possessed (inherited) their father's, grandfather's or even great-grandfather's settlement; this is derivative settlement.

Continuing economic and social difficulties in the 1840s led to repeated calls for the reform of settlement law. Suggestions included making the union the unit of settlement and granting the guardians sole responsibility for removal decisions; allowing those who had been resident for some time in a parish immunity from removal; and simplifying the law by making birth in a parish the sole basis of acquiring a settlement (this last was never introduced). As a result of these pressures, the Poor Law Commission's *Ninth Annual Report* of 1843 considered possible reforms. In response to its recommendations, the government introduced the Poor Removal Act 1846. The terms of this Act conferred irremovable status upon those paupers who had lived in any parish continuously for five years.[84] This status of irremovability differs from the previous common law use of the term which referred to those non settled poor who, after 1795, were deemed irremovable from their residence parish until they actually sought poor relief. In that earlier situation, responsibility to relieve always lay with the settlement parish. After 1846, financial responsibility for the poor was transferred to the parish in which they lived and had acquired the new legal status of irremovability. It was this residence parish and not the pauper's settlement parish which now became liable for the costs of their relief. This was 'residence' without settled status. In turn, these irremovable poor could not confer any new settlement upon their descendants. The general and legal effects of this amendment resulted in further restrictions to those purposes and function of settlement both for the parish and the poor.

In short, the consequences of this new status of irremovability were to sever certain legal rights and obligations between paupers and their settlement parish for these irremovable poor. It therefore represents a significant step in the demise of their personal legal rights. Poor relief became increasingly embedded within this new administrative law process rather than a common law right. Once aid was severed from the parochial basis of settlement it became easier for relief to be 'understood' as public [law] generosity rather than a private [law] right. For the irremovable poor, the terms of the 1846 and subsequent acts conferred no legal rights. If they moved elsewhere and lost irremovable status they become subject to removal to their settlement parish, not to where they lived and were formerly legally irremovable. Families thus lived and died in places where they were irremovable and even received relief but acquired no settlement. In addition, as we shall see below, those financial problems 'created' by settlement obligations were simply transferred elsewhere. Finally, these changes have been described as generous to the poor but they did not confer settlement. The outcome of this is, as settlement appeals from the mid-nineteenth century demonstrate, many families had not achieved settlement status since the early nineteenth century (see an example of this p. 89). This explains why the attempted abolition of derivative settlement in the Divided Parishes Act 1876 was unsuccessful, to the extent that large numbers of exceptions emerged within the case law, providing legal evidence of how difficult it still remained for many of the labouring classes to acquire a new settlement.

The introduction of irremovability was precipitated by the economic crises of the 1840s, resulting in increased numbers of removals and escalating parish legal costs still born by the poor rate.[85] In consequence, parishes were required to contribute more to the common fund of the unions, assessed every three years in arrears. Yet, despite the opposite intention, some local financial difficulties were exacerbated by the implementation of the terms of the 1846 Act. Prior to this date it was predominantly rural parishes that were under financial stress as they supported those settled poor who had left to live and work in the towns five years or more previously.[86] After the introduction of irremovability, urban parishes and townships found themselves unable to recoup their non-resident poor relief costs from those rural settlement parishes. As a result, their poor law costs rapidly increased and, worse, although one term of the Act stipulated that time spent in receipt of poor relief could not count in calculating irremovability in the future, it remained unclear whether this new provision was to be retrospective. These problems led to the setting up of a Select Committee in 1847 to investigate the operation of the law and the legal issue before the Committee concerned those conflicting interpretations of these provisions.[87] The relevant section of the 1846 Act states that the provision renders non-settled poor of five years' residence in a parish irremovable. The presumption by local guardians was that this provision was intended to operate retrospectively as well as prospectively. However, the law officers of the Crown took an opposing view, holding that the section was not so intended and this opinion was circulated to all poor law unions. Nevertheless, a large proportion of poor law guardians declined to follow this advice. They argued that the opinion, although persuasive, did not have the authority of legal precedent. The problem for the Select Committee was that no legal authority was likely to be established for at least two years, such being the shortest time before any relevant appeal could be heard at the Court of Queen's Bench due to current delays in the processes of law.[88]

These legal problems were circumvented by the passing of Bodkin's Act 1847 whose terms charged the costs of the irremovable poor to the common fund of the union. The Act was confirmed and extended in 1848 (11 & 12 Vict. *c*. 110). Further amendments allowed paupers to achieve irremovable status after three years' residence in a parish; these were contained in the terms of the Poor Removal Act 1861. Three further statutes were passed amending and clarifying processes for removing the Irish (see Chapter 8) along with a technical Act in 1864 for calculating the time necessary to achieve irremovability.[89] These reactive reforms demonstrate the difficulties faced by those who wished to amend settlement. Any changes in the rules still operated in the context of the substantial body of legal precedent and this invariably produced unforeseen results. The members of the Select Committee of 1847 believed that the current system was unjust and that the power of removal should be abolished, but they disagreed over the feasibility of any system adopting the union as the unit of settlement and rating. In consequence, they made no recommendation to Parliament. A Select Committee of 1861, reporting in 1864, recommended making the cost of all the poor in each union chargeable upon the common fund of the union.[90] Finally, s. 1 of the Union Chargeability Act 1865 established that one year's residence rendered a pauper irremovable. All poor relief costs were to be chargeable upon the common fund of the union and the basic tenets of settlement law, the autonomy and obligations of a parish to its settled poor, were thereby largely but not completely subsumed within a national bureaucratic system. This was achieved without conferring any legal rights upon the poor and reducing those local legal rights, duties and obligations formerly possessed by parishes and their ratepayers. Settlement law now operated as a cost-allocation mechanism between unions, with the right to remove a threat hanging over the irremovable and non-settled pauper, largely severed from those personal rights that settlement had once represented.

To sum up, the terms of the 1865 Act took most of the powers surrounding settlement and rating from parochial jurisdiction and transferred them to the guardians of the poor law unions. Until this date, the right to institute the removal process was vested solely in parish officials. As a result, although after 1834 the guardians of the poor law unions could instruct parish officials to remove a pauper, they could not force them to do so.[91] Such remained the legal position whatever limitations upon the opportunities to exercise those powers had been introduced by irremovability. An attempt to amend this was set out in s. 2, Poor Removal Act 1862: '[S]uch warrants of removal shall be granted in England only on the application of the relieving officer, or other officer of the guardians of the union or parish.' This failed however and sole legal authority to initiate removal was only successfully transferred to the poor law guardians by s. 2 of the Union Chargeability Act 1865.[92]

In consequence of all the above, by 1865 settlement law, although unchanged in its cases and legal authorities, occupied a very different legal position under the new poor law; a transformation achieved by incidental accretions rather than the purposive route often ascribed to other legal developments. After a history of more than 260 years, parochial autonomy, obligations and discretion were marginalised within the poor law system. However, the 'system' retained one element from that fading parochial autonomy; each parish elected its own guardians. As we shall see in Chapter 7, those guardians retained a greater social and financial interest in their parish as ratepayers than in their roles as guardians. In addition, rating and its intimate origins within the settlement entitlement continued to have legal and economic force; settlement until abolition in 1948, rating continues today. In summary, the momentum of such a massive body of law continued even when its original purposes were gone. By 1865 although the Law of Settlement and Removal was largely unchanged, statutory amendments had rendered many people irremovable but unfortunately unable to gain a settlement where they lived. Thus that law was still a live legal matter should those individuals lose their irremovable status and then fall into destitution. But for the most part, this was a matter between unions and not a personal relationship between pauper and parish.

This legal transformation may also serve to explain how the right to relief, so closely attached to possessing a legal settlement, has come to be forgotten and hence denied today. From their perspective, the greatest changes for the able-bodied poor in 1834 were the 'abolition' of out-relief and the loss of a personal right to apply to Justices for such relief payments. From the perspective of the poor, this perceptible severing of those rights that settlement had long protected, left only the punitive mechanism of removal; exercised as always for the financial benefit of ratepayers. The developments within irremovability, the creation of the union as the unit of settlement and the establishment of a common fund in each union to pay for poor relief marked the end of settlement in its incarnation of localism with common law rights, duties and obligations. It is at this point in time that poor law may be understood as administrative law, primarily concerned with governmental control and financial preoccupations. However, that fundamental legal right of the poor to be relieved continued even if now within a union workhouse; that right remained under the overarching legal authority of the 1601 Act.

One other aspect of poor relief post 1834 requires consideration; the continuation of out-relief payments; specifically in the form of non resident relief consisting of payments to those settled paupers who were living away from their settlement parish. Close readings of the sections of the 1834 Act reveal that the able-bodied poor and their families must in future only receive aid in a union workhouse. The frail, elderly and ill were technically exempt from these rules although by the end of the nineteenth century members of this group constituted the majority of residents in workhouses. As a result, where it is paid, non-resident relief is in breach of both the spirit and the terms of the Act. However, the legal position of such payments is complex. In what constitutes recognition of the likelihood of delays in implementing all of the proposed changes, s. 52 of the 1834 Act permits the Poor Law Commissioners by Order or Regulation, to declare to what extent and under what conditions out-relief might be administered to able-bodied persons or their families. All relief (except in an emergency) given contrary to such an Order is declared to be unlawful.[93] This latter was somewhat optimistic for, as many historical reconstructions reveal, 'out-relief' continued to be paid in many parishes. Furthermore, the Commission's continuous activity in issuing Orders indicates persistent and unsuccessful attempts to control this situation. To that end, on 21 December 1844 the Commissioners issued an Out-door Relief Prohibitory Order, binding all the unions listed in the Schedule to the Order (mainly in the South of England). This was not successful and worse: even after obtaining a Removal Order, union officials for various reasons sometimes decided not to remove those same non-resident poor. Recognising even if deploring that *status quo*, Article 77 of the General Consolidated Order of 24 July 1847 as amended instructs that if guardians wish to give relief to non-settled poor resident in their unions, and also claim payments back from their settlement parishes: 'every such undertaking must be made in conformity with the rules and regulations of the Poor Law Board', successor to the Commission in 1847 after the scandal of paupers found existing in near starvation at Andover workhouse. Horrifically such institutional neglect still occurs, as at the time of writing the media are reporting that six disabled patients have died of starvation through neglect in NHS hospitals.[94]

Bowing to the inevitable, the Order of 1847 sets out details of how non-resident payments are to be made through the Post Office and provides an accounting format. In reality, the Poor Law Board possessed no legal authority to compel boards of guardians to work together in the administration of non-resident relief. In consequence, that 1847 Order somewhat optimistically declared that if unions did decide to cooperate then the Regulations were binding and must be observed. We can assume this too failed as in their circular dated 9 December 1868 the Board further impressed upon guardians the importance of strict compliance with the Order, as does a letter of 21 March 1894 from the President of the Local Government Board (successor in 1871 until 1919 when it was replaced by the Ministry of Health); clearly some unions never complied. Numerous historical reconstructions support this conclusion as they reveal the extent and duration of non-compliance within the localities after 1834. Chief amongst these was an unofficial administrative derogation as unions and individual vestries continued payments of non-resident relief. This derogation remained of considerable social and economic importance especially in northern industrial towns.[95] For example in 1845, 68 unions have accounts with Bradford to pay the costs of relief for their settled paupers. The same pattern is repeated in Leeds. This obviates the need for removing those paupers and saved Leeds and Bradford substantial legal costs. There are detailed records of such payments from Kirby Lonsdale, recorded by Garnett the overseer.[96] His letters and general correspondence indicate that this money is paid directly to large families who are resident elsewhere, as a supplement to wages or for rent. Garnett, like many parish overseers, did not simply pay on trust but only to save his township money.[97] Such payments were largely minimal, just sufficient to keep those families *in situ*; in cases of utter destitution pauper families are faced with no alternative but to return or be removed to their settlement parish. In Manchester, too, settlement parishes relieved a considerable number of the non-settled poor.[98]

This option was simply not available in the depressed agricultural South of England where the Assistant Commissioners had strong control and strictly enforced those prohibitions against the payment of non-resident relief. However, the Commission conceded that:

> [T]here is nothing in the statutes which prohibits it, or is directly inconsistent with it, and they think that the legality of this mode of relief has been impliedly recognised by the courts in several decided cases ... [whose principle appears to them to be] that the overseers of the parish (and consequently the guardians) may, if they think fit, give relief to a person settled in a parish but residing out of it.[99]

The only legal restraint upon parishes was a risk that such payments to any pauper resident elsewhere would raise a strong presumption that the pauper possessed a settlement in the paying parish, settlement by estoppel.[100] The net consequence of this practice, born of a mix of legal autonomy and economic pressure, is that in spite of repeated central efforts to the contrary, out-relief payments became increasingly common in the North of England. Their accounts still survive, listed on printed standard forms which indicate the extent of the practice. There were two versions of this formalised local practice. One involved a settlement parish agreeing to pay relief to their paupers resident in another parish, thus forestalling their removal and return. The advantage to the settlement parish was that the period of destitution may be brief (caused perhaps by a trade slump or temporary illness) and afterwards the family may recover financial independence. Unions that refused to make payment risked the removal and hence return of these families as permanently pauperised and a perpetual burden upon the ratepayers. The second variety of non resident relief consisted of a wage supplement paid to settled paupers resident and employed elsewhere. It is apparent that after 1834 and well into the twentieth century these expressions of local poor law legal autonomy, although far from the spirit and intention of the 1834 Act, continued at both union and later at County administrative level.

The remaining history of poor law as administrative law stands outside the remit of this legal reconstruction, but is here briefly summarised. The workhouse system continued into the twentieth century and in December 1905, a Royal Commission on the Poor Law and Unemployed was appointed. It took four years to investigate the workings of the poor laws, producing both a *Majority* and a *Minority Report* (led by Beatrice Webb) in 1911, but no new legislation was introduced until the codified Poor Law Act 1927. This Act consists of 99 poor law statutes redrafted into one statute of 244 sections. Two years later some aspects were repealed and more amended when the terms of the Local Government Act 1929 transferred poor law functions to Local Councils and County Boroughs, abolishing the poor law unions and their boards of guardians. The Poor Law Act 1930 represents a further codification. Most of these changes were administrative, some cosmetic as poor law institutions became Public Assistance institutions, but the principle under which relevant relief was given, and always so stated, is the legal authority of the 1601 Act. This remained the position until the Beveridge reforms after the Second World War. The National Health Service Act 1946, which came into force on 5 July 1948, finally abolished the poor law replacing it with the Welfare State.

Coda: poor law as administrative law

Returning to juristic considerations, further evidence for the evolution of common law welfare into poor law as administrative law may be reconstructed within contemporary legal texts. The earliest of these reveal that the Law of Settlement and Removal and issues surrounding local rates are at the heart of the subject. Michael Nolan's *A Treatise of the Laws for the Relief and Settlement of the Poor* (1805) is the most comprehensive and authoritative and is extensively quoted and sourced for the next 150 years. A close reading reveals that Nolan's work contains 400 pages on settlement but only 14 on the law concerned with relief payments. The topics of poor law are discussed in a structure which states the principles and sets out the relevant precedents. Volume I, 400 pages long, begins with the setting and collecting of poor rates, considering both the legal principles and the operation of the law. Then the origins of settlement and the heads of settlement are examined. Volume II (some 400 pages of text plus 200 pages of relevant statutes) continues the discussion of the heads of settlement, certificates, parish officials, parish accounts, the removal processes and poor relief. The material is complex and presumes both legal knowledge and legal skills in the reader. This text can be compared with Herbert Davey's *Poor Law Settlement and Removal* (1908), which has a similar structure but isolates settlement and the removal process, the common law material. Poor relief is not included; there is no discussion of parish officers or of the funding via a poor rate. That material can be found in texts such as W.C. Maude's *Poor Law Handbook* (1903). In 188 pages, only 20 concern settlement and removal in a summary form, the rest of the work is concerned with administrative matters such as meetings of guardians, indoor relief, medical relief and so on. The effect of the 1834 reforms may be seen in these works: Nolan demonstrates that settlement was poor law, Davey, that settlement was not repealed and Maude that settlement was marginalised in poor law processes.

By the 1930s this transformation from private law right to public law duty is complete. The codification Poor Law Acts 1927 and 1930 appear in legal textbooks annotated by a plethora of case references.[101] For a further example, one which demonstrates the changes that occurred in the fundamental nature of settlement and poor law it is only necessary to consult E.J. Lidbetter's *Handbooks for Public Assistance Officers, – I. Settlement and Removal* (1932). The author explains that his purpose is to supply a simple textbook for students studying for the certificates of the Poor Law Examination Board, in order to qualify as County and Borough Council officials performing: 'the daily routine of [poor law] administration'.[102]

He continues:

> The days of gladiatorial contests of settlement officers are, happily ended. It is therefore unnecessary, in a textbook on settlement and removal, to produce a compendium of high technique ... with its elaboration of rare and peculiar points calculated to stimulate the litigious mind.[103]

Lidbetter understands poor law as a matter of public administration and explains that lay officers need not concern themselves with matters of settlement appeals as authorities maintain professional departments as part of their normal organisation to deal with such matters. This is poor law as public law.

Other works, such as John Clarke's *Social Administration including the Poor Laws* (1935) are produced in an environment of social improvement. The introduction by Arthur Greenwood MP explains the now purposive context of poor law as a branch of social services:

> I take the view that there is a moral responsibility on the community to ensure that its members are fitted to undertake the heavy responsibilities of citizenship and parenthood ... through collective effort and a deliberate attempt on the part of the nation to create an inspiring social environment for itself, to protect its members from anti-social influences, and to remove the canker of insecurity ... from the lives of millions of our people.[104]

These fine aims are to be achieved through social engineering; they represent a total disconnection from poor law origins as a common law right. The element of local autonomy is also missing. The Poor Law Act 1930 may have moderated the worst horrors of the new poor law and its workhouse test, but the rights dimension that once informed relief practices exists only in the continuing legal authority of the 1601 Act. There is no discussion by Clarke of the legal rights of the poor. Aid is discussed as a government contribution towards improving both the people and their lives, granted within a framework of condescending paternalism.

Such is the legacy of poor law's administrative bureaucratic turn. In 1946 that direction was rejected as Parliament passed the legislation to introduce a new Welfare State. Nevertheless, that earlier juristic shift to public law guaranteed that this new direction followed a bureaucratic administrative route. However, in spite of this path and a continuing lack of any consistent conceptual agreement as to the purposes and function of welfare in modern Britain, it is always 'understood' that the poor will be relieved. It is heartening to reflect that the cultural weight of a 450-year-old juristic norm ensures that the 'spirit and intention' of the 1601 Act constitutes the slowly beating heart of welfare's twenty-first century behemoth.

Notes

1 Sir Frederick Morton Eden, *The State of the Poor*, 3 vols, 1797, A.G.L. Rogers (ed.), London: Routledge and Sons Ltd, 1928.
2 Robert C. Palmer, *English Law in the Age of the Black Death, 1348–1381. A Transformation of Governance and Law*, London and Carolina: University of North Carolina Press, 1993.
3 Lorie Charlesworth, 'Justices of the Peace' (English Common Law), Stanley M. Katz (ed.) *Oxford International Encyclopedia of Legal History*, New York: Oxford University Press, 2009.
4 Brian Tierney, *Medieval Poor Law*, Berkeley and Los Angeles, CA: University of California Press, 1959, pp.7–10.
5 Ibid., pp. 69–80.
6 For a full list of local records available to researchers see: W.E. Tate, *The Parish Chest. A Study of the Records of Parochial Administration in England*, 3rd edn, Cambridge: Cambridge University Press, 1969.
7 Tierney, *Medieval Poor Law*, pp. 80–83.
8 Neil S. Rushton, 'Monastic Charitable Provision in Tudor England', *Continuity and Change*, 16, 1, May 2001, 9–44.
9 W.W. Mortimer, *The History of the Hundred of Wirral*, Manchester: E. J. Morten, 1847, pp. 310–15.
10 J.M. Neeson, *Commoners: Common Right, Enclosure and Social Change in England, 1700–1820*, Cambridge: Cambridge University Press, 1993.
11 For a full discussion of the history of custom as law, see: Theodore Plucknett, *A Concise History of the Common Law*, 5th edn, London: Butterworth and Co., 1956.
12 Ibid., p. 313.
13 Andrea C. Loux, 'The Persistence of the Ancient Regime: Custom, Utility, and the Common Law in the Nineteenth Century', *Cornell Law Review*, 79, 1993, 183–218, at 183.
14 G.W. Oxley, 'The Administration of the Old Poor Law in the West Derby Hundred of Lancashire 1601–1834', 1966, unpublished thesis, University of Liverpool, Chapter 6.
15 Eamonn Duffy, *The Voices of Morebath*, New Haven and London: Yale University Press, 2001.
16 Richard Burn, *History of the Poor Laws with Observations*, London: H. Woodfall and W. Strachan, 1764.
17 Ibid., p. 62.
18 The Thomas Berri Charity is the oldest in operation on the Charity Commissioners lists. A commemorative plaque in the church spells the donor's name from the bottom up, its tone reflects the religious upheavals of the time. The author wishes to thank the Rector of Walton on the Hill, the Reverend Trevor Latham for supplying this information:

> In God the Lord put all you truste
> Repente your of your formar wicked waies
> Elizabethe our Quene moste juste
> Blesse her O Lorde in all her daies
> So Lord encrease good councelers
> And preachers of His most holie worde
> Mislike of all papistes desirers

O Lord cut them off with thy sworde
How small soever the gifte shall be
Thank God for him who gave it thee
XII penie loves to XII poore foulkes
Give everie sabothe day for aye.

19 Michael Nolan, *A Treatise of the Laws for the Relief and Settlement of the Poor*, 2 vols, 2nd edn, London: A. Strahan, 1805, reprint, New York and London: Garland Publishing Inc., 1978, vol. II, 168, and Chapter XXIX.
20 Nick Wikely, *Child Support Law and Policy*, Oxford: Hart Publishing, 2006.
21 Burn, *History of the Poor Laws*, p. 93.
22 Michael Dalton, *The Countrey Justice*, London: The Society of Stationers, 1618; reprint, Norwood, NJ: Walter J. Johnson Inc., 1975, pp. 75–76.
23 Michael Dalton, *Country Justice*, London: Henry Lintot, 1727, p. 227; Nolan, *Treatise*, vol. I, p. 137.
24 *Margaret Brown's Case*, 7 Car 3 (1631).
25 *Suckley v Whitborn*, 2 Bulstrode 357 (1649).
26 Nolan, *Treatise*, vol. I, pp. 141–43.
27 Lorie Charlesworth, 'Readings of Begging: The Legal Response to Begging Considered in its Modern and Historical Context', *Nottingham Law Journal*, 15, 1, 2006, 1–12.
28 Nolan, *Treatise*, vol. I, p. 139.
29 35 Geo.III *c*. 101, (1795).
30 *R v All Saints, Derby* (1849), 14 Q.B. 207.
31 F.C. Montague, 'The Law of Settlement and Removal', *Law Quarterly Review*, XIII, 1888, 40–51 at 41.
32 Herbert Davey, *Poor Law Settlement and Removal*, London: Stevens and Sons, 1908, p. 1; Nolan, *Treatise*, vol. I, pp. 7–19.
33 *R v Knaresborough* (1851), Q.B. 446.
34 *R v All Saints, Derby* (1849), 14 Q.B. 207.
35 Nolan, *Treatise*, vol. I p.151.
36 The best description of the rules of settlement, reproduced in the Appendix, can be found in Montague, 'Settlement and Removal', p. 50.
37 See: James Burrows, *A Series of the Decisions of the Court of King's Bench upon the Settlement Cases from … 1732*, London: Her Majesty, 1768, p. 124.
38 Nolan, *Treatise*, vol. II, pp. 141 and 147.
39 For an example of a 'decayed gentleman' see: J. S. Taylor, *Poverty, Migration and Settlement in the Industrial Revolution; Sojourners' Narratives*, Palo Alto, CA: The Society for the Promotion of Science and Scholarship, 1989, p. 39.
40 Joanna Innes, 'Parliament and the Shaping of Eighteenth Century Social Policy', *Transactions of the Royal Historical Society*, series, 40, 1990, 63–92, at 67.
41 Griffiths, *The Politics of the Judiciary*, London: Fontana Press, 1991.
42 Innes, 'Parliament,' p. 74.
43 M.E. Rose (ed.), *English Poor Law 1780–1930*, Newton Abbot: David & Charles, 1971, p. 19.
44 P. Clarke, 'Migration in England during the Late Seventeenth Century and Early Eighteenth Century', *Past and Present*, 83, 1979, 57–90, at 72.
45 Tate, *Parish Chest*, p. 200.
46 *Hayes v Bryant*, 1 H. Black 215, at 253.
47 Nolan, *Treatise*, vol. II, pp. 226, 232.
48 Ibid., pp. 169–70, 227–32.
49 J.F. Archbold, *A Summary of the Law Relating to Appeals, against Orders of Removals against Rates etc*, London: S. Sweet, Steven and Sons, 1826, p. 8.

50 *R v Higworth* (1717) 93 E.R. 32; *R v Manchester* (1714) 88 E.R. 702; Ross Cranston, *Legal Foundations of the Welfare State*, London: Weidenfeld & Nicolson, 1985, p. 31.
51 *R v North Shields* (1780) 99 E.R. 213.
52 Jonathan Healey, 'Poverty, Deservingness and Popular Politics: The Contested Relief of Agnes Braithwaite, 1701–6', *Transactions of the Historic Society of Lancashire and Cheshire*, 156, 2007, 131–56.
53 Archbold, *Summary of the Law*, 1826, p. 8.
54 *R v Eastbourne (Inhabitants) (1803)* 4 East 103 at 107; 102 E.R. 769 at 770.
55 Nolan, *Treatise*, vol. II, p. 257.
56 *Tawney's Case* 1 Bott, 343, Pl 373: Nolan, *Treatise*, vol. II, p. 260.
57 Nolan, *Treatise*, vol. II, p. 264.
58 W. Ivor Jennings, *The Poor Law Code*, 2nd edn, London: Charles Knight and Co., 1936, pp. 97, 158–59.
59 Nolan, *Treatise*, vol. II, p. 120.
60 Ethel M. Hampson, *The Treatment of Poverty in Cambridgeshire 1597–1834*, Cambridge: Cambridge University Press, 1934, pp. 273–89.
61 Dalton, *Country Justice*, 1742, p. 170.
62 Hampson, *Treatment of Poverty*, p. 287.
63 *Rex v Wensley* 5 Terms Rep. 154; William Golden Lumley, *A Popular Treatise on the Law of Settlement and Removal*, London: Shaw and Sons, 1842, pp. 139–44.
64 *Rex v Lillington*, 1 East 488.
65 *Rex v Newington*, I Term Rep. 354; Nolan, *Treatise*, vol. II, p. 126.
66 Taylor, *Poverty*.
67 Nolan, *Treatise*, vol. II, p. 118.
68 *Rex v St Ives*, Sett Cases 153, A motion for *mandamus* to a parish to grant a certificate was rejected as a strange attempt.
69 Nolan, *Treatise*, vol. II, p. 131.
70 Ibid., p. 147, citing *Great Bedwin v Wilcot*, 2 Str. 1158.
71 After 1795 pregnant unmarried women were still deemed to be chargeable, 'constructive' chargeability though not requiring relief. This was repealed in s. 69 Poor Law Amendment Act 1834.
72 There is evidence of their issue after 1795: D. Gowing, 'Migration in Gloucester 1662–1865. A geographical evaluation of the documentary evidence related to the administration of the Law of Settlement and Removal,'1979, unpublished thesis, University of Southampton, p. 42 n. 9; Song examines 405 certificates issued between 1751 and 1834 by seasonal distribution, but he does not indicate how many were issued after 1795: B. K. Song, 'The poor law and labour markets in Oxfordshire, 1750–1870', 1996, unpublished thesis, University of Oxford, p. 178; Oxley states that 37 settlement certificates were issued between 1795 and 1837: G.W. Oxley, 'The administration of the old poor law in the West Derby Hundred of Lancashire 1601–1834', unpublished thesis, University of Liverpool, pp. 391 and 397.
73 *R v Inhabitants of Rislip* [1669] I Ld. Raym 394.
74 *R v Eastbourne (Inhabitants) (1803)* 4 East 103 at 107. 102 E.R. 769.
75 Section 6, the Poor Relief Act 1722states that the purchase of an estate of less than £30 did not allow the purchaser to acquire settlement; s. 8, neither did paying highway taxes; s. 8, churchwardens or overseers of the parish were required to give reasonable notice to the removing overseers for any appeal against Removal Orders: 'The reasonableness of which notice shall be determined by the justices of the peace at the Quarter Sessions to which the appeal is made'.
76 On the detail and complexity of the appeal process see: Nolan, *Treatise*, vol. II, pp. 266–384.
77 The preamble of the Quarter Sessions Act 1731, refers to cases: 'set aside upon exceptions or objections to the form or forms of the proceedings without hearing or examining the truth or merits of the matter in question between the parties concerned'.

78 M.E. Rose, 'Settlement, Removal and the New Poor Law', in Derek Fraser (ed.) *The New Poor Law in the Nineteenth Century*, London: Macmillan, 1976, p. 27.

79 J.R. Poynter, *Society and Pauperism. English Ideas on Poor Relief 1795–1834*, London: Routledge and Kegan Paul, 1969, p. 7.

80 Only Docking Poor Law Union in Norfolk chose to do so. The union consisted of a collection of widespread 'close' parishes: Anne Digby, *Pauper Palaces*, London: Routledge and Kegan Paul, 1978, p. 92.

81 Rose, 'Settlement', p. 27.

82 Lorie Charlesworth, 'Consumer Protection in Sale of Goods Agreements; An Ancient Right in Modern Guise', *The Liverpool Law Review*, XVI, 2, 1994, 167–86.

83 Gertrude Himmelfarb, *The Idea of Poverty. England in the Early Industrial Age*, London: Faber & Faber, 1984, p. 183.

84 Widows were irremovable for the first 12 months after their husband's death, as were those who applied for temporary relief on account of sickness or accident.

85 David Ashforth, 'Settlement and Removal in Urban Areas, Bradford 1834–71', in M.E. Rose (ed.) *The Poor and the City*, Leicester: Leicester University Press, 1985, p. 78.

86 Rose, 'Settlement', p. 40.

87 *Report of the Select Committee to Enquire into the Operation of the Law of Settlement and the Poor Removal Act*, 1st Report and Minutes of Evidence, 1847, PP 82, X1.1.

88 Ibid.,'p. 6. A contemporary legal opinion states: 'Although the position has not been expressly decided, it has been virtually affirmed by the Queen's Bench, that it is to be read *retrospectively*', E.W. Cox, *The Practice of Poor Removals*, London: J. Crockford, 1848, p. 15.

89 When calculating a pauper's time of residence to acquire irremovability status, time in another parish of the same union could be included: 27 & 28 Vict. *c.* 105, (1864).

90 *Report of the Select Committee on Poor Relief*, PP 1864, IX.

91 Lumley, *Popular Treatise*, pp. 154, 156.

92 W.A. Holdsworth, *The Handy Book of Parish Law*, 3rd edn, London: George, Routledge and Sons, 1872, p. 248.

93 W.C. Maude, *The Poor Law Handbook*, London: Poor Law Officers' Journal, 1903, p. 87.

94 *The Independent*, 25 March 2009.

95 Ashforth, 'Settlement,' pp. 69–71.

96 'Township Letters, 1809–36': Cumbria Record Office, Kendal, Kirby Lonsdale WPR/19: in J.S. Taylor, 'A Different Kind of Speenhamland: Non resident Relief in the Industrial Revolution', *Journal of British Studies*, 30, 1991, 183–208, at 195.

97 Ibid., p. 197.

98 In the 1840s numbers equalled that of payments to the settled poor. The costs quintupled between 1847–48, probably as an effect of the 1846 Act: City of Manchester. Cultural Services, Central Library, Churchwardens' Accounts. 1809–48, M3/3/4/6A & B, in: Taylor, 'A Different Kind', p. 200.

99 However the Commission's General Prohibitory Order, in force in 412 unions, prohibited such payments with some exceptions; for discussion of these see: Lumley, *Popular Treatise*, pp. 146–47.

100 Unless payment could be shown to have been given through error or mistake: 'it will go far to conclude all question as to the settlement', Ibid., pp. 147–48.

101 Technically, the 1662 Act was repealed by and restated in the Poor Law Act (1927) and the Poor Law Act (1930) which codified poor law cases and statutes from 1601. The law remained unaltered: E.J. Lidbetter, *Handbooks for Public Assistance Officers.-I. Settlement and Removal* London: Law and Local Government Publications Ltd, 1932, pp. 3–4; Jennings, *The Poor Law Code*, pp. 7–8.

102 Lidbetter, *Settlement and Removal*, p. 1.

103 Ibid.

104 John C. Clarke, *Social Administration including the Poor Laws*, 2nd edn, London: Sir Isaac Pitman and Sons, 1935, p. viii.

Chapter 4

Deconstructing from the negative: a critical historiography of legal [mis]conceptions

As previously noted, it is becoming a convention for legal scholars to include elements of 'history' within their texts. Occasionally historicist in tone, nevertheless these reconstructions perform both normative and validating roles to that scholarship whilst constituting a welcome injection of history to the discipline of law.[1] However, such accounts of the poor law in welfare texts unfortunately perpetuate misunderstandings of the legal past and continue to mislead and distort aspects of modern scholarship. Chapter 1 considered a recent example drawn from welfare rights theory and others will be touched on below. This raises certain questions: Why are these accounts misleading and from where are they drawn? The previous chapter addressed the first question to provide a doctrinal account establishing the existence of the right to relief and the role of settlement as the legal foundations of poor law. This chapter concerns the second question and addresses the persistence of incorrect views of welfare's past in legal scholarship, engendered by reliance upon poor law historians' reconstructions as accurate and complete representations of the law. Those who rely upon such accounts include scholars in the United States who acknowledge the English poor law system as foundational in the establishment of North American welfare systems. This is problematic as welfare debates both in Britain and the United States are grounded within these incorrect legal accounts of welfare's pedigree.

Conventionally, that pedigree does not include recognition of the right to relief guaranteed by settlement; it is rather reduced to a linear narrative of non-legal poor law, dominated by its post-1834 ideology. In consequence, even John Gillom's masterly study (2001) of the treatment and experience of 'welfare mothers' in Ohio is contextualised within a teleological description of 'conventional' negative English poor law history.[2] The Foucaultian nightmare world of control and observation he exposes thus has an inevitable quality; it is a logical conclusion to poor law's negative 'principles' reconstructed from his sources, poor law histories. As a result, his study lacks awareness of those legal elements that would support his critical analysis of Ohio's punitive, modern welfare system, contextualised as it is in an incorrect understanding of the past. Such historicist accounts of 'undeserving' (no rights) poor, relied upon by Gillom and others, reflect continuing negativities towards the poor. These are expressed, for example, in government advertising campaigns to encourage good British citizens to do their public duty and shop their neighbours as 'welfare cheats'. Meanwhile, insufficient money is expended in funding welfare advisors to ensure that all citizens obtain the benefits to which they are entitled.

In summary, this chapter is intended as a corrective to those negative influences upon welfare scholarship produced by incorrect law in historical reconstructions. In this context, historical readings of poor law have developed conventions and orthodoxies that [mis]understand its legal nature, arrived at by extensive archival study conducted without legal knowledge. This chapter constitutes a critical analysis of those academic writings that either create or perpetuate these inaccuracies in poor law reconstructions. It examines the historiography of poor law to reveal where this occurs, concentrating predominantly on reconstructions concerning settlement and rights. As a full critical historiography would occupy half this book and the writer has produced more elsewhere, this chapter will focus upon those long-established works that are conventionally accepted and cited as authoritative and consider their influence.[3] In particular, it revisits a debate concerning settlement whose lack of resolution seems to have discouraged further reconstructions.

It is unsurprising that poor law reconstructions fall into error: their legal subject is no longer in practice or in legal memory. Moreover, there has not been a 'legal history' of poor law since P.F. Aschrott's *English Poor Law System Past and Present* was published in 1902.[4] After all, historians are not lawyers and if they sometimes seek to understand law by throwing assorted statutes into an intellectual mix, this is a logical if not a legal approach. It is therefore understandable if a lack of 'law-mindedness' leads some scholars to minimise the power and effect law may have upon human behaviour, both individually and collectively. In summary, although there is an enormous body of scholarship reconstructing welfare's past, little of it is contextualised within a doctrinal legal framework. As a result, vital ingredients for our understanding of the operation of poor law are missing and many reconstructions of poor law history make fundamental legal errors in their recreations of that past. It is in order to correct some of those errors that what follows constitutes a juristic critique of the work of professional historians of the poor law. To this end, as this work necessitates a re-evaluation of current social histories via a socio-legal analysis, this chapter challenges that absence of accurate legal discussion in the works of historians, all of whom use records generated by aspects of the law of settlement and removal.

Settlement's contemporaries were well aware of the legal status of poor law. Lawyers wrote poor law textbooks, lawyers worked for the Poor Law Commission and lawyers gave evidence before Select Committees. In their evidence, lawyers explained the intricacies of settlement law, the implications of removals for the poor and indulged in complex and fascinating esoteric discussions upon settlement technicalities with members of Select Committees. Little of this may be found in poor law reconstructions. In fact analysis of the writings of early twentieth century poor law historians does not reveal any enthusiasm for settlement or understanding of its connection with rights. Sydney and Beatrice Webb, with their interest in public administration, largely understood poor law from their perspective, challenging current administrative solutions to the 'problem' of poverty.[5] Dorothy Marshall and Ethel Hampson, writing in the 1920s, demonstrate little sensitivity to poor law as law.[6] In short, these and other historians are writing as settlement cases are being appealed to higher courts but poor law's cultural status is largely negative. After the Second World War and the abolition of poor law, the powerful scholarly influence of the administrative concerns of the Webbs continued, but publication in 1963 of Mark Blaug's poor law research influenced historians to concentrate upon researching poor law as part of wider social and economic history, an approach that continues today.[7]

The following discussion adopts an hermeneutic approach to published work; it measures the correctness, accuracy and validity of historians' words against legal doctrines, principles and cases set out in the previous chapter. This methodology is manifestly unfair from the perspective of some of those scholars' stated aims and objectives, but is necessary to progress legal analysis. This critical approach, although largely negative, is not intended as a rejection of historical reconstructions. On the contrary, all the work reviewed below reveals the extent and range of legal records, the complexity of the operation of law in action and much more. It has been an extraordinary experience as a legal scholar to approach the study of an area of law from the perspective of its effect upon the lives of those subject to its rigours. Unfortunately, also because of the labours of historians, the study of this area of law has become grounded largely within the experience of its 'victims' rather than its beneficiaries, the settled poor, for reasons explored below.

Historians and the 'nature' of poor law

Current historical reconstructions of settlement maintain the negative perceptions and conclusions produced by the Webbs.[8] Marshall and Hampson shared this negativity as did J.L. and B. Hammond.[9] There have not been any subsequent studies of either poor law or settlement itself which successfully challenge that perspective. In consequence, awareness of and sensitivity to the legal rights of the poor has generally not been a factor in historians' work, with the honourable exception of E.P. Thompson.[10] Accordingly, in 1964 when Philip Styles produced the first specific account of settlement consisting largely of a linear narrative of statutes, there is no discussion of the legal and, therefore, social significance of settlement's role in underpinning poor law rights. Subsequently, in 1968 Blaug's reappraisal of poor law history did not extend to a consideration of law.[11] In summary, with the exception of the debate discussed below, for most historians settlement has lost its legal role. As a result, little published to date on this subject accurately reflects the legal character and relationship between settlement and poor relief or the academic implications of using these records without any legal analysis. The debate about the legal context of poor law has not been opened and without that debate the nature of poor law remains imperfectly understood, as the legal explanation for much poor law practice remains invisible to so many researchers.

The current approach in poor law reconstructions is to emphasise the harm settlement caused. The Webbs argued that it created a bureaucratic puzzle, which burdened Justices of the Peace, parish officers and the poor, and that it hindered social mobility.[12] This assertion is no longer accepted as subsequent research has revealed extensive mobility amongst the poor. Although this has stimulated debate between historians as to what settlement records reveal, this has not been extended to a technical legal analysis and legal solecisms are entrenched within historical reconstructions. For example, some historians incorrectly state that the power of removal began with the 1662 Act and all now refer to it incorrectly as the 'Settlement Act'.[13] There are certain characteristics within most poor law reconstructions where settlement is concerned: it is usually separated from archival findings, there are lists of statutes, the writings of contemporary reformers are quoted, sometimes Justices' manuals are named but rarely legal texts.[14] Finally, historians cite few cases and those that are mentioned are generally miscited, obscure, irrelevant, incorrect and/or misunderstood. Few reconstructions trace settlement to its abolition, even fewer (except Lynn Hollen Lees) reveal awareness that settlement remained law until 1948.[15] It is not surprising therefore that the development and legal significance of settlement has become intellectually detached from poor law reconstructions. This results in scholarship that privileges 'poor law' as an amorphous, if contested, subject and relegates settlement to an awkward sub-text.

As a result of this bracketing out, historians are able to reconstruct 'poor law' from any perspective: social, political, cultural, feminist, economic, geographical or local. But what exactly is this 'poor law' they reconstruct? Absent recognition of the law that led to their creation, historians are playing decontextualised intellectual games with a fabulous collection of surviving local and national records. It is therefore unsurprising that historians have not moved far from those negative accounts of settlement in early reconstructions. The Hammonds wrote that the laws of settlement: 'were in practice ... a violation of natural liberty'.[16] The Webbs, in turn, defined settlement as: 'a framework of compulsion and repression'.[17] There is no recognition here of the role played by settlement in delineating and upholding the rights, duties and obligations of the poor. This negative perspective is constant within the historiography where errors of legal interpretation and, hence, understanding abound. This is evident, for example, within J.R. Poynter's work reconstructing contemporary theories of poor relief. He dismisses settlement as purposive, as jealously 'restricting' the responsibility of administering poor relief to a local level and he describes a 'perpetual' settlement war between parishes as a: 'national sport'.[18] His observations emphasise litigation and local autonomy, but lose sight of the larger legal picture. For Poynter, the 1601 Act 'gradually' became the basis for: 'a tradition of local practice'; not recognising its status as *the* legal authority underpinning all poor relief in England and Wales. In brief, Poynter displays a post-Beveridge purposive preoccupation with welfare that retains the negativity engendered by the 1834 reforms. In consequence, he assumes the existence of an early 'national' poor law, damned by a 'failing system' of national control. In reality, what he reconstructs as 'failing' is a locally run and funded 'system' operating within an overarching common law structure. This 'failure' thesis recurs in much poor law history supported in part by a continuing acceptance of the Webbs' 100-year-old accounts.

The sheer weight of those voluminous poor law texts by the Webbs provides one explanation for their continuing authority; no serious poor law historian can afford to neglect them. Indeed for a considerable period they were held to be so complete that it only required a series of local studies to complete poor law research.[19] In spite of this, they are no longer accepted uncritically and have been accused of bias due to suspicion engendered by their socialist political affiliations and their involvement in poor law reform, including Beatrice Webb's participation in the drafting of the *Minority Report* for the Royal Commission of 1905–9 noted earlier.[20] However, no challenge on the grounds of accuracy has been raised concerning their dismissal of settlement. Indeed close readings of most subsequent historical reconstructions reveal that their sources on the effects and nature of settlement law can be tracked either directly or indirectly via other publications to the Webbs' monumental tomes. As that work continues to influence current scholarship in both history and law, as recently as 2008 in the case of Paz-Fuchs, their work requires further scrutiny. In this context, the Webbs took a particular view of the role of the parish; they incorrectly assert: 'the entire body of the manual-working wage earners of the kingdom, together with their families, were legally immobilised by the settlement act [sic]',[21] and, bizarrely, that anyone who visited their relatives in another place could be removed by order of the Justices.[22] For the Webbs, the purposes of the 1662 Act constitute: '[an] attempt to immobilise, in the parishes to which they "belonged" the nine-tenths of the population who were subjected to the law of settlement and removal'.[23] Their legal assumptions are many and odd, they include: that removal warrants were issued as a matter of course, that the pauper was the 'victim' of settlement and that settlement law developed as: 'the lawyers … getting [sic] new principles [sic] established by the Court of King's Bench'.[24] Finally, there are numerous inconsistencies within their text. For example, having stated that all wage earners were subject to the tyranny of settlement law,[25] a few pages later they write: 'only a few wage earners were subject to the law because of loopholes [sic]'.[26]

The Webbs' reconstruction of the new poor law, published in 1929, narrates piecemeal amendments to minor aspects of the settlement laws, recognising that the terms of the 1834 Act left settlement law substantially unchanged.[27] However in declaring that the Union Chargeability Act 1865 'solved' the problem of settlement they suggest: 'During the 60 years which have elapsed since [the] ... act ... comparatively little has been heard of the law of Settlement and Removal, down to 1927 it still nominally existed.'[28] This is contradicted a few lines later as they record that in 1907, 12,000 persons were removed from one union to another in England and Wales.[29] Such inconsistencies reflect either poor editorial control of their many research assistants and/or the authors' negative perceptions of settlement. This position may in part be traced to their reliance upon Marshall, whose 1926 work also introduces the use of the local study to inform discussions of settlement law.[30] However she does not recognise the legal rights of settled paupers to receive poor relief, although she makes a number of astute observations about the operation of settlement. She identifies the increasing legal complexity of the settlement process and she records several instances where the Justices sitting at the Quarter Sessions in Cambridgeshire could not reach a decision and referred the matter for the [legal] opinion of the Judges of Assise.[31]

Nonetheless, Marshall's overall conclusion is that settlement is coercive. In her study she acknowledges that not all 'strangers' were removed, although she does not use the term 'discretion'. She concludes reasonably that: 'the overseers concentrated their efforts on securing the removal of those classes of persons whom experience had shown to be the least capable of maintaining themselves without relief', and that parish officers: 'tended to leave strangers alone if they neither attempted to gain a settlement ... nor appeared likely to become chargeable in the near future'. She contrasts this with the speed of action to remove a family if the chief breadwinner became incapacitated or died.[32] In her turn, Hampson refutes one of the Webbs' incorrect statements, that a removal warrant was granted as a 'matter of course' and she provides the first detailed example of a pauper case study, that of Argent Keenish.[33] However, Hampson portrays settlement in action rather as a large fishing net for ever trawling unsuspecting victims and she portrays the poor as preoccupied with avoiding that net. Her purposive, negative understanding of the operation of law further directed poor law reconstructions towards a reading that settlement is something which happened to the poor; not the source of rights or the expression of parochial duties and obligations. This remains so even as Hampson reconstructs parish decision-making procedures, relating minutes of vestry meetings where decisions whether to begin removal proceedings or to appeal Removal Orders were taken.

However, Hampson's sweeping opening condemnation of settlement ends on a more nuanced analysis of her research findings, concluding the existence of a more tolerant, parish-based system and that the poor were not driven and controlled by coercive legislation. Nevertheless the later 1934 volume repeats these contradictions and glosses the gap between evidence and law:

> Whilst doubts may be thrown upon the extent to which able bodied labour actually was rendered immobile, the act (of 1662) was in truth the origin of many of the evils which poor law inflicted on the country in the course of succeeding generations.[34]

This negative reading of settlement is one that still dominates poor law reconstructions more than 70 years later.

Reconstructions after Blaug: settlement despised

In 1963, Blaug renewed scholarly interest in the nature of English poor law by concluding, after testing various hypotheses, that relief under the old poor law was essentially a response to population increase, low wages and a shortage of work rather than its cause.[35] Peter Solar extended this argument in 1995; after examining research on the economic consequences of English poor law he concludes that poor relief played an integral and autonomous part in England's economic development.[36] These scholars demonstrate that poor law had value for England's economic development and that the economic analyses by poor law reformers were therefore wrong. Following Solar's conclusions suggests that settlement as foundational within poor law aided economic development and some subsequent research has examined this. In 1990 George Boyer reviewed economic theories concerning the consequences of the operation of poor law. These comprise the traditional, neo-traditional and revisionist positions from the Webbs and Hammonds to Eric Hobsbawm and the revisionist school of Blaug, Anne Digby and Derek Fraser, who reject the hypothesis that out-relief had disastrous consequences upon the long-term labour market.[37] Starting from the position that no theory as to the economic effects of poor relief is totally correct, Boyer tests them all empirically. He examines settlement but from a particular context, that of industrial cities which he states use poor relief as unemployment insurance [sic] between 1795 and 1834.[38] This purposive view of a labour subsidy neglects legal rights or legal entitlement. However, he makes the point that the composition of the parish vestry had a significant effect upon the administration of poor relief; an observation of parochial legal autonomy, although not presented as such.[39] In southern parishes Boyer believes that the widespread use of out-relief was because vestries were largely composed of farmers, who would benefit from a wage subsidy paid to their workers. He does not consider the right to relief, rather perceiving such payments as supplementary income. Later in the work, Boyer assumes that workers make migration decisions based upon overall income, but does not include the significance of having or acquiring (and thereby losing the previous) settlement in his economic model.[40] Boyer suggests that the traditional interpretation of the poor law's effect upon economic growth needs to be revised, but his conclusions avoid legal aspects and do not consider elements of that discretion not to act in removing non-settled poor.[41]

The first major piece to concentrate specifically upon settlement 'law' is by Philip Styles.[42] Published in 1964 its stated purpose is to: 'consider the legal and administrative background and the relation of the act of 1662 to the Tudor poor law'. Styles reconstructs Elizabethan statutes and local practices from the 1570s onwards and deduces that their aim is to restrict newcomers in urban and agricultural areas.[43] From this perspective, he concludes that the 1662 Act is symptomatic of a growing preoccupation with the settlement and removal of poor people. That this is a negative perception may be seen as he emphasises that 'decisions' (uncited) of Judges in Assise purposively built up a body of case law between 1601 and 1662: 'to afford protection to the migrants and restrain the endeavour of parish officers to rid themselves ... of potential paupers'.[44] This unlikely reading is explained as an effort to curb local practices. This is 'unlikely' as such purposive law-making by judges is an ahistorical inaccuracy. Moreover, the overall tendency in this period is a reduction in the time qualification for achieving a settlement, from the earlier 'three years' to 40 days. It is unclear from Styles' work whom he believes appealed cases to the Quarter Sessions and he mis-states legal procedures and grounds for appeal where he states: 'Only those settlement cases came before the Quarter Sessions in which the facts were uncertain or the overseers, perhaps, were unusually strict or unrelenting.'[45] Although much of his work on certificates is illuminating in its detail, it is unhelpful for a legal understanding of the relevant law.

By 1969 this approach to poor law reconstructions is well established, placing the relief of poverty in its wider political, social and economic contexts. The legal aspects of settlement are of less interest, perhaps it was believed that nothing was left to be said on the subject. Specialist studies concentrate upon settlement documents only to establish the accuracy of various theories concerning migration, economic developments and local practices. Generalist analyses place poor law and its nineteenth century reforms into their broader social and political context. Chief amongst the latter were the writings of Poynter and later Himmelfarb.[46] However, G.W. Oxley returned poor law studies to a narrower context. He does discuss settlement, but opens his discussion of 'legal' aspects somewhat confusingly by intertwining threads of vagrancy and poor relief.[47] Oxley does not mistake the complexity of the legal material for confusion, rather he perceives: '[t]he smoothness and efficiency with which the law was generally put into operation'.[48] He uses a broad range of settlement records to reveal parochial decision making processes and is aware of the differences between parishes in the issuing of certificates, in keeping (or not) of records; or in spending: 'several years' maintenance costs to prove a: 'settlement elsewhere'.[49] He unfortunately and typically views settlement as resultant: 'the settlement laws were an inevitable consequence of a localised system of poor relief', adding: 'as a unit of administration the parish was at best a compromise'.[50] It is these misunderstandings of the legal position that make his work, too, unhelpful for a legal reconstruction.

From the 1970s historians use settlement records to develop a number of discrete themes. These include the social and economic effects of both the old and the new poor law; the nature and economic effects of open and close parishes; settlement and out-relief payments. Consequently, a considerable body of research has been produced by historians as they reconstruct the social effects of settlement under the old poor law. Amongst these, J.S. Taylor's 1976 work on settlement is regarded by historians as one of the most authoritative pieces concerning law.[51] Taylor's own authorities include the works of earlier historians and some contemporary texts but his legal account of settlement law is incorrect. His stated purpose is to: 'provide a historical framework in which to view the law'.[52] Somewhat obscurely, he opens his discussions with a technical legal question couched in the form of a contemporary song sourced from an 1805 edition of Burn's *Justices' Manual*, although it dates from Sir James Burrows' 1768 casebook.[53] This delightful piece of arcana is presumably for effect as the author does not provide any explanation of its legal significance. What then follows contains a number of legal errors. One such is Taylor's statement that settlement (he refers to it as 'Law') was of legal significance only between 1691 and 1834. Another is that the 1662 Act is: 'virtually abandoned' by 1691. This conclusion is so incorrect that it is worth considering how Taylor could have arrived at it. Perhaps he adopts this view because the terms of the 1662 Act refer specifically only to settlement by renting a tenement. Taylor appears unaware that settlement by estate and birth predate the Act and were unaltered by it (see Appendix). The 1691 Act adds technical details to settlement concerning hiring, parish officers and rating, etc. but has no other legal effect. This error is then compounded: 'Finally, without exception, the importance of the backward-looking, largely transient and ineffective Settlement Act [sic] of 1662 has been largely exaggerated.'[54] In consequence of all the above, Taylor's closing remark is disingenuous: 'No effort will be made to subject the law itself to detailed exposition for there are many excellent legal treatises that do this well enough.'[55]

In 1991, Taylor returns to the question of settlement and develops some aspects of Boyer's economic study to consider non-resident relief, payments to settled poor who have moved elsewhere.[56] Here again he misunderstands and misinterprets the legal framework; the right to relief, the rights, duties and obligations of the parishes and parochial discretion. For he boldly and wrongly states: 'The system was not established by law, has no identifiable point of origin and was not centrally controlled.'[57] Taylor continues that this is: 'the consequence of innumerable individuals seeking personal advantage and local officials pursuing two commonsense goals – the avoidance of trouble and expense'. He recognises that: 'at the heart of the matter were the laws governing pauper settlement', but not how. Even as he concedes that settlement law has largely escaped study, he oversimplifies and slips further into legal inaccuracy, particularly confusing rules through time.[58] He deduces that enforcement of settlement rules is 'occasional', missing both the legal explanation for parochial discretion and its role in the right to relief for the settled poor. In reality Taylor largely, but less accurately, covers the same territory as M.E. Rose's 1976 article.[59] He does examine specific case studies, apparently to deduce a principle behind payments to non-resident paupers, but does not arrive at the correct legal explanation. As with most of the work discussed, Taylor attempts to deduce answers about migration, economic pressures and general tendencies from settlement records that record legal problems posed by personal life circumstances of individuals. Such an exercise requires an awareness of the fundamental principles of the law of settlement and removal, not present in this work.

In totality, there are hundreds of articles, textbooks, dissertations and monographs drawing upon local settlement records. What few of these studies recognise or acknowledge is how misleading legal records are when removed from their legal context. Especially as these records largely represent the negative side of settlement, the pathology of legal process, and their use reinforces pathological conclusions about settlement law that are resoundingly negative; a bias noted but not developed by Lees.[60] It is this aspect that has dominated poor law reconstructions. Pathological because resorting to the courts is a desperate and expensive remedy, only adopted when a problem emerges that requires legal adjudication and there is a legal remedy available. Otherwise, for settlement obligations as with any other legal obligation, in normal circumstances local officials considered and paid up as was their legal duty and the settled pauper's right. Only *in extremis* does and did one bring in the lawyers. The sheer volume of poor relief paid out without recourse to law through the long survival of the poor law demonstrates this. And still the positive side of possessing a settlement, its legal guarantee to a share of parish poor relief, is marginalised and rejected in poor law studies. Perhaps this is because relief payments appear as a plethora of small amounts of money in most vestry accounts without accompanying details and thus do not possess the glamour of those other legal records. However, these ordinary everyday payments are recorded because they represent the performance of parochial legal duties and obligations to the poor and must be accounted for annually to the Justices (see Chapter 7). Many historians take these uncontested payments for granted and thus do not see what it is these payments reveal, as they appear over and over again, recorded within all surviving sets of vestry minutes in England and Wales; that the settled poor possess a legal right to relief. Perhaps, too, this law-blindness is reinforced by an academic tendency to understand 'critical analysis' as deconstructing from the negative.

From all the above the reader will correctly deduce that most historians avoid technical legal analysis and those who attempt to do so often mis-state the law, but this is only one aspect of the picture. What is evident is that historians' reconstructions illuminate settlement law in action in a rich and varied scholarship. Unfortunately, it is problematic to read this research from a legal perspective when the law is so often mis-stated or absent. It is worse as the consequences have coloured a conventional view of settlement law only as oppressive. Removal was harsh but the concept of freedom of movement is still contested in modern British society, particularly when applied to migrants and refugees. That observer of the poor, William Cobbett, wrote in 1830 about country people to whom the next village might be unvisited alien territory, but he did not decry those people as narrow.[61] It is possible that many poor labourers and others did not wish to move away from their homes but external pressures sometimes forced them to seek employment elsewhere. Settlement did not prevent this, but many must have felt anxiety on leaving the security of their settlement parish. However, possessing a settlement guaranteed that if such a move failed they could return, or be returned and relieved in that place. Charles Dickens provides one illustration of this in *Bleak House* (1853); unfortunately for the poor, after 1834 removal increasingly meant incarceration in a union workhouse.[62]

The common law right to relief embedded within the possession of a settlement no longer survives, but it constitutes the most important 'forgotten' element missing from reconstructions of the operation of poor law in England and Wales. However, there have been some attempts to address the problem of what 'role' settlement played in poor law, what it 'meant'. The following section will examine an academic debate between two historians who specifically claim to write about settlement as law and who disagree profoundly.

The Snell–Landau settlement debate[63]

The debate originated in an article by Keith Snell in 1981 suggesting that a survey of settlement examinations could reveal seasonal patterns of unemployment. In 1990 Norma Landau contested this position, stating that her work upon settlement examinations produced in rural, eighteenth century Kent demonstrates that these were carried out as a means of general surveillance. She concludes that their timing did not have the significance ascribed by Snell. Amusingly, given the minimal doctrinal content of their work, Roger Wells has characterised their debate as: 'bogged down in the very extensive case law built up across the late seventeenth and eighteenth century'.[64] Wells considers that the crux of their differences lies in Landau's 'belief' that the terms of the 1795 Act radically changed settlement enforcement, whilst Snell disregards the Act believing it left settlement largely unchanged. Through their archival research these two scholars arrive at irreconcilable conclusions, yet both claim those conclusions harmonise with comparable materials they have consulted.

In spite of the following discussion, Snell does demonstrate legal acuity. In 1991, refuting Landau's assertions he explains that the purpose of his earlier (1985) work, *Annals of the Labouring Poor*, is to use selected pauper biographies contained within the settlement documents to discuss aspects of rural life and poverty. Unlike almost any other poor law historian except M.E. Rose and sometimes Taylor (see below), Snell emphasises the relationship between the settlement entitlement and the right to poor relief, citing Nolan, Steer and Shaw (contemporary law-text writers) as authority to underline the legal nature of settlement activity within parishes. His definition of settlement is that of a lawyer except where he describes settlement law as increasingly redundant after the mid-nineteenth century, a perspective not supported by the burgeoning case law.[65] Snell's dismissal of Landau's work is based upon a fundamental rejection of her purposive view that the settlement laws were enacted in order to monitor population movement (immigration). In 1988 Landau responds with this creative piece of legal interpretation:

> That parish officers monitored immigration should not be surprising. After all surveillance is what parliament both intended and assumed when it enacted settlement laws.[66]

She modifies this statement slightly in 1991: '[E]ighteenth century settlement laws were the legal structure which channelled inter parochial migration ... they struck a fine balance between open and close parishes.'[67]

Interestingly, subsequent research illuminates migration from a different perspective. In his 1996 doctorate, Song examines distances between parishes concerned in removing their poor to establish migration patterns in Oxfordshire.[68] He makes the valuable point that settlement documents were not direct evidence of actual migration, rather the tension between parishes over the costs of poor relief.[69] He deduces certain factors which illuminate Landau's work: poor people moved from their homes when distances to new employment opportunities were just too far to walk and when they held certificates. The author's conclusions from his work upon the Oxfordshire settlement records are that, first, a large proportion of the productive workforce moved within two miles and, second, that the less productive members of the labouring poor moved an average of ten miles.[70] Thus his explanation of migration focuses upon those concerned and suggests that the better workers are snapped up.

Although always focusing upon her narrow, purposive understanding of settlement, Landau draws upon settlement records to 'understand' the nature of settlement law. Her thorough research and conclusions deduced from primary bottom-up sources have a logical and coherent appearance. Unfortunately, as these are legal records generated by the operation of law her method remains problematic. Lawyers read law top down; its application and decisions are arrived at by applying relevant legal authorities to specific situations.

Historians draw upon primary sources, here local records, to deduce historical truths. If these sources are legal records as here, then there is a dissonance where archival research collides with lawyers' primary source, the law. The solution is to interpret local settlement records within a context of what is lawful, what the law permits, but this does not happen; Landau does not place her analysis of parish officials' actions in questioning, certificating and removing paupers within that context. In consequence, she appears unaware that, although there was wide discretion not to act, in removing paupers and appealing against Removal Orders to Quarter Sessions, a parish could only act within the legal framework of what that law permitted. No settled or irre-movable pauper could be removed and, significantly, no appeal could succeed if a settlement could not be legally challenged by the receiving parish.

Landau's other legal interpretation, which she uses to substantiate her theory that settlement law was primarily to control immigration, is extre-mely problematic. She states that changes in settlement introduced in the terms of the 1795 Act, that poor people could only be removed when 'chargeable' rather than 'likely to be chargeable' is fundamental.[71] In fact, settlement law remains as before, as we have seen only the pre-condition to action is amended. In spite of this, Landau asserts that this alteration in pre-condition 'proves' that settlement law is exclusively concerned with the supervision of migrants. In reality this amendment had the opposite effect as it removed parish officials' discretion to remove non-settled poor (not pau-pers), thus the Act restricted parochial control. If settlement law is primarily intended to control immigration, as Landau asserts, then this amendment makes no sense at all. Landau's narrow and legally incorrect interpretation colours all her work and thus serves in some way to explain the criticism it has received, albeit generally not upon these technical legal grounds. It must be noted that local officials could use settlement enquiries to monitor inco-mers if they wished but investigations, both practical and legal, plus a formal settlement inquiry in a court hearing would cost the parish and require payment out of the poor rates. Officials must in turn answer for such expenditure to the ratepayers at vestry meetings. From the examples cited by Landau this does indeed appear to be the situation in her source parishes, but such a conclusion cannot be extrapolated to include all applications of set-tlement rules in every parish in England and Wales; a criticism supported by Snell.[72] Moreover, Landau's work may concentrate upon settlement records because they are so extensive and uniform. There is clearly a temptation to use them statistically and that confers a spurious certainty upon the resulting conclusions. Nevertheless this is misleading as there are of course no com-parable records to reveal how many non-settled poor are not formally ques-tioned, a matter of significance if the researcher wishes to ascertain the motives behind the exercise of lawful parochial discretion by parish officials.

There are other issues raised by Landau's publications but this work will concentrate upon one in particular.[73] This concerns her use of case law; the only case she discusses in detail, a likely source of Well's comment above. Perhaps it is included to confer legal gravitas to the discussions, if so its appearance is a disaster. The case is *Rex v Ferry Frystone*,[74] but it appears in Landau's article as: '*Rex v Frystone*, M 42 George 14', a non-existent citation and hopefully a proofing error. Landau suggests this decision: 'may have altered overseer's practice'.[75] Case law as it filtered back to the localities through the advice of local attorneys would undoubtedly have done so. However, it is improbable that this particular example chosen from tens of thousands had much effect; it concerns the consequences of pauper death before a court issues a Removal Order. The case adds a minor detail to an equally minor rule. That rule states that neither *ex parte* settlement examinations under oath before two magistrates nor removal examinations constitute evidence admissible to prove a settlement in the absence of or insanity before the removal hearing concerning that pauper or their family.[76] The case adds a pauper's death to that list. Landau deduces that this case establishes a rule that after death a settlement was no use to dependants. This constitutes both an incorrect reading of the decision and a mis-statement of the law. As we shall in an example below, a Removal Order establishes a legal settlement and constitutes proof for dependents and for descendants claiming derivative settlement. The case cited by Landau is in fact a product of two all too common features of legal process: the adjournment of hearings and the law's perennial delays. In summary, Landau's view of settlement is fundamentally negative, informed by her conviction that its purpose is control. Moreover her use of these pathological sources, settlement enquiries and Removal Orders, simply reinforces that perspective. Landau does not demonstrate any awareness that settlement underpins the right to poor relief.

This is not true of Snell's work: he describes settlement as providing: 'a framework of economic security' and discusses the importance to the labouring classes of their ability to gain a settlement.[77] Landau's narrow focus upon migration control ensures that she does not consider settlement as a body of rights, duties and obligations centred on the parish. In consequence, her assertion that law supports her conclusion lacks substance.

Although Snell disagrees strongly with Landau's basic premise, he utilises a similar methodology in analysing settlement records in order to deduce patterns of seasonal unemployment. His work demonstrates an understanding of aspects of settlement but does not discuss legal doctrine. He appears unaware that in the matter of settlement enquiries, only the non-settled and unsettled poor came within the remit of parish officials and thus not all parish poor. He also misquotes Nolan on the interpretation of the pre-1795 rule of 'likely to be chargeable'. However, in *Annals of the Labouring Poor*, Snell emphasises the positive aspects of settlement in considering that for a poor family settlement represented an heirloom, a guarantee of parish relief.[78] He further observes that the poor continued to view relief as their privilege long after reformers took a different view. He does not develop these perceptions into recognition of the legal right to relief. However, Snell demonstrates considerable understanding and appreciation of the significance of settlement as law. There are minor technical difficulties in his accounts, unsurprising in a legal subject no longer in practice. However, Snell makes a telling point in identifying settlement and poor relief as part of what Thompson describes as the 'moral economy' of the poor.[79] This work suggests that such rights in fact represent a legal economy.

There is an additional issue in this historiographical survey that requires addressing; the absence of legal language in these reconstructions. This work opened by underlining that poor law is law and, as scholars are aware, law encompasses numerous linguistic dimensions. One of the most basic of these recognises that over the long development of the common law, words have acquired particular legal meanings thus giving them legal force. Just as case law must be cited correctly, statutes given correct titles and so on, correct terms must be used. Unfortunately, poor law historians are frequently guilty of rejecting correct legal language for other vocabulary they prefer. Sometimes this practice serves to load reconstructions of welfare's past towards the agenda of the writer; a favourite is 'pension' for relief payments (see p. 93), a term that appears in pauper letters personally asking the Justices to order relief and in overseer's responses but rarely in case law. Sometimes, incorrect language use underlines a lack of legal understanding. For example, 'pauper' is the legal term for a poor person in receipt of relief, in the twentieth century the legal term became 'poor person', but earlier 'poor person rsquo; means a person vulnerable to destitution; 'vagrant' is a poor person convicted of vagrancy, but appears additionally in nineteenth century Parliamentary Papers where 'vagrants' generally means the 'casual poor'. It must be underlined here that the imperative that dictates the use of correct legal language is not an issue of personal whim or academic debate but of legal convention.

Naturally, the discipline of History possesses linguistic imperatives. Historians dispute terms, as in the Snell–Landau debate, where Snell protests at Landau's 'anachronistic' use of the term 'immigrant'.[80] Even though Landau believes this to be an accurate and helpful way of describing a particular group in relation to settlement law, its constant repetition undoubtedly loads her discussions in support of her intellectual position. This is emphasised by an idiosyncratic definition of the settled poor as: 'immigrants ... who could never be impeded by settlement laws'.[81] Confusingly, elsewhere it is 'immigrants' who are subject to removal.[82] The term has no legal status in settlement and Landau's adoption of the term as authoritative leads to such incorrect statements as: '[I]f the immigrant employed an apprentice or servant in the new parish ... [they] ... gained a settlement.'[83] This is only true in law of a settled apprentice master or employer. The correct legal terms are settled, non-settled (possessing a settlement elsewhere), irremovable (not settled but not able to be removed) and unsettled (not possessing a settlement in England

and Wales); this is how they are always used and understood both within and without the operation of poor law.

Snell is not immune from this criticism. He too has adopted an idiosyncratic term to describe those poor people who appear in the settlement records: 'sojourner'. This description is not appropriate and its use is legally inaccurate. 'Sojourner' is one of a number of terms that appear in the 1662 Act to describe categories of settled poor. Taylor also gives weight to the term, stating that it is used in documents to define a person living away from their settlement parish.[84] It is unclear to which 'documents' Taylor refers, the term does not appear in Nolan, Justices' Manuals or case law. However, it does appear in Burn, *The History of the Poor Laws with Observations* (1764) not a legal text *per se*, used descriptively in discussing an unrelated matter appertaining to a person of indeterminate status between stranger and inhabitant who possessed no legal settlement in the parish.[85] The use of 'sojourner' by Taylor and Snell is another example of historians according formal status to non-legal terms. Thus, in Snell's idiom, paupers who were removed could comprise sojourners, strangers and inhabitants who possessed no legal settlement. This is incorrect and mis-leading; the correct term here is non-settled poor. To underline the point: there is no legal term to define the poor; they are defined by their settlement status and thus their settlement rights. Much confusion could be avoided, plus a tendency to distort academic arguments, if the correct legal terms are always applied. Snell adopts another term which, although a further drift from legal accuracy, has interesting resonance for contemporary welfare theorists; he describes settlement as a form of citizenship.[86] That he does so whilst admit-ting it is an anachronism is unhelpful. His stated purpose is to explain the concept of settlement, but his attempt serves only to compound the historians' drift from law. Settlement is settlement, there is no alternative term for this body of law and its name encompasses all its legal authority.

In order to illustrate some of the above, what follows is an account of one appeal case drawn from thousands. Significantly, this 1878 case underlines that settlement and removal remain a live legal matter long after 1834. More immediately, this example illuminates one of the saddest aspects of these cases, that families had long histories of vulnerability to poverty and removal, some for generations. In what follows, poverty stands revealed alongside the possession of a settlement as a pauper's inheritance. *The Guardians of Barton Regis Union v The Overseers of Liverpool* contains the following narrative concerning John Davis, 'the pauper':

> In 1810 an Order for the removal of Richard Davis, the pauper's grand-father, was made by the Justices of Gloucester, adjudging that his last place of settlement was then in the parish of Bedminster in the Bed-minster Union.[87] This Order was not appealed against. John Davis, the pauper's father has acquired no settlement to the present time. On the 17th November 1842 the pauper was born in the appellant's union.[88]

The law report explains that on 30 November 1875 an Order for removing the pauper from Liverpool to the appellant's union was issued. It is that union that is appealing. This case demonstrates that Davis, then living in Liverpool, aged 31 and receiving relief when the case is first heard in 1875, has not acquired any settlement during his life in his own right, neither had his father; 65 years in total. Davis' grandfather's settlement was established by Removal Order in 1810 having also sought relief. That settlement may have been inherited in turn from his father, or his birthplace if illegitimate; the possibilities and permutations are endless. To describe Davis as an 'immigrant' or 'sojourner' is legally meaningless. His status is that of non-settled pauper in Liverpool and settled pauper in the Bedminster Union (at that date the unit of settlement). In short, Davis possesses a derivative settlement in that parish to which his grandfather was removed in 1810; proof of the same was the Removal Order.

Similar details may be found in many of the cases and in all local records. These provide that rich source discussed above that is used to great effect in poor law reconstructions. One such example, despite criticisms above of his 1976 settlement article, is Taylor's *Poverty, Migration, and Settlement in the Industrial Revolution; Sojourners' Narratives* (1989), which contains a full and varied selection of these brief pauper biographies. His study is invaluable for its illustrations of law in action even though Taylor underestimates the legal complexities, perceiving settlement as purposive, concerned only with removal. However, in this work he states at one point that settlement rests upon the principle that each person possessed a right to relief, but he does not develop this point.[89] In spite of this positive element, Taylor's work is not a socio-legal account, but as an historical reconstruction of paupers' experience of settlement enquiries and the removal processes his work is the classic text.

In spite of some positive indications within the works of Snell, Taylor and also M.E. Rose, who, if not acknowledging the right to relief *per se*, closely identify relief and the settlement entitlement, few other historians recognise the significance of the legal role of settlement in poor law and therefore deny the existence of the right to relief of the settled poor.[90] Worse, there are signs that this orthodoxy of denial is hardening. Contributions to Martin Daunton's 1996 edited volume typify negative perceptions of settlement in poor law reconstructions.[91] In addition, some of these scholars read modern welfare preoccupations into that past. For example, Richard Smith compares parish officials with socially discriminating welfare fund managers and discusses the poor rate as: 'one manifestation of the collectivity'.[92] He considers vagrants as part of the 'undeserving poor', although a vagrant is a poor person convicted of the criminal offence of vagrancy. In addition, whilst acknowledging poor relief is based upon the parish he incorrectly describes local discretion in amounts and manner of relief, lawful within the legal framework, as a: 'considerable local or regional deviation from a national norm'.[93] This 'norm' is not clarified and Smith oddly refers to statutory 'theory'. Colin Jones, another contributor to Daunton's volume, manifests the continuing separation of law and history even as he develops the concept of 'community' as the main social framework in his reconstruction of charity and welfare. After noting that in England 'community' has tended to mean 'parish', he continues:

> Though utterly logical and comprehensible to most English historians, given the parish-ional (ibid) cadre within which England's poor laws operated, the choice is based more in institutional fiat than on cultural meaning of community to which parishioners may have subscribed.[94]

Thus Jones elegantly subsumes law within 'institutional fiat'. Although aspects of charity appear in these reconstructions, generally law is neglected or incorrectly discussed.

Another edited collection published in 1997 by Tim Hitchcock *et al.* drills down into a wide selection of settlement records to recreate the lived experience of the poor contextualised within their localities.[95] This work is packed with detailed pauper biographies in a series of local studies. This self-described 'history from below' aims to explore 'social relationships' between the poor and those in authority over them, but misses the larger legal framework of rights, duties and obligations. In following E.P. Thompson (1991) to develop the theme of 'paternalism', this work moves further away from law, whilst 'law in action' manifests itself unremarked by the authors within richly illustrated chapters.[96] These vivid reimagined lives do not aid our understanding of legal rights, for the editors and contributors reject the right to relief. This right is [mis]understood throughout; for example, the: 'sheer solidity and strengths of the poor's belief in their right to relief' is not explored in law but from narrative descriptions of *status quo* local circumstances. Worse there are errors: '[T]he parish was not, of course legally bound to come up with this package of a regular pension.'[97] Here the writers miss the legal obligations of the parish and express their conclusions through the mind-set and language of modern welfare provision; meanwhile both firmly and incorrectly repeating throughout the text that poor relief is a 'customary right'. The editors suggest that: '[T]he complex local triangles of negotiation between magistracy, vestry and labouring poor still await their historian.'[98] What the 'triangles' need is a lawyer. This volume devotes much discussion to the poor's belief in their right to relief but as is the convention rejects the existence of the legal right.

It is therefore unsurprising that Lees should choose an unfortunate title for her 1998 work *The Solidarities of Strangers*. Her title encapsulates a convention that rejects legal rights, yet in reality it is upon the solidarities of settlement, of neighbours and of fellow ratepayers that the poor depend.[99] However, her work is founded upon other 'rights' in a thread that runs through the work. Unfortunately, at each point where law might clarify Lees' discussion, she slips into 'customary forms' and 'popular culture' for

explanation.[100] This language frames her broader dialogue that, as in the
volume above, concentrates upon how the poor 'understood' their rights. In
discussing such perceptions, Lees draws upon E.P. Thompson's work and also
the works of sympathetic contemporaries John Clare and William Cobbett
(see Chapters 5 and 9).[101] Although Lees devotes a section to the right to
relief, she does so in order to concentrate upon popular culture and the poor's:
'conviction of the legitimacy of relief ... [and] ... a strong defence of their
social rights'.[102] There are technical legal errors, for example, in her use of an
untraceable case *King v Carlisle* 1767 [sic].[103] This case is not as significant as
Lees believes. According to her explanation of its facts and decision it is an
example of overseers successfully challenging a Justices' Relief Order thus
forcing the pauper subject of this action into the house if she wishes to receive
aid; a legal avenue closed to parish officials in 1780.[104] However, Lees provides a sympathetic account contextualised within culture and society, framing poor law within the poor's sense of rights. It is fascinating to speculate
how this work would read had Lees accepted and included the legal right to
relief as part of its heady intellectual mix.

In a more recent publication, *On the Parish?*, Steve Hindle (2000) rejects
the legal right to relief outright.[105] His work follows what is now the
established academic convention in poor law historical reconstructions: discrete sections concerning 'law'; inaccurate 'legal' discussion; separation of
archival findings from the law that generated them; and a denial of legal
rights. In spite of this, Hindle's archival reconstructions support a legal
interpretation of settlement law developing over time. When read from a
legal perspective, Hindle's research reveals vestry compliance with legal
obligations and rights plus legal local autonomy, illuminating the vital
importance of settlement as it underpins the operation of poor relief. Hindle's work confirms, however, that the denial of a legal right to relief is
established orthodoxy. In is within this context of denial that Hindle devotes
a discrete section of his book to an historiography of reconstructions of denial
of this right. Unlike Lees, he concentrates upon historians' accounts; those
who 'suggested' and accepted the right to relief, how this is now rejected
and he even suggests that Snell and others confuse the matter by introducing
settlement into their debates.[106] Hindle does not consult legal texts; he
reconstructs 'law' from the work of other historians to arrive at his 'legal'
conclusions. Nonetheless, the existence of this section has significance; for it
appears that even the suggestion of a legal right to relief must be refuted. In
short, acknowledgement of this right destabilises poor law histories, mar-
ginalises long-held beliefs, invalidates conclusions and disturbs academic
reputations that have invested in denial. In such manner it seems the door is
firmly shut and new interpretations are not required, for historians have
decided. However, this preoccupation with denial places discussion of the
right to relief at the centre of poor law academic orthodoxy and a clear target
for reappraisal and hence revision of such inaccurate conclusions.

Hindle is not responsible for the *status quo*, it is one he inherited, but he thoroughly accepts it. As a result within his work the legal reader finds incorrect conceptions and interpretations of law; a few of the more striking will be considered below. The first is Hindle on settlement. He begins with a technically incorrect statement: 'Until 1662, the only statutes that stipulated minimum periods of residence for a migrant to secure settlement and by implication eligibility for collection [sic] were those against vagrancy.'[107] What then follows is conjecture as Hindle interprets the 'meanings' of assorted statutes largely concerned with vagrancy, an entirely separate legal matter. In his archival reconstructions, however, Hindle uncovers fascinating source material from seventeenth century Quarter Sessions to illuminate how judges consider relief and settlement matters in their annual meetings. These dialogues demonstrate the complexities involved for the local judiciary as they attempt to interpret and apply the developing doctrines and principles of settlement within their localities. There is in short much detail, but none of the broader legal framework that informs and, therefore, explains this material. For example, Hindle asserts that it was a 'local' strategy to draw up lists of 'migrants', nonetheless listing the poor formed a term within a number of early poor law statutes.[108] There are numerous other examples where local activity takes place within a legal framework that is not apparent to the author. Hindle does, however, vibrantly illuminate a poor law 'system' coming into being; the role of Justices and judges in overseeing that birth and a surprising level of compliance with that settlement imperative, the right to relief. Finally, Hindle concentrates upon the non-settled poor who dominate the records and perpetuates that inherent bias towards the negative aspects of settlement.

Additionally, Hindle demonstrates another convention, the use of non-legal terms to describe matters of law. In his text poor relief is generally referred to as a 'pension', a term with inherent entitlement connotations and available for sailors and soldiers, however not from the poor rates. It appears from a close reading of Hindle's work that he is responding to a sense of entitlement by the poor, an entitlement he agrees they felt, even though he rejects the existence of any legal right. This dichotomy produces tensions within the text; most notably in a section of the work where Hindle considers refusal of relief by parish officials and hence the role of Justices in ordering aid as: 'the penal withholding of relief'.[109] Here his use of language acknowledges a legal dimension linking law, relief and its refusal; although blurred by that writer's detour into criminal justice. This is most apparent where Hindle characterises the withholding or ending of relief as: 'discretionary punishments'.[110] As we have seen in Chapter 3, although officials may be fined for wrongfully withholding relief, there is parochial discretion concerning its amount and manner. Much of this confusion concerning law, legal entitlement and developing legal doctrine is grounded in Hindle's denial of legal rights. This leads him into legal error as he asserts: '[S]ettlement was, therefore not the guarantor of entitlement; it was merely the principle means through which entitlement was regulated.'[111] He does not clarify that 'entitlement', but custom and morality appear variously in his work as potential explanations.

It is impossible to deduce legal principles from archival sources alone. Equally when understood doctrinally, the law of settlement and removal manifests an eloquent lucidity that conceals both the messy, confused way it operated in the real world and its less than smooth development over time. Although Hindle lacks a lawyer's clarity in approaching law, he does acknowledge its importance; if not directly then by implication for there is a lot of 'law' in his work. However, in spite of much legal confusion, his work is a revelation of poor law in action. That author's legal errors in no way minimise his scholarship in reconstructing the lives of those who experienced poor law. This includes those who received or were denied that aid; parish officials and those Justices and Judges at Assize who oversaw the system according to legal principles, including the right to relief of the settled poor. This last remains the correct legal reading of the proceedings he reconstructs, even as he denies it.

Lawyers and poor law reconstructions

This final section considers the manner in which the above conventions in historical reconstructions of the poor law influence and mislead current welfare texts. The three most significant are: no accurate doctrinal legal discussions; reliance upon 'legal' conclusions contained within other historians' reconstructions; and an almost universal and incorrect denial of the existence of the legal right to relief for the settled poor. One example of this was considered in Chapter 2, more will be examined below in order to establish the extent of this drift from legal accuracy and its implications for legal scholarship.

The first of these is by Ross Cranston (1985), who in examining the legal foundations of the welfare state devotes a chapter to the poor law. Much of Cranston's reconstruction is grounded in doctrinal legal analysis and contemporary textbooks. He also discusses the legal relationship between American welfare roots and English poor law. Cranston's reconstruction fully acknowledges the continuing legal authority of the 1601 Act until 1948 and takes a broad and scholarly overview of legal and juristic developments in England in the eighteenth and nineteenth centuries. Unfortunately, his section on settlement begins with the conventionally negative perceptions of contemporary poor law reformers and in spite of his extensive use of legal textbooks including Nolan for other aspects of poor law, he does not draw upon their sections on the right to relief. As a result, he mischaracterises the role and nature of settlement, relying upon the statement below upon Holdsworth's *History of English Law* (1936), whose poor law section in turn mis-states the law:

> Briefly, the law of settlement developed because the poor law placed the obligation on local areas to provide poor relief. The practice developed that a locality would receive only those 'settled' there and might

physically remove others if they applied for relief ... Once subject to a Removal Order, individuals had no right to go elsewhere, even if they would have been accepted, for the law only recognised their place of settlement.[112]

Cranston reconstructs aspects of various heads of settlement within their doctrinal framework and notes that disputes were between parishes. He recognises that persons [sic] could not be forcibly removed by poor law authorities from a locality without a Justices' Order, but then claims (without evidence) that this rule was often ignored in practice.[113] Cranston follows this with a discussion of the rule that a poor person also possessed the legal right to appeal against their Removal Order and how their destitution made this unlikely. Cranston mis-states the rules of settlement to deduce the 'hardship' for families divided by removal as possessing different settlements (a legal impossibility), then continuing: 'although in theory [sic] this was not supposed to occur so as to separate husband and wife or where young children are involved'.[114] Subsequently Cranston, although writing from the discipline of law, examines the 'right to relief' from a non-doctrinal perspective. He notes that:

> Before the welfare state, the 'social rights' of the poorer section of society consisted mainly of their claims to 'relief' (benefits and services) under the poor law. In the early nineteenth century there was a body of opinion which asserted that the Elizabethan poor law conferred an enforceable legal right to relief, but that this right was severely threatened by proposals leading to the new poor law.[115]

Cranston gives three possible sources for this 'body of opinion'. His first is that it is grounded in natural law, citing as authority Lord Ellenborough's 1803 anti-positivist stance in *R v Eastbourne (Inhabitants)*; a clever suggestion but correct for legal and not those jurisprudential reasons stated.[116] Second, Cranston cites Blackstone to suggest that poor relief is based upon mutual obligations between members of society. Finally, Cranston proposes that the right to relief may be found in the language of the 1601 Act. Unfortunately, having arrived at the correct legal position, Cranston undoes himself. He notes that cases such as *Hays v Bryant* indicate that there were 'judicial remarks' that poor law officials had a legal obligation to provide poor relief without any need for a Justices' Order. But then he demurs from this: 'as there seems to be no decision involving a direct claim by a poor person'.[117] Here Cranston is apparently unaware of Orders issued at the request of settled poor.

Cranston's legal deductions, although leading him towards the correct answer, collapse under the pressure of historians' denial of the right to relief. In short, Cranston abandons the conventions of legal interpretation to misconstrue the two cases above. At this point it seems appropriate to repeat that *Hays v Bryant* both confirmed and restated the right to relief and is so cited in all subsequent case law.[118] In addition, still misled by the weight of historical reconstructions, Cranston cites a legal textbook supporting the existence of the right to relief: 'The law of England requires that every destitute person who is in want of any necessary of life … shall receive immediate relief.' Unfortunately, he bows to historians' consensus and dismisses this as the 'rhetoric of a right to relief'.[119] The quotation is from William Golden Lumley's 1842 publication on settlement, a legal text not 'rhetoric'.[120] In summary, although there is much of legal interest in Cranston's reconstructions, he skirts the right to relief again and again and finally rejects it in his reconstruction of welfare's past. It is for this reason that his work is presented here as an example of the pernicious influence of those decades of denial in poor law histories. This is an orthodoxy that has led legal scholars to abandon their legal instincts and skills in an unfamiliar area of law that has passed from legal memory.

It is this orthodoxy that, in an otherwise sophisticated and nuanced legal account, leads Nick Wikely, in 2006, to the same conclusion: there was no legal right to relief.[121] He notes that this writer takes the opposite position but the historians win the day: '[H]owever, the historical orthodoxy seems to be rather that parishes had a duty to relieve the deserving poor, rather than the poor had a right to relief as such.'[122] Similarly Wikely acknowledges this writer's research findings, citing: '[I]n legal terms, poor law was largely settlement law.'[123] However, he too turns from a legal analysis to the social historians' reconstructions. He privileges Hindle's 'method' of statutory interpretation over that expressed in contemporary texts and cases to conclude that: 'the Elizabethan statutes did not in themselves confer entitlement. The right to relief, rather, was negotiated in the course of local practice'.[124] In short, although Wikely considers and presents both socio-legal and historians' reconstructions concerning this right, he remains another casualty of historians' misunderstanding of poor law as law. All too frequently as this chapter illustrates, the weight and 'authority' of their conclusions concerning 'law' ensure that denial of the right to relief has become orthodoxy, and not just amongst historians.

This denial, as we saw with Gillom earlier, has travelled to the United States where it influences American understandings of welfare's past. This is unsurprising as many elements of poor law are foundational in United States' welfare law, although certain legal elements could not be incorporated.[125] Amongst those that persist are funding mechanisms largely based upon and within parochial (local state) structures and remnants of the legal authority of the 1601 Act.[126] However, currently American welfare is a far from universal system which makes the transmission of historians' negativity all the more damaging; forgetting or denying those legal rights to relief that are part of a common legal heritage supports negative political agendas. This orthodoxy, whose roots, as we have seen (p. 19), may be traced from those early British writers, the Webbs,

Marshall and Hampson, is evidenced for American and British welfare law scholars particularly in the work of Jacobus tenBroek. For example, Wikely cites tenBroek's 1965 series of articles which reflect upon poor law origins in Californian welfare law. These make incorrect legal assumptions; for example, on apprenticeship, and are very sketchy on that long poor law past.[127] Moreover, tenBroek extends the negative position taken by historical reconstructions; he understands the Elizabethan poor law itself as purposive, concerned with control (particularly financial) and not legal rights, duties and obligations. It is this position that influences American legal academics.[128]

Nevertheless, even in an intellectual climate that perceives settlement negatively, tenBroek's malign view of the 1601 Act requires exploring. The first and most powerful rationale is that tenBroek blames an English past for the injustices of the American present: 'Among the images of poverty bequeathed to us by the Statutes of Elizabeth was the invidious stereotype of the poor and disabled as all but invariably the victims of their own vices.'[129] For tenBroek this translates into a legislative inevitability that the poor are responsible for their poverty and the consequent stigmatising of the poor in: 'a welfare law of crimes'.[130] This is a post-1834 attitude rather than one drawn from the seventeenth century. The second possible rationale is tenBroek's conflation of poor law and vagrancy (see Chapter 8). The third is settlement itself, as it manifests itself in modern America via a perceived direct transmission from Tudor England; it is disliked intensely by tenBroek: '[S]ettlement rules have been established as a condition of eligibility for aid.'[131] This is particularly problematic as tenBroek perceives settlement as undermining Constitutional Rights, particularly freedom of movement. It is how he comprehends these historical 'survivals' that so perturbs tenBroek, for he reads the failures of the present as a direct consequence of that poor law past, referring to: 'the custodialism of old-fashioned poor relief'.[132] Finally, it is unfortunate that tenBroek was unaware of the rights dimension contained within the legal history of poor law, for he desires a system promoting social equality and personal dignity. That is truer of poor law's legal origins than of a Californian welfare system he believes to be constructed in the image of English origins he despises. tenBroek's work remains influential in legal scholarship but his historical 'understanding' largely reflects the negative tone of poor law reconstructions. To take two further examples from American scholarship: in a comparative study of the growth of the American welfare system in 1988, Daniel Levine specifically states there was no right to relief under the English poor law.[133] This trend continues today. In his comparative study of *Poverty in World History* (2007), Steven Beaudoin notes the early establishment of a poor relief system in England and its 'mandatory nature'; that is a compulsory system of poor rates.[134] Nevertheless he emphases the control of begging, misses settlement completely and mischaracterises poor law as a system based around the 'deserving poor'; there are no legal rights in his brief reconstruction.

However, not all reflections upon the poor law are so destructive. Although academic lawyers and others have followed historians' scepticism concerning the 'forgotten' right to relief, the same is not true of the judiciary. For, although poor law is abolished, its cases survive as precedents within a common law system that exists continuously with[in] the past. It is within this juristic framework that the Court of Appeal heard a judicial review in 1996.[135] That hearing challenged a decision by the then (Conservative) Secretary of State who, it was alleged, misused powers conferred on him under statute to create regulations. These regulations excluded asylum seekers designated 'economic migrants' from claiming urgent case payments amounting to 90 per cent of the normal income support level.[136] Counterfactually, they had no right to relief. The applicants for judicial review of those regulations contended that these were not within the powers conferred under the relevant act. The Divisional Court dismissed the appeal; the Court of Appeal upheld it. Simon Brown LJ considered the relevant legislation including the European Convention on Human Rights but also cited as legal authority for his decision the reasoning of Lord Ellenborough in *R v Eastbourne (Inhabitants)* (1803), cited earlier:

> As to there being no obligation for maintaining poor foreigners before the statutes ascertaining the different methods of acquiring settlements, the law of humanity, which is anterior to all positive laws, obliges us to afford them relief, to save them from starving.[137]

And thus as his lordship in 1803 confirmed for the right to relief for foreigners, so did his twentieth century successor. The same right that is the 'forgotten past' of this book, denied by historians, doubted by legal academics but drawn upon as legal precedent by law lords.

In conclusion, this extraordinary twentieth century use of a poor law precedent, applied in a liberal and humanitarian manner destabilises negative perceptions of welfare's legal past and underlines the need to rebalance contemporary perspectives. What is more, the use of this case underlines the legal significance of the right to relief, both in the past and for today. This is of consequence as juristic analysis of welfare law relies upon incorrect reconstructions of that legal past drawn from the discipline of history. Those historians pass incorrect judgement upon matters of legal doctrine deduced from archival research and not from the discipline of law. Fortunately, Simon Brown LJ based his legal judgement upon law and legal principles and not historical reconstructions.

Notes

1   For a critical analysis of historical reconstructions within the discipline of law see Lorie Charlesworth, 'On Historical Contextualisation: Some Critical Socio-Legal Reflections',

Crimes and Misdemeanors: Exploring Law and Deviance in Historical Perspective, 1, 1, 2007, 1–40.

2 John Gillom, *The Overseers of the Poor*, Chicago: University of Chicago Press, 2001.

3 For a full discussion on this see: Lorie Charlesworth, 'Salutary and Humane Law, A Legal History of the Law of Settlement and Removal, *c.* 1795–1865,' 1998, unpublished thesis, University of Manchester, pp. 71–152.

4 P.F. Aschrott, *The English Poor Law System Past and Present*, 2nd edn, London: Knight & Co., 1902.

5 S. Webb and B. Webb, *English Local Government, Vol. 2, The Manor and the Borough*, Parts 1 and 2, 1908, reprint, London: Frank Cass and Co., 1963; — , *English Poor Law History, Part I, The Old Poor Law*, 1929, reprint, London: Frank Cass and Co., 1963; — , *English Poor Law History. Part II, The Last Hundred Years*, 1929, reprint, London: Frank Cass and Co., 1963.

6 Dorothy Marshall, *The English Poor in the Eighteenth Century; A Study in Social and Administrative History*, London: George Routledge and Sons Ltd, 1926; Ethel M. Hampson, 'Settlement and Removal in Cambridgeshire 1662–1834', *Cambridge Historical Journal*, II, 1928, 273–89; — , *The Treatment of Poverty in Cambridgeshire 1597–1834*, Cambridge: Cambridge University Press, 1934.

7 Mark Blaug, 'The Myth of the Old Poor Law and the Making of the New', *Journal of Economic History*, XXIII, 2, June, 1963, 151–84.

8 S. Webb and B. Webb, *English Local Government,Vvol, I, The Parish and the County*, 1906, reprint, London: Frank Cass and Co, 1963; — , *The Manor and the Borough*; — , *The Old Poor Law*; — , *The Last Hundred Years*.

9 Marshall, *The English Poor*; Hampson, *The Treatment of Poverty*; J.L. and B. Hammond, *The Village Labourer, 1760–1832*, 2 vols, 1911, reprint, Stroud: Alan Sutton Publishing Ltd, 1995.

10 E.P. Thompson, *Whigs and Hunters*, London: Penguin Books, 1990; — , *The Making of the English Working Class*, London: Penguin Books, 1982; — , *Customs in Common*, London: Penguin Books, 1991.

11 Philip Styles, 'The Evolution of the Law of Settlement', *University of Birmingham Historical Journal*, IX, 1964, 33–63; Blaug, 'The Myth of the Old'; — , 'The Poor Law Report Re-examined', *The Journal of Economic History*, XXIV, 1968, 229–45.

12 Webbs, *The Old Poor Law*, pp. 326–33.

13 B.K. Song, 'The Poor Law and Labour Markets in Oxfordshire, 1750–1870', 1996, unpublished thesis, University of Oxford, p. 204.

14 Sir Frederick Morton, Eden, *The State of the Poor*, 3 vols, 1797, A.G.L. Rogers (ed.), London: Routledge and Sons Ltd, 1928; Sir George Nicholls, *History of the English Poor Law*, vol. 1, 1851, vol. 2, 1860, vol. 3 published posthumously, all reissued, London: P. S. King and Son, 1904; Michael Nolan, *A Treatise of the Laws for the Relief and Settlement of the Poor*, 2 vols, 2nd edn, London: A. Strahan, 1805, reprint, New York and London: Garland Publishing Inc., 1978.

15 Lynn Hollen Lees, *The Solidarities of Strangers. The English Poor Laws and the People, 1700–1948*, Cambridge: Cambridge University Press, 1998.

16 Hammonds, *Village Labourer*, vol. I, p. 111.

17 Webbs, *The Old Poor Law*, p. 327.

18 J.R. Poynter, *Society and Pauperism. English Ideas on Poor Relief 1795–1834*, London: Routledge and Kegan Paul, 1969, p. xx.

19 Alan J. Kidd, 'Historians or Polemicists? How the Webbs Wrote their History of the English Poor Law'. *Economic History Review*, 2nd series, vol. XL, 3, 1987, 400–417, at p. 401.

20 M.E. Rose, *The Relief of Poverty 1834–1914*, London: Macmillan, 1972, p. 56; M.E. Rose. (ed.) *English Poor Law 1780–1930*, Newton Abbot: David & Charles, 1971, p. 324.

21 Their sources include all those in Richard Burn, *History of the Poor Laws with Observations*, London: H. Woodfall and W. Strachan, 1764; Webbs, *The Old Poor Law*, p. 314.
22 This statement has no basis in law: Ibid., p. 321.
23 This statement is also incorrect in law: Ibid., pp. 322–23.
24 Ibid.
25 Ibid., p.317.
26 Ibid., p. 334.
27 Webbs, *Last Hundred Years*, p. 240.
28 Ibid., p. 431.
29 Ibid.
30 Marshall, *The English Poor*.
31 Ibid., p. 169.
32 Ibid., pp. 164–65.
33 Hampson, 'Settlement and Removal'; – *Treatment of Poverty*, p. 278.
34 Hampson, *Treatment of Poverty*, p. 125.
35 Blaug, 'Myth of the Old', pp. 151–84.
36 Peter Solar, 'Poor Relief and English Economic Development before the Industrial Revolution', *Economic History Review*, XLVIII, 1995, 1–22, at 2.
37 George R. Boyer, *An Economic History of the English Poor Law. 1750–1850*, Cambridge: Cambridge University Press, 1990, p. 23.
38 Ibid., pp.11–18.
39 Ibid., p. 94.
40 Ibid., p.174.
41 Ibid., p. 191.
42 Philip Styles, 'The Evolution of the Law of Settlement', *Historical Journal*, IX, 1964, 33–63.
43 This includes the practice of issuing bonds (with named guarantors) to migrants, who gave security, with one or two other persons, to either the corporation, or after 1671, to churchwardens, often for quite considerable sums.
44 Styles, 'Evolution', p. 43.
45 Ibid., p. 44.
46 Poynter, *Society and Pauperism*; Gertrude Himmelfarb, *The Idea of Poverty. England in the Early Industrial Age*, London: Faber & Faber, 1984.
47 G.W. Oxley, *Poor Relief in England and Wales, 1601–1834*, Newton Abbot: David & Charles, 1974, pp. 15–16.
48 Ibid., p. 21.
49 Ibid., p. 42.
50 Ibid.
51 J.S. Taylor, 'The Impact of Pauper Settlement 1691–1834', *Past and Present*, vol. LXIII, 1976, 42–74.
52 Ibid., p. 45.
53   A woman having a settlement
        Married a man with none:
          The question was, He being dead,
          If that she had was gone?
        Quoth Sir John Pratt – Her settlement
        Suspended did remain,
        Living the husband: But, him dead,
        It doth revive again.
          Taylor, Ibid., p. 42.
    The original source for the poem is Sir James Burrows, *Decisions in the Court of King's Bench upon Settlement Cases*, 3 vols, London: His Majesty, 1768, p. 124. Burrows states

that the poem refers to two cases which he remembers but which he cannot find in the printed reports, *Shadwel*, and *St John's Wapping, c.* 1740.

54 Taylor, 'The Impact of Pauper Settlement', p. 44.

55 Ibid., p. 45.

56 J.S. Taylor, 'A Different Kind of Speenhamland: Nonresident Relief in the Industrial Revolution', *Journal of British Studies*, 30, 1991, 183–208.

57 Ibid., p. 184.

58 Ibid., pp.186–87.

59 M.E. Rose, 'Settlement, Removal and the New Poor Law' in D. Fraser (ed.) *New Poor Law in the Nineteenth Century*, London: Macmillan, 1976.

60 Lees, *The Solidarities of Strangers*, p. 49.

61 William Cobbett, *Rural Rides*, 1830, George Woodcock (ed.), republished, London: Penguin, 1967, p. 292.

62 In this novel, Dickens bases a plot twist around settlement. Thus the poor brickmakers and their families in London reappear in the vicinity of Bleak House. There, they are the cause of the heroine, Esther Summerson, becoming infected and scarred by smallpox. The labourers and their families return from London because they have no work. A contemporary reader would have perfectly understood that they needed to return to their settlement parish in order to obtain relief. This unexplained legal point is lost on the modern reader.

63 Norma Landau, *The Justices of the Peace 1679–1760*, Berkeley, CA: University of California Press, 1984; – 'The Laws of Settlement and the Surveillance of Immigration in Eighteenth Century Kent', *Continuity and Change*, vol. 3, 1988, 391–420; – 'The Regulation of Immigration, Economic Structures and Definition of the Poor in Eighteenth Century England', *Historical Journal*, 33, 3, 1990, 541–71; – 'The Eighteenth-century Context of the Laws of Settlement', *Continuity and Change*, vol. 63, 1991, 417–39; K.D.M. Snell, 'Agricultural Seasonal Employment, the Standard of Living, and Women's Work in the South and East, 1690–1860', *Economic History Review*, XXXIV, 3, 1981, 407–37; – *Annals of the Labouring Poor. Social Change in Agrarian England 1660–1900*, Cambridge: Cambridge University Press, 1985;—, 'Pauper Settlement and the Right to Poor relief in England and Wales', *Continuity and Change*, 63, 1991, 375–415; — , 'Settlement, Poor Law and the Rural Historian; New Approaches and Opportunities', *Rural History*, 32, 1992, 145–72.

64 Roger Wells, 'Migration, the Law and Parochial Policy in Eighteenth and Early Nineteenth Century Southern England', *Southern History*, 15, 1993, 87–139, at 90.

65 Snell, 'Pauper Settlement', p. 378.

66 Landau 'The Laws of Settlement', p. 409.

67 Landau, 'Eighteenth-century Context', p. 429.

68 B.K. Song, 'The Poor Law and Labour Markets in Oxfordshire, 1750–1870', 1996, unpublished thesis, University of Oxford, p. 171 n. 54.

69 Ibid., p. 151.

70 Ibid., pp. 173–75, 185. For a table showing the status of those certificated and the distance they moved: Ibid., p. 175.

71 Landau, 'The Laws of Settlement', pp. 391, 415; — , 'The Regulation of Immigration', p. 541; — , 'Eighteenth-century Context', pp. 419, 430.

72 Snell, 'Pauper Settlement'.

73 Charlesworth, 'Salutary and Humane', pp. 134–46.

74 *Rex v Ferry Frystone* 2, East 54.

75 Landau, 'The Laws of Settlement', 419, n. 55.

76 Nolan, *Treatise*, vol. I, p. 305.

77 Snell, *Annals*, pp. 72–73.

78 Ibid., pp. 72–74.

79 Ibid., p. 112.

80 Snell, 'Pauper Settlement', p. 380.
81 Landau, 'Law of Settlement', p. 410.
82 Ibid., p. 392.
83 Ibid., p. 410.
84 J.S. Taylor, *Poverty, Migration, and Settlement in the Industrial Revolution; Sojourners' Narratives*, Palo Alto, CA: The Society for the Promotion of Science and Scholarship, 1989, p. 8.
85 Richard Burn, *The History of the Poor Laws with Observations*, London: H. Woodfall and W. Strachan, 1764, p. 107.
86 Snell, 'Pauper Settlement', p. 400.
87 In 1878, the date of this hearing, although the pauper possesses a settlement in a specific parish, the unit of settlement is the Poor Law Union in which the parish is situated.
88 *The Guardians of Barton Regis Union v The Overseers of Liverpool* (1878) 2 QBD 295 at 296.
89 Taylor, *Poverty*, p. 169.
90 Rose 'Settlement, Removal', pp. 35–38.
91 Martin Daunton (ed.), *Charity, Self-Interest and Welfare in the English Past*, London: UCL Press, 1996.
92 Richard Smith, 'Charity, Self-Interest and Welfare: Reflections from Demographic and Family History', in Ibid.
93 Ibid., p. 30.
94 Colin Jones, 'Some Recent Trends in the History of Charity', in Daunton (ed.), *Charity, Self-Interest*.
95 Tim Hitchcock, Peter King and Pamela Sharpe (eds), *Chronicling Poverty; The Voices and Strategies of the English Poor, 1640–1840*, London: Macmillan, 1997.
96 Ibid., pp. 1–4.
97 Ibid., p. 10.
98 Ibid., p. 11.
99 Lees, *Solidarities of Strangers*.
100 Ibid., pp. 31, 74–75, 79, 162, 176.
101 Ibid., pp. 73–79.
102 Ibid., pp. 162–65.
103 Ibid., p. 31.
104 *R v North Shield* (1780) 99 E.R. 213.
105 Steve Hindle, *On the Parish? The Micro-Politics of Poor Relief in Rural England c.1550–1750*, Oxford: Clarendon Press, 2000.
106 Ibid., pp. 398–405.
107 The earliest of numerous statutes stipulating time is that of 1503: Ibid., p. 306.
108 Ibid., p. 313.
109 Ibid., p. 397.
110 Ibid., p. 397.
111 Ibid., p. 404.
112 Ross Cranston, *Legal Foundations of the Welfare State*, London: Weidenfeld & Nicolson, 1985, pp. 22–23.
113 Ibid., p. 24.
114 Ibid. This incorrect statement is cited as being from *R v Leeds* (1844) 114 E.R. 1493.
115 Ibid., p. 29.
116 *R v Eastbourne (Inhabitants)* 102 E.R. 769 at 770; Ibid.
117 *Hayes v Bryant* (1789) 126 E.R. 147; Ibid., p. 30.
118 *Hayes v Bryant*, 1 H. Black 215 at 253.
119 Cranston, *Legal Foundations*, p. 32.
120 William Golden Lumley, *A Popular Treatise on the Law of Settlement and Removal*, London: Shaw and Sons, 1842.

121 Nick Wikely, *Child Support Law and Policy*, Oxford: Hart Publishing, 2006, p. 38.
122 Ibid., p. 39. Citing but rejecting this writer's position.
123 Ibid., p. 43; citing: Lorie Charlesworth, 'A Brief History of English Poor Law', *Journal of Social Security Law*, 2, 1999, 79–92, at pp. 80, 90–91.
124 Wikely, *Child Support*, p. 44; citing: Hindle, *On the Parish?*, p. 446.
125 Cranston, *Legal Foundations*, p. 26.
126 Jacobus tenBroek, 'California's Dual System of Family Law: Its Origins, Development and Present Status', Parts 1–2 of 3, *Stanford Law Review* 16, 1964, 257; 17, 1964, 614.
127 Wikely, *Child Support*, p. 43, citing: tenBroek, 'California's Dual System', 16, 1964, p. 284.
128 tenBroek, 'California's Dual System', 17, 1964, pp. 676–77, 681–82.
129 Jacobus tenBroek and Floyd W. Matson, 'The Disabled and the Law of Welfare', in Jacobus tenBroek (ed.) *The Law of the Poor*, San Francisco: Chandler Publications, 1966, p. 508.
130 Ibid., p. 508.
131 Ibid., p. 510.
132 Ibid., p. 516.
133 Daniel Levine, *Poverty and Society: The Growth of the American Welfare State in International Comparison*, New Brunswick and London: Rutgers University Press, 1988, pp. 17, 278.
134 Steven M. Beaudoin, *Poverty in World History*, London and New York: Routledge, 2007, pp. 52–53.
135 *R v Secretary of State for Social Security, ex parte Joint Council for the Welfare of Immigrants* (1996) All E.R. 385.
136 The Secretary of State acted under powers conferred on him by ss. 135(1)(2), 137(2)(a) and 175(3)(a) of the Social Security Contributions and Benefits Act 1992. He made the Social Security (Persons from Abroad) Regulations 1996. Regulation 8 amended the Income Support (General) Regulations 1987, which by Regulation 70 had enabled persons seeking asylum in the United Kingdom who were not eligible for income support to claim urgent cases payments amounting to 90 per cent of the normal income support.
137 *R v Eastbourne (Inhabitants)* (1803) 4 East 103 at 107; 102 E.R. 769 at 770. Simon Brown LJ in *R v Secretary of State for Social Security, ex parte Joint Council for the Welfare of Immigrants* (1996) All E.R. 385 at 401.

Chapter 5

Lived experience: the poor 'speak'

Amongst the most fascinating and highly valued sources for historical reconstructions are witness accounts, broadly construed; for example there is a tradition in Holocaust scholarship that draws upon witness statements, personal
memories and trial material.[1] Poor law historians follow a similar methodology, using settlement records and other material including contemporary literature and diaries. Those works deconstructed in the previous chapter
demonstrate this methodology and, in particular, how historians place stress
upon the poor's own often recorded, widely held belief in their 'rights'.
Almost unanimously, those historians who consider this matter have concluded that the poor are expressing cultural and social norms, not legal rights.
Admittedly personal testimony can be problematic, but both groups of historians incorporate the voices of their 'witnesses' into their texts. However, it
is at this point that these two sub-disciplines of history demonstrate a fundamental methodological split. Holocaust historians argue for the value and
'truth' of remembered accounts, as Friedlander says of survivors remembering
their lives before 1940: '[T]heirs were the only voices that conveyed both the
clarity of insight and the total blindness of beings confronted with an entirely
new and horrifying reality.'[2] There are elements of respect and decency in this
perspective; moreover many of these witnesses are still alive. Perhaps this
difference is why poor law historians do not seem able to 'believe' their witnesses; if so this is poignant, regrettable and misleading. For the poor were
more than a static and abstract element of the historical past, poor law is their
story and the rights they claim are legal rights. Thus what follows is based
upon recognition that the poor often meant rights much as we do today;
something to which they were entitled – legal rights.

This perspective is adopted to underline one aim of this work; returning law
and legal rights to the heart of poor law studies. To that end, the voices of
witnesses, particularly the poor, provide vital evidence of how that law was
understood. Significantly, they remind us that law is an integral part of society,
both a constituent and a reflection of cultural norms and a mechanism for protection as well as of control. Perhaps historians, in common with many others,
understand 'law' as predominantly part of the criminal justice system. If so, this

is unfortunate as law is pervasive in society and performs many functions – not least the protection and guarantor of rights. However, if the law-minded reader, fully aware of poor law's legal rights, obligations and duties, reads poor law reconstructions he or she will find much evidence of law in action unrecognised by their authors. It is within that spirit this chapter reconstructs some aspects of the lived experience of the poor to reveal how the poor and others viewed the relief 'systems', including those of the manor, in order to reveal their awareness of legal rights. It will briefly consider the expectations and social opinions of the various participants of the poor law system and how these individuals behaved towards, and understood, each other's legal rights. In addition, it is important to note that the poor law reforms of 1834 expressed a cultural shift in economic and social relations within English society in the late eighteenth and early nineteenth century. This changing social context provided a pre-condition for the creation of a punitive welfare system, whose *grundnorm* was mistrust of a large section of the poor who many believed, and some still do believe, are responsible for their own destitution.

That mistrust was part of a world view increasingly held by sections of the gentry, a class group who held political power through interests in property and thereby the legal possession of the franchise. It must be emphasised that England is far from a democracy during this period, women do not possess the vote, neither do the labouring classes. Voting reforms in 1832 began the change, but were far from enfranchising the entire population and this was also a time of increasing public protest and disorder. In consequence, an increasing mistrust of the labouring classes by those who wielded both local and national power forms part of a dichotomy of contemporary beliefs which at the same time accepts (with criticism from some quarters) that the poor will be relieved. This dichotomy is fundamental to the local operation of the law of settlement and removal; relieving the settled poor whilst strangers ('others') and non-settled poor are to be excluded by operation of law or by other available and permitted methods. These may include: restricting new tenancies, apprenticing children in other parishes, 'encouraging' unmarried pregnant women to marry men from other parishes, issuing certificates and so on. Settlement itself possesses its antinomies, protecting and excluding; after 1834 this crystallises into a negative totality expressed within implementation of the new poor law. From that point, the right to relief is nuanced by the administrative requirement that such relief should only be given in the workhouses of the national system of poor law unions. It is that negativity, so long surviving, which made the poor law hated and whose memory, it is suggested, continues to colour historical reconstructions of poor law.

Poor law, customary law and enclosure

Not all aid to the poor came from the parish rates, for customary support provided within manors continued long after 1601. Although the terms of the Statutes of 1601 and 1662 are legal authority for relieving the settled poor under the common law, they were not the sole mechanism for the provision of aid in England and Wales. Manorial systems continued to provide base subsistence for those settled in a manor insofar as manorial rights could do so. This remains the case until manors are enclosed and thus cease their existence as a collection of legal rights concerning a defined area of land. Settlement for occupants of surviving manors encompassed manorial and poor law rights, so it is unsurprising that officials of a manor, a discrete legal unit, took action to prevent new settlement. Evidence confirms that these actions continued until enclosure, although any action was limited to those available in the manorial courts, such as fining tenants for taking in lodgers and so on. It may be obvious but it is worth emphasising that all manors sat within at least one parish and thus residents were liable for the poor rate and serving parish office, whilst also possessing a settlement and hence the right to relief derived from their settlement entitlement. Therefore, although poor law is not customary law, social, administrative and legal connections between manor and parish continue until the enclosure of these customary lands.[3] Granting tenancy on a manor, therefore, might qualify for parish settlement which conferred a legal right to relief, potentially a costly double liability, first for the manor and second for the parish. Thus manorial authority permits a second layer for controlling and/or restricting the possibilities of a poor person acquiring a parish settlement.

Local studies, concentrating here upon G.W. Oxley's 1966 research in the records of the West Derby Hundred, Lancashire, confirm that customary actions to control strangers continue after 1662 and those of the manor ran parallel to common law settlement actions.[4] As manors are not always geographically precisely co-extensive with the settlement units of a parish and manors are not 'places maintaining their poor' within the meaning of the acts, this is a complex relationship. It might be argued that as the common law develops so customary aid fades, but this does not appear to be so as actions taken to prevent non settled labourers acquiring a parochial settlement continue in the manorial courts until enclosure. Oxley's research demonstrates that the courts of the manors of Upholland, Scarisbrick and Little Crosby amerced those who took non-settled lodgers and that these actions continued throughout the eighteenth century.[5] In 1736 Ashton Court announced that a fine of 39 shillings would be imposed on those who:

> lodged and entertained wandering and idle persons and sturdy beggars ... [since] ... such practices were so disadvantageous not only to the Lord but also to the tenants [ratepayers].[6]

Other measures to prevent such arrivals were introduced by manorial courts, Little Woolton court in 1668 prohibited the letting of estates under £10 per annum to any stranger without the consent of: 'three or four sufficient men of the township'.[7] Some individuals provided bonds for their security. In the manor of Atherton in 1680, newcomers were bound to Lawrence Rawsthorn who was Lord of the Manor in his wife's right.[8] After 1690 these bonds stated that they were to the overseers. Oxley believes that this continuity of practice continued in the West Derby Hundred throughout the seventeenth century.[9]

His research demonstrates both continuation and transition of preoccupation with settlement from the mechanisms of manorial customary law to the common law jurisdiction of the Justices and the Sessions Courts. The juries of many manorial courts appointed inmate inspectors throughout the eighteenth and early nineteenth centuries to check if non-settled poor were being lodged by the residents of their manor and to bring those residents before the manorial court.[10] Offending manorial tenants were amerced and if they refused to pay, the action was transferred to the Justices for fining under the common law. It is the amercement that was transferred, not the action complained of. Poor law is not customary law, but there are social, administrative and legal connections between the two, as the possession of customary rights was an integral and important part of the economic structure for many of the poor. Oxley, in looking at court records, is concentrating on the pathology of those rights, the negative, 'top-down', control–exclusion aspects of the legal framework. This should not be allowed to obscure the corollary to this pathology, that for those settled residents who possess manorial rights the manor and its courts guarantee subsistence and therefore security. In this context, Neeson notes that the jury of Wigston in the late eighteenth century would not allow individuals who did not possess legal [parish] settlement to glean after harvest.[11]

It might be argued that this matter of manorial rights is insignificant compared to the overarching poor law 'system' covering England and Wales, but it is worth noting that in medieval England half of the land was unen-closed open fields, operating under a largely manorial system. As a result a huge section of the population was supported in traditions that parallel the later settlement poor law entitlement for the destitute.[12] This situation changed quite dramatically and by 1914 only five per cent of land was not enclosed, much as today.[13] Nevertheless, before enclosure use of those common fields and common land were regulated by regular meetings of manorial and local courts, by the decisions of juries and by field orders and fines for those who wasted the commons.[14] Enclosure was achieved as a commercial matter for profit, both in land use and in land ownership and the losers were the cottage farmers, smallholders and those who eked a marginal living with the benefit of the commons and wastes.[15] These joined the ranks of the landless labouring poor.[16] Those who lost legally enforceable cus-tomary rights of common lost the possibility of eking out a basic existence by the various shifts traditionally available to them, providing a modicum of self-sufficiency. Neeson's analysis of the effect of enclosure and the loss of common rights points to a further explanation for negative perceptions of settlement. It is evident that settlement frequently operated in a social framework where customary rights played an important economic role in the lives of many of the rural labouring classes, protecting and assuring a share of those rights to the settled poor. In consequence, after enclosure the protective element of settlement is more difficult to identify and much more so after the implementation of the terms of the 1834 Act.

Law protected and protects customary rights. It must have been traumatic to those whose manorial rights were removed to find themselves denuded of that protection which local law had formerly afforded. This was harshest for the occupiers of small cottages who were no longer able to enjoy the customs they had formerly been able to assert as of right, with the support of the manorial courts, vestry and occasionally the Justices to enforce fines. Lawful rights became unlawful via legal process. Neeson does not fully recognise the legal nature of these aspects pre-enclosure and, although acknowledging that enclosure brought loss, she follows the orthodoxy of denial even as she emphasises that if others spoke of privileges, these were 'rights', meaning a matter of personal belief not law, to those who enjoyed them:

> [T]he evidence of usage before enclosure, suggests that many commoners valued the common, not only the poorest. This is important because it means that common usage of commons was not a charity for the weakest in the village, it was a resource for almost everyone.[17]

An absence of legal analysis ensures that this sympathetic summing up still constitutes an example of the victim's voice being heard but not fully understood, not believed.

Productive commons were insurance, a reserve and the oldest part of an ancient legal economy, which allowed commoners to live simply with less need of poor relief. Their destruction destroyed a way of life; Cobbett describes the poverty of rural labourers living on the Isle of Thanet, Kent now the land was enclosed:

> The labourers' houses, all along through this island, beggarly in the extreme. People dirty, poor-looking. The cause of this ... in this beautiful island every inch of land is appropriated by the rich.[18]

What Cobbett mourns is the loss of a world governed by manorial customs. These comprised regulations governing the use of common fields and the practices of customary courts which provided opportunities for parishioners to build relationships of mutual obligation between the labouring classes, even the poorest, the farmers and gentlemen. Such customary activities as collecting wild fruit or cutting and selling turves served to foster reciprocity in local relationships and permit a sense of mutuality to be perpetuated. Seasonal shared activities associated with the produce of the commons allowed contact and developed familiarity, exchange and respect as a basis for a sense of fairness between villagers.[19] This local culture of mutuality diminished and vanished after enclosure. Agricultural practices became more private as differentiated specialised forms replaced shared use rights and the collective regulation of pasture.[20]

Neeson's study vividly illuminates the effect and value of common rights to those who possessed them, even if she does not completely locate these rights within their legal framework. Her work serves as a corrective to earlier work that consider those rights as vestigial, for example Eric Hobsbawm and G. Rude in *Captain Swing*.[21] Neeson's extensive local study adds a further layer to the picture of life for the poor at the end of the eighteenth and early nineteenth centuries. Her work serves to explain both why poverty became so desperate for many during that period and how this loss of rights for the poor became a distinctive feature of English law-making. The discontent of the poor in the early nineteenth century coupled with a fear of revolution, a larger political matter outside the remit of this work, created a climate of social uncertainty where those who had influence in the localities often feared the poor, even when sympathising with their desperate plight. Worse, a cry of 'rights' by the poor became something to be feared as a prelude to civil disorder. The increased social and economic divisions between the poor and the rest of society led inevitably to a loss of compassion. The poor were perceived as a problem and not as part of society and this, in turn, created a climate where control became more politically important than protecting rights. This situation has modern relevance where 'society' fears the refugee, the immigrant, the 'stranger'; these along with the poor and dispossessed are increasingly perceived as disconnected from society.

E.P. Thompson's moral economy as a legal economy

Enclosure was resisted by the poor who faced loss of both legal and economic rights, but as this is a local issue, so protests are local too. Thompson places the protests of the labouring classes against enclosure within a social tradition of resistance and rebellion as part of a larger popular culture.[22] He points to a strong sense of rights and fairness amongst this group, but in adopting a 'cultural' explanation underplays the legal aspects of those 'rights'. A further problem with Thompson's legal perspective is his use of the term 'custom' broadly construed; comprising both legal rights and folk customs, such as 'rough music' where local disapproval was expressed on a more social level. Although he discusses and explicitly states the difference, he does not always clearly differentiate the two in the text for the 'custom' under discussion.[23] However, Thompson's 'rebellious traditional culture' viewed through the lens of law is a reactionary culture, resisting the modernisation (by abolition) of customary rights.[24] From elements of his argument it appears that Thompson's preoccupation with class and inequality may have led him away from law. As he is unaware of the legal right to relief so he fails to consider that the 'gentry' as ratepayers retain a legal obligation to pay for the support of their neighbours, the settled poor. Thompson's 'fiercely independent' rural artisans thus may also be understood as fiercely 'dependent' when it came to understanding and obtaining their legal rights to poor relief. He notes the significance of a loss of security stemming from an increased penal enforcement of the criminal justice system, but perhaps underplays the loss of legal rights, including that post-1834 curtailment of the personal legal right to enforce the payment of poor relief. Nonetheless, the huge amount of evidence on protest and custom that has been produced by historians has testified to the high levels of local unrest both before and after 1834. If this is placed within the context of equally extensive evidence that the poor are well aware of their 'rights', accepting their words it is reasonable to suggest that it was the loss of legal rights that contributed to their discontent, rather than solely a culture of rebellion.[25]

Witness statements: listening to poor voices

What is clear is that historians have not understood poor law as law and make a fundamental category error in denying the legal existence, fully attested in case law and legal texts, of the right to relief for settled poor under the common law. This has coloured both their research conclusions and their readings of 'evidence' presented in historical reconstructions of the poor law to date. In what follows it is suggested that historians have not believed the voices of the poor to understand that 'rights' means rights that can be enforced, have a 'real' existence and are *legal* rights. In this context, contemporary writings, particularly diaries, have proved a valuable guide to how the poor perceived these 'rights' and have been a great resource for historians. For example, the Reverend William Holland's *Diaries* (1799–1818) are often cited in historical reconstructions: they provide evidence of how the poor are relieved and their attitude to that relief. However, less well observed is that they illuminate the right to relief in action.[26]

It is, therefore, suggested that the following extracts should be read in their legal contexts. These include: church charity is discretionary, but clergymen have a duty to disperse it; the settled poor have a legal right to relief but the manner and amount are at parish discretion. This is another aspect of the 'conditionality' that appears to confuse modern understanding of those legal rights. However, no matter how 'difficult' individual settled paupers are, even if some become subject to the criminal justice process, they still must be relieved and they know it. Hence Holland records:

> The poor came for meat and corn this cold weather and against Christmas Season. Some very thankful and some almost saucy. If a man had

not some object beyond the gratitude of his fellow creatures he would never do a Charitable Act as long as he lived: [23 December 1799].

Holland took over the vicarage and parish church of Over Stowey, in Somerset, in 1779. He kept a diary from that year until his death. Holland did his 'duty', but in his diaries demonstrated little sympathy for some of the parish poor. This is not surprising: those poor knew their place and it was not always the place Holland wished them to occupy. On occasion, the overseers resisted their claims and refused relief; but the poor knew their legal rights and applied to the Justices and were sometimes successful. Holland thoroughly disapproved of this situation.

In addition, the settled poor of Over Stowey know how important the appointment of parish officials are to their comfort and peace of mind, for they naturally wish and require that the exercise of parochial discretion in the amounts and manner of relief be in their favour. Thus Holland bitterly recounts an annual vestry meeting:

> But the Poor of the Parish got intelligence of it and crowded upon us in such a manner that we scarce knew what to do. The Overseers are harassed to death and summoned every day before a Justice, this will never do. Our Poor Rates are four times the sums they were two years ago. The Justices attend to every complaint, right or wrong, and every scoundrel in the Parish croud to make their complaint ... they expect to be kept in idleness or to be supported in extravagance and drunkenness ... They grow insolent. Subordination is lost and make their demands on other people's purses as if they were their own: [13 October 1800].

This passage reflects the increasing costs of poor relief during this period and the personal annoyance of an aggrieved ratepayer who is angry that the Justices will enforce the legal right to relief. Holland knows that the parish must relieve the settled poor when destitute and worse, that the poor know it. It is not surprising he is so angry; he is frustrated, out of pocket and powerless to prevent these claims.

Worse, the paupers don't behave well when relieved, as events in the poorhouse the following year reveal:

> Mr James Rich and Mr John Poole doing something in the Poor House. What I cannot tell. I suppose examining it, it is in sad repair and those two villains who dwell there tear everything to pieces: [24 January 1801]. I understand there will be a bustle in the Poorhouse tomorrow as a Special Warrant has been issued against many of them. Indeed it is a sad set of thieves. Such people left to themselves will never do, they corrupt one another. Every Poorhouse ought to have a Governor to keep them in order: [26 January 1801]. I find that the Constables have been at the Poorhouse

and carried off three of them, viz Porter the fellow who pretends to be seized with fits now and then when it suits his purpose and Rich a woman of a very bad character in many respects and Bet Carter who turns Evidence and the worst of the lot. Another little woman, Bet Pierce, confirms the evidence of the former but that hardened villain William Hill as they call him stays behind and Porter's wife. The first is an old and experienced rogue and will not go out to plunder with the rest lest they should discover, and now he hugs himself in his Superior Sagacity. But I trust he will be found out when he least expects it as his haunts are pretty well known: [27 January 1801]. There has been a bustle in the Poorhouse ... Some of them had beat down a partition and got into the Sunday School and stole some wood from thence: [1 February 1801].

Unfortunately, the next four diary notebooks are missing, so we do not know the outcome for all concerned although Porter does continue to cause Parson Holland grief. What we can deduce is that matters are so out of control that those paupers named above will be appearing before the Justices and possibly sentenced to prison. If Hill is drinking and/or gambling, he could be convicted of vagrancy (see Chapter 8). What we can know is that convicted or not, on return they are going to be relieved when destitute. The test is destitution not character and this bad lot, well known in the village, will still receive aid. They are settled, it is their legal right and hence the explanation for that relief is not the various suggestions made by historians, which include 'monitoring immigration', 'control', 'negotiation', 'custom', 'culture' and 'politics of survival'.

What is evident is that the poor responded to law on their own level within the context of their own culture. E.P. Thompson and Douglas Hay have examined local practices that were on the cusp between 'folk' and 'enforceable' custom, such as local gentry tolerating moderate game poaching in times of dearth; noting that the poor rate costs were kept down when the poor had access to such 'resources'.[27] They uncover the manner in which 'formal' law destroys customary 'rights and assumptions'.[28] It can be argued that the weakening of traditional legal jurisdictions facilitated this process and allowed the erosion of non-legal, but formerly tolerated activities. A strong 'system' would have resisted the criminalising of traditional pursuits, for although poaching and trespass were always punished within the customary manorial system and the criminal law, this was generally done according to local usage and within the context of local need and knowledge. Thompson acknowledges that compared with the horrors of slavery, or those inflicted by the Third Reich, perhaps it is over-reacting to be so passionately concerned with rights lost by the poor through the operation of law but concludes:

I am disposed to think that it does matter ... the law when considered an institution ... may very easily be assimilated to those of the ruling class ... But all that is entailed "in the law" is not subsumed in these institutions ... what was often at issue was not property, supported by law, against no property; it was alternative definitions of property-rights ... when it ceased to be possible to continue the fight at law, men still felt a sense of legal wrong: the propertied had obtained their power by illegitimate means ... For law was often a definition of actual agrarian practice, as it had been pursued 'time out of mind', ... this law, as definition, or as rules ... was endorsed by norms, tenaciously transmitted through the community.[29]

Although Thompson is referring to local non-legal customs, how much more powerfully his words resonate when the right to relief is factored into his assertions.

Not all the gentry match Thompson's picture of class war as thoroughly as the bitter Parson Holland, admittedly exposed to the 'rougher elements' professionally; others took a kindlier stance. One such is Dorothy Wordsworth, living in Cumbria with her brother in considerable poverty. In her diary she records a number of poor people whom she encountered and those she assisted:[30]

> At Rydale, a woman of the village, stout and well dressed, begged a half-penny; she had never she said done it before, but these hard times! [14 May 1800].

This is clearly a respectable woman, 'well dressed' and well nourished, who has fallen on hard times. Dorothy provides another example:

> On Wednesday evening a poor man called, a potter – he had long been ill, but was now recovered, and his wife was lying in of her 4th child. The parish would not help him, because he had implements of trade, etc. etc. We gave him 6d. [20 June 1800].

What is evident is that the potter has not satisfied the overseer's test of destitution; he is not ill and has the means to work. Thus the parish have no legal obligation to relieve, yet still Dorothy and William are moved to assist him. William illustrates another aspect of poor law in 1802. 'Alice Fell; or Poverty' concerns a distressed pauper child he met travelling at night alone at the rear of a post-coach.[31]

> 'My child, in Durham do you dwell?'
> She checked herself in her distress,
> And said, 'My name is Alice Fell;
> I'm fatherless and motherless.'
> 'And I to Durham, Sir, belong.'

Again, as if the thought would choke
Her very heart, her grief grew strong;
And all was for her tattered cloak!

The poet tells us that he gave some money to the innkeeper to replace her cloak and:

Proud creature was she the next day,
The little orphan, Alice Fell!

Sentiment aside, this is a settlement story. A contemporary reader would understand this as the story of a child being returned to her settlement parish to be relieved. There is a hint she might be illegitimate (perhaps to make the poet look more virtuous) for the settlement rules at that date state that a bastard child is the legal responsibility of their birth parish and thus is to be returned there once they reach the age of seven. Modern cynicism aside, this may appear an odd theme for a 'Romantic' poet. That is the point; the Wordsworths illustrate the dichotomy of poor law in expressing an alternative cultural norm that is sympathetic to the poor and in the case of the poet, inviting the reader to share that perspective. This is William the Radical, the believer in rights. Paternalist this may be, but a very different paternalism to that of Parson Holland.

The final voice is that of a very different poet, it belongs to John Clare. Although an almost contemporary of the Wordsworths, he was born into great poverty. His poem *The Parish*, written between 1823–26, relates the 'story' of Clare's settlement parish where he and his parents, mired deeply in poverty, were subject to what he voices as abuse of power by vestry and local officials.[32] Clare exemplifies bottom-up evidence. He was born into a near illiterate peasant family in the village of Helpston, situated in the Northamptonshire fens where, having learned to read, he stole time away from his labouring work to read and later write in secret. His poetry protests against the exploitation of the poor and against the enclosure of land.[33] By 1820 he had achieved fame in the literary circles of London, met Coleridge, Hazlitt, Charles Lamb and others.[34] Sadly, he subsequently developed serious mental illness. Although he is often referred to as 'the hedgerow poet', this is a misleading description. *The Parish* is no jolly bucolic romp in a rural idyll and unsurprisingly was not published during the author's lifetime. Written as Clare first achieved fame, it consists of 2,202 lines of bitter, satirical, passionate spleen, without full stops or commas, the angry outpourings of a man denouncing the cant and hypocrisy he has witnessed and experienced in local village life. Clare wrote at a time of great social upheaval where traditional ways of life were under political challenge from the Whigs, under commercial threat from economic pressure and cultural threat from the zeitgeist.[35] Old rural ways of life are changing, with clear winners and losers.

Clare records these transformations and expresses very eloquently that sense of loss and how the poor experienced treatment by parish officials. Thus the overseer:

> treats the poor oer whom he rules as slaves
> And stints the pauper of his parish fare. (lines 1026–1027)

Clare's condemnation of those whom he believed had lost sight of their role in society sits in the tradition of Chaucer's *Canterbury Tales* and, like Chaucer, Clare attacked the worldly clergy (hunting parsons) whilst lamenting the loss of the 'good old Vicar' who cared for the parish poor. Clare was not, however, a dilettante lamenting a lost golden age. He writes as one of the labouring classes whose life before literary success lay in the hands of the parish and its officials. Those officials had extensive power and influence over the lives of the labouring classes through their legal roles in the operation of the poor law. Clare's voice puts flesh on these legal bones. His 'Parish' is his settlement parish where he and his parents are subject to the power of the vestry and local officials. In 1819 his crippled father became totally destitute. Clare senior had been breaking stones for a small wage, possibly parish work as part of the package of measures taken by vestries to enable the poor to remain partially self-funding. Clare himself took a series of labouring jobs to assist his family whilst he wrote his poetry.[36] He earlier attempted to become a lawyer's clerk but was rejected on sight. In his autobiography Clare writes that, as his fame spread, he had to endure many insults from local magistrates, shopkeepers and farmers. The village of Helpston, more or less owned entirely by the Fitzwilliam family, was what contemporaries describe as a close parish.

In short, Clare was born in the worst of all possible worlds, traditional but without dignity and respect for the poor. And yet, he too knows his rights and mourns the changes. His poem opens in rage:

> The parish hind oppressions humble slave
> Whose only hope of freedom is the grave
> The cant miscalled religion in the saint
> And Justice mockd while listening wants complaint
> The parish laws and parish kings and queens
> Prides lowest classes of pretending things. (lines 1–7)

When Clare's father was no longer able to work, he was faced with the prospect of the workhouse for himself and his wife, losing the room he rented and his possessions being sold towards the cost of their keep; in line with the legal position requiring destitution to trigger the right to relief. In addition, it was a legal requirement for a son to pay towards his parent's relief in the workhouse.[37] Fortunately for Clare, his first volume of poetry, *Poems Descriptive of Rural Life and Scenery* was published in 1820 and it became an overnight success. He was able to keep his parents out of the workhouse, but continued to struggle financially for some time.

The value of *The Parish* as a primary source for a socio-legal reconstruction of welfare's past lies in the subtleties of Clare's ambiguity about his poverty, revealing dichotomies and antimonies embedded within poor law to a modern reader. *The Parish* concerns a local vestry under the old poor law. There, a settled pauper denied aid could assert his common law right to relief by applying in person to a magistrate; as noted earlier, if an Order is issued but not obeyed the overseer may be indicted, although courts disliked fining these unpaid officials.[38] Meanwhile, the manner of that aid and the attitude by officials to the poor remained local, externally unsupervised and culturally led. In short, we cannot know how it felt to those driven by refusal to ask the Justice for aid, to face the overseer in court and be argued over as a thing. Aid was a legal right, but how much public humiliation was involved in enforcing that right?

> Tho justice Terror who the peace preserves
> Meets more of slander than his deeds deserves
> A blunt opinionated odd rude man. (lines 1400–1402)
> Tho pleading oft meets with harsh replies
> And truths too often listened too as lies
> Altho he reigns with much caprice and whim
> The poor can name worse governers than him. (lines 1406–1409)

And how did the overseer respond when called to account for not obeying the Order? And more, was the pauper grateful?

> He pleads bad times when justice chides his ways
> Tho justice self is ill deserving praise. (lines 1954–1955)

Although relief is a legal right for the destitute settled poor, Clare's Justice did not perhaps always fulfil that duty, or sufficiently control the overseers' reluctance to pay that aid. Holland expected gratitude, Clare's parish officials perhaps did too; Clare shows how little gratitude is deserved.

In his rage, Clare castigates doctor, farmer, clergy, spinster and all who form part of village life and society from 'quacks' and 'knaves' to the vice ridden and the drunk. Reading the poem today enables the reader to experience that world from a sharp and critical perspective. Clare stands behind the reader's shoulder, prodding with his pen to make us understand his words as he speaks of law:

> Heaven shield thee England in thy ancient cause
> From tyrant governments and broken laws. (lines 1000–1001)

No reader can doubt that Clare's satirical references to a land of liberty cloak a passionate belief in freedom, in rights and in traditional values. He castigates all parish officials but reserves particular venom for the 'Clerk' whose role in collecting the poor rate extends to the poor for they too are liable for rates. This official, as was his legal duty, 'claims' the property of the poor to ensure that they pay or, if they appear likely to fall on the parish:

> Tasking the pauper [his] labours to stand
> Or clapping on his goods the Parish Brand
> Lest he should sell them for the want of bread
> On parish bounty rather pind than fed. (lines 1278–1281)

Clare is our witness that by the 1820s the poor are relieved but law is experienced punitively, that they are being humiliated as their legal right to relief is grudgingly 'honoured' and worse. They are fully aware that the legality of their settlement relief entitlement is disrespected and thus diminished in the eyes of officials and magistrates.

Social historians have recovered much evidence from the records of the poor processed through the poor law; historians of gender have recovered valuable sources to inform their writings, but if socio-legal history is to achieve at least part of its purpose it needs very particular sources in order to provide the context within which an academic analysis may be constructed. Ideally, the historian of law seeks the voices of those who spoke specifically of law, preferably from their own experience, in this case of how poor law as law impinged upon their daily lives and opportunities. Much negative material can be found in the Parliamentary Papers of the period, written largely by those who advocated reform of the poor law. In contrast to these, there are other commentaries written by those more sympathetic to the plight of the poor, ranging from the writings of William Cobbett to those of Nathaniel Hawthorne in the 1860s.[39] Charles Dickens' novels and journalism provide astute observations upon poor law. His novels contain much evidence that poor law as law surrounded and directed the life choices available to the poor. All these contemporary sources provide rich evidence of the role poor law as law played in the lives of the poor.

Nevertheless, John Clare's poem *The Parish* provides something very special for a socio-legal historical reconstruction. The crucial value of *The Parish* lies in its author's self-awareness. It is easy to find horrors in poor law records, reconstructions of settlement concentrate upon its negative aspects and the works of Thompson and others are out of fashion with revisionist historians. Today poor law historians examine the legal records and deduce the purposes of law from non-legal perspectives. However, the presumptions within Clare's poem illuminate the erosion of rights; how 'law' explicitly within the text was mocked by parish officials and thus eroded by corruption and change as payments of relief degrade recipients in the parish world-view. What matters too is that Clare tells us in a clever linguistic turn, 'justice' still supports the poor, saying of his 'Justice': 'The poor can name worse governers than him' (line 1409). Clare makes that degradation of the poor explicit, he shows us how grudgingly those legal rights and duties are performed in his settlement parish in order (he feels) to humiliate the poor and he permits and invites us to share his grief and his rage. In short, John Clare's poetry, mediated through his personal experience and pain, provides the reader with a sense of shared experience, a context for experiencing the operation of the poor law unlike any other. There is an immediacy in the work which gives a quality of reportage to the text, the reader stands in the shoes of a poor man and feels the slights, the righteous anger of the writer and the hypocrisy of the village 'kings and queens'. *The Parish* is written by a poet who knows he will never be allowed to forget his family's pauper status.

There is something else here too, an echo of that worldview that E.P. Thomson spent his life reconstructing and analysing, his moral economy that may also be understood for the relief of poverty as a legal economy. John Clare provides us with further evidence to support this perception; his voice is witness to a world of legal rights under threat. Clare wrote of how things were, of a time of mutuality when the priest shared what little he had, the farmers shared their homes with their labourers, before the 'parish huts', where the poor are housed, fell into decay.[40] Although some commentators on Clare's work have dismissed this sentiment as a yearning for a mythical golden age with its 'folk memory' elements, yet there is external evidence to support his view: not just in the works of Thompson, Peter Linebaugh and others, not only in contemporary records but also in the reality of those legal rights in his words.[41] These writers have reconstructed ample evidence that the poor possessed their customs, both traditional and legal, and that without exaggerating the position had as important a part to play in village life as any other group. By 1820 the traditional English rural way of life is in decline and Clare's poem is a witness statement recording that decline and he provides us today with evidence of the distress individuals suffer as positive social customs and legal rights are eroded.

It is far from my purpose to reduce Clare's poem to a poor law critique. Clare deserves more from his readers than this plundering for academic purposes but his words, his perspective, have relevance not just for reconstructing poor law's legal past but also for his twenty-first century reader concerned with the alleviation of poverty. For those who do not acknowledge the legal rights of the poor that were for so long part of our legal culture, this witness John Clare shames us:

> The rich man is invisible
> In the crowd of his gay society
> But the poor mans delight
> Is a sore in the sight
> & a stench in the nose of piety.[42]

Notes

1 Most notable is that adopted by Christopher Browning, *Ordinary Men: Reserve Police Battalion 101 and the Final Solution in Poland,* New York: HarperCollins, 1992, and subsequently, rather less stringently, by Daniel Goldhagen, *Hitler's Willing Executioners; Ordinary Germans and the Holocaust,* New York: Alfred A. Knopf Inc., 1996.
2 Saul Friedlander, *Nazi Germany and the Jews, Vol. 1, The Years of Persecution, 1933–1939,* New York: Phoenix, 1997, p. 2.
3 W.E. Tate, *The English Village Community and the Enclosure Movements,* London: Victor Gollancz Ltd, 1967, pp. 31, 45.
4 G.W. Oxley, 'The Administration of the Old Poor Law in the West Derby Hundred of Lancashire 1601–1834', 1966, unpublished thesis, University of Liverpool, pp. 136, 154–56.
5 Ibid., pp. 136–37.
6 Liverpool Record Office (hereafter LRO). DD Li; Ibid.
7 Oxley, 'Administration', p. 139.
8 LRO, PR/1776; Oxley, 'Administration', p. 141.
9 Ibid., p. 142.
10 Ibid., pp. 154–56. Noting that in the North of England parishes were generally large so were sub-divided into townships for poor law administration. These townships generally follow the pre-existing manorial structures. Thus Tranmere on the Wirral was based upon the manor of Tranmoll.
11 J.M. Neeson, *Commoners: Common Right, Enclosure and Social Change in England, 1700–1820,* Cambridge, Cambridge University Press, 1993, p. 324.
12 Robert Allen, 'Agriculture during the Industrial Revolution', in R. Floud and D. McCloskey (eds) *Economic History Since 1700, Vol. 1, 1700–1860,* 2nd edn, Cambridge: Cambridge University Press, 1984, p. 97.
13 Neeson, *Commoners.*
14 Ibid., p. 134.
15 E.P. Thompson, *The Making of the English Working Class,* New York: Pantheon Books, 1963; E.J. Hobsbawm, *Industry and Empire: An Economic History of Britain,* 2nd edn, London: Abacus, 1968; Frank Sharman, 'An Introduction to the Enclosure Acts', *The Journal of Legal History,* 10, 1989, 45–70.
16 G. Rogers, 'Custom and Common Right: Waste Land Enclosure and Social Change in West Lancashire', *The Agricultural History Review,* 41, 1993, 137–54, at 152–53. For a full discussion of the legal processes involved, see: Sharman, 'An Introduction'. Mingay notes that one of the problems created by enclosure was that compensation for loss of rights was given to the owners of property, the right attaching to the property not the person and thus not to the tenants who used those rights: G.E. Mingay, *Parliamentary Enclosure in England,* London: Longman, 1997, p. 125.
17 Neeson, *Commoners,* p. 174.
18 William Cobbett, *Rural Rides,* 1830, George Woodcock (ed.), republished, London: Penguin, 1967, p. 206.
19 Neeson, *Commoners,* p. 182.
20 Ibid., p. 255.
21 E.J. Hobsbawm and G. Rude, *Captain Swing,* New York: Lawrence and Wishart, 1968.
22 E.P. Thompson, *Customs in Common,* London: Penguin Books, 1991. see also: — , *Whigs and Hunters* 1975, reprint, London: Penguin Books, 1990; —, *The Making of the English Working Class,* London: Penguin Books, 1982; D. Thompson (ed.), *The Essential E.P. Thompson,* New York: The New Press, 2000; Douglas Hay, John Rule, Peter Linebaugh and E.P. Thompson, *Albion's Fatal Tree,* London: Allen Lane, 1975.
23 Thompson, *Customs,* pp 3–6.
24 Ibid., p. 9.

25 B. Bushaway, *By Rite, Custom, Ceremony and Community in England 1700–1880*, London, Junction Books, 1982; A. Charlesworth, 'The Development of the English Rural Proletariat and Social Protest, 1700–1850: A Comment', in M. Reed and Roger Wells *Class, Conflict and Protest in the English Countryside, 1700–1880*, London: Frank Cass, 1990; Hobsbawm and Rude, *Captain Swing*; Mingay, *Parliamentary Enclosure*; Neeson, *Commoners*; Rogers, 'Custom'; M.E. Rose, 'The Anti Poor Law Movement in the North of England', *Northern History*, vol. I, 1966, 70–91; J. Rule, *The Labouring Classes in Early Industrial England 1750–1850*, London: Longman, 1994; E.P. Thompson, 'The Moral Economy of the English Crowd in the Eighteenth Century', *Past and Present*, vol. 50, 1971, 76–136; — , *Making of the English*; — , *Whigs and Hunters*; — , *Customs*; Wells, R., 'The Development of the English Rural Proletariat and Social Protest, 1700–1850'; 'Social Conflict and Protest in the English Countryside in the Early Nineteenth Century: A Rejoinder', in Reed and Wells (eds) *Class, Conflict*.

26 Jane Ayres (ed.), *Paupers and Pigstickers The Diary of William Holland A Somerset Parson, 1799–1818*, Stroud: Allan Sutton Publishing, 1984.

27 Thompson, *Whigs and Hunters*, pp. 261–63. Thompson opens this book with a discussion of the foresters whose customary rights were being eroded and closes with the Whigs whom he held responsible. See also: D. Hay, J. Rule and P. Linebaugh, *Albion's Fatal Tree*, London: Allen Lane, 1975.

28 D. Sugarman, 'Theory and Practice in Law and History: A Prologue to the Study of the Relationship between Law and Economy,' in B. Fryer, A. Hunt, D. McBarnet, and B. Moorhouse (eds) *Law, State and Society*, London: Croom Helm, 1981, pp. 86–88.

29 Thompson, *Whigs and Hunters*, pp. 260–61.

30 Dorothy Wordsworth, *Lakeland Journals*, London: HarperCollins Publishers Ltd, 1994.

31 William Wordsworth, *Collected Works*, New York: Oxford University Press, 2000, p. 241.

32 Eric Robinson (ed.), *John Clare: The Parish*, London, Penguin Books, 1985, p. 11. For a fuller poor law reconstruction of this poem, see: Lorie Charlesworth, 'John Clare's *The Parish*, a Rural Idyll?' *Liverpool Law Review*, 2/3, 2001, 167–78.

33 Roy Porter, *Enlightenment. Britain and the Creation of the Modern World*, London: Penguin Books, 2001, p. 75.

34 Robinson, *John Clare*, pp. 9–10.

35 See: Thompson, *Making of the English*; *Customs*; Neeson, *Commoners*.

36 These included field-labourer, gardener and lime burner: Robinson, *John Clare*, p. 11.

37 This common law duty was restated in the terms of the Poor Law Amendment Act of 1834.

38 Ross Cranston, *Legal Foundations of the Welfare State*, London: Weidenfeld & Nicolson, 1985, pp. 31–32.

39 Randall Steward (ed.), *Nathaniel Hawthorne: The English Notebooks*, Oxford: Oxford University Press, 1941.

40 Recent research has demonstrated the longevity and extent to which farm servants lived with their employers: Steve Caunce, 'Farm Servants and the Development of Capitalism in Early English Agriculture', *Agricultural History Review*, 45, 1997, 45-60; Gary Moses, 'Proletarian Labourers? East Riding Farm Servants', *Agricultural History Review*, 47, 1, 1999, 78-94; Alun Howkins and Nicola Verdun, 'Adaptable and Sustainable? Male Farm Sservice and the Agricultural Labour Force in Midland and Southern England, c. 1850-1925', *The Economic History Review*, 61, 2, 2008, 467-495.

41 E.P. Thompson and Peter Linebaugh, *The London Hanged; Crime and Society in the Eighteenth Century*, London: Allen Lane, 1992; Hay *et al.*, *Albion's Fatal Tree*; Peter Linebaugh and Markus Rediker, *The Many-Headed Hydra*, London: Verso, 2000.

42 Robinson *John Clare*, p. 25. This is the final verse of an anonymous poem, entitled 'Rich and Poor; Or Saint and Sinner', published in *Drakard's Stamford News*, 20 July 1821, believed to be the work of John Clare.

Chapter 6

Paupers as textual analysis: exploring the settlement entitlement through *Little Dorrit*

The previous chapter proposes that the voices of the poor should be heard and believed for they speak of well-established legal rights. This chapter adopts a doctrinal legal technique in order to reconstruct a further dimension of the pervasiveness of settlement law; namely the manner in which precise details of each pauper's life have consequences for his or her settlement entitlement. It underlines how settlement is contingent upon the life story of each individual, that it is truly a personal legal right. In order to do so this chapter puts on the robes of a nineteenth century attorney and, as near as is possible in hindsight, reconstructs the settlement entitlement of two individuals. Sir John Baker, taking a doctrinal approach, argues that this is impossible and only a contemporary practitioner could truly understand: 'what was the law'.[1] This chapter represents a challenge to Baker's pessimistic assertion by taking an innovative approach. It explores those settlement implications contained within the life stories of Amy Dorrit and Arthur Clennam, lead protagonists in Dickens' novel *Little Dorrit*. Perhaps over-extended as a metaphor, this constitutes as much a literary conceit as doctrinal legal analysis, however it permits this fictional couple to serve as a trope of contemporary life and a base upon which the application of this repealed law may be mapped. Although this methodology has counter-factual elements, in form it echoes a classical teaching technique, that of the student case study; long established within the discipline of law from the earliest apprentice training at the Inns of Court to modern university law schools. Traditionally, common law teachers tell a story, a fiction of people and events that students are required to deconstruct. Those students must identify the legal issues and discuss them fully, not to produce a 'right' answer or one solution, but to note all ambiguities and difficulties. As academics, we ensure that such case studies do not provide sufficient factual detail to allow an easy solution; rather we omit and even mislead to test the legal skills of the student.

This case-study method forms part of the rationale for this choice of methodology, as does the nature, content and purposes of those hundreds of thousands surviving first-instance poor law legal records. At first glance, these appear a valuable resource as most are concerned, directly or indirectly, with the settlement and possible removal of an individual pauper (and their family). In addition, they contain biographical details of age, occupations, residence patterns and life circumstances. However, this depth is illusory. These records are taken at a specific moment in time and such biographical details are brief. It is also extremely difficult to obtain further family histories of such poor individuals. In consequence, they would not be appropriate as a teaching tool, neither do they provide the rich tapestry of fact and obscurity found within the chosen literary source, *Little Dorrit*. Indeed, one could set the novel as a legal assignment on a course in poor law. Furthermore, the novels of Charles Dickens are still widely read and celebrated for expressing concern for the poor; they contain full biographies of contemporary fictional individuals who either potentially or within the novels 'experience' poverty. Additionally, although *Little Dorrit* was written in the mid-nineteenth century the narrative falls within the time scales of both the old and the new poor law. This permits a reconstruction of the law of settlement and removal in action at a time of significant legal transition and illuminates how little that law changed.

Reading *Little Dorrit* through the lens of law offers a methodology that illuminates legal doctrine, it is not a literary critique aiming to produce fresh insight into the novel. It is conceded that *Little Dorrit* is not an obvious choice, for other novels such as *Oliver Twist* deal more graphically with poverty. However, for a lawyer, the circumstances of the lives of Arthur and Amy, the twists and turns from destitution to riches and back again, provide examples of a rich variety of possible/potential settlement problems. Furthermore, despite a lack of detailed poor law narrative, *Little Dorrit* does express concern for the plight of the poor. It is noteworthy, for example, that the first part of the novel is titled 'Poverty'. For our present purpose, the novel contains detailed biographies of Arthur Clennam and Amy (Little) Dorrit, who marry at its conclusion. Between them their stories illustrate many of the issues relevant to those poor law officials who needed to decide if a pauper possesses a settlement in their parish and is therefore legally entitled to poor relief. Dickens provides the reader with sufficient clues to deduce some of the poor law solutions and leaves enough gaps in the narrative to present a lawyer with the sort of problems contemporaries would face. In addition, the book is well known and this permits readers to follow the legal arguments without requiring too many biographical explanations.[2]

In this context, there is evidence within the novel of Dickens' own legal knowledge and experience.[3] One aspect of that evidence has a settlement resonance. Arthur Clennam was illegitimate, legally a 'bastard'; such a child in 1857, the year in which Dickens published his novel, was: 'considered (in law) the offspring of no one'.[4] This theme is subtly nuanced within the novel. Dickens shows Arthur Clennam describing his own emotions as that of 'nobody's' as he reflects upon his own unworthiness in falling in love with the daughter of his friends, the Meagles. This subtle legal irony, a lawyer's joke, reflects both the importance of Arthur's illegitimacy for the plot of the novel and lets the reader into a secret that is always kept from Arthur. It is a rather cruel joke. Certainly, chapters in Book One emphasise this theme: Chapter XVII is titled 'Nobody's Rival' and Chapter XXVI 'Nobody's State of Mind'. This issue concerning the legal status of those born outside marriage has, as we shall see below, important implications when establishing a pauper's settlement. In summary, the information available in the novel provides the reader with enough biographical details to permit the reconstruction of many of those questions necessitated by the legal doctrines of settlement law that would so have exercised overseers, lawyers and Justices of the Peace. Some of these questions concerning a pauper's personal life history would have been asked every time relief was sought. As such, this study must stand for the thousands of settlement enquiries that took place in courts in England and Wales each year. In addition, it illuminates the legal problems raised as vestries fought each other to avoid the ascription of legal and hence financial responsibility for maintenance of the destitute poor. For the primary motive for all this legal activity over hundreds of years was financial. Any prudent ratepayer would wish to minimise poor rate costs and establishing that a pauper family possessed a settlement elsewhere was the only method of doing so.

The sections of the chapter reconstruct first Amy Dorrit's and then Arthur Clennam's settlement entitlement at each stage of their 'life' histories in a linear manner. This entails a close textual reading of the novel to link their stories with the legal doctrines of settlement law. Where relevant, that narrative will analyse how the legal position altered during the nineteenth century. An historian seeking to answer questions raised by the study of poor law archival sources will find some solutions in those legal issues raised by personal details within each pauper's biography. Hence, each pauper in receipt of aid has approached the officials of a specific parish and demonstrated their destitution and the first question a responsible parish official was duty bound to ask was: does this person possess a settlement here? It must be emphasised that the law was not concerned with the character of the pauper; if they were 'deserving' or not, simply did they possess a settlement in this named parish?

The first section of this chapter concerns Amy, her story and its settlement implications, including a discussion of the settlement of her father, William Dorrit, 'Father of the Marshalsea'. It examines Arthur's life in the same way, for once he and Amy marry, she takes his legal settlement. Then the chapter moves beyond the novel to provide a brief exemplar of how the overseers of any parish where a pauper family applies for relief approached the question of their settlement. This is the reverse of the earlier legal textbook analysis. The overseers' investigation begins (after 1795) at the moment the pauper seeks aid. If no settlement is proved in the residence parish and, as here, it concerns a married couple, the overseers trace the husband's life story backwards chronologically and geographically until a place of settlement is established. Once a provable settlement is discovered, the investigations end.

Legal advice may be taken and the legal process begun. This requires that the overseers apply to the Justices and start a formal settlement inquiry in a process described below. If a Removal Order is granted, then the couple and any dependent children are taken to that place established as their father's lawful settlement, even if he has never lived there.

As settlement is a detailed and complex matter, this reconstruction will only briefly cover aspects of those heads of settlement relevant to each party's situations. There are two legal points that require underlining. The first we have met often, that the legal basis for relieving poverty is the authority of the 1601 Act, always so stated in the case law. The second is that the legal basis of most of the statutory settlement qualifications, namely hiring and service, serving a parish office and apprenticeship, etc., was that each established residence in a parish for 40 days. Satisfying these 'rules' provided the necessary qualification of 'notice' required under the terms of the 1662 Act. These 'rules' underpin the following reconstruction.

Establishing Little Dorrit's settlement

Our eponymous heroine's story opens as she cares for her father in the Marshalsea in London where they are both living.[5] This was the small debtors' prison of the King's Court of Westminster where Amy Dorrit was born and her father imprisoned for debt. William Dorrit remained in prison for 23 years until it was discovered that he was heir to a fortune and he bought his freedom. Dickens sets the novel in his past, some: 'thirty years ago'.[6] This places the opening scenes in c. 1826,[7] an historical solecism as the Marshalsea moved to the site of the old Surrey County Gaol in 1811. Dickens' father, with some of the family, were imprisoned there for debt in 1824 when Dickens was a child and perhaps that is too sharp a memory for the novel.[8] However, a textual explanation suggests that as Amy's father had been in the prison since 1804, factual accuracy would disrupt the plot.

We can deduce from the novel that Little Dorrit was born in prison in 1804, that her mother died soon after and Amy lived and grew up in the prison. Therefore, by the start of the narrative she is 22. Sometime in the following year her father's inheritance is revealed, he settles his debts and leaves the prison as William Dorrit of the 'Dorrits of Dorsetshire' (c. 1826–7). Amy and Arthur marry in 1828 when she is 24 and he 42. The number of sub-sections below reflects the relevant settlement issues that surround their personal circumstances. It is worth noting that paupers are not passive within this legal process. Despite the complexities of the legal questions surrounding settlement entitlement there is evidence that paupers are aware how their factual evidence could affect their legal status. Historians have illustrated how some demonstrate legal sophistication in answering settlement questions and this is evident within surviving settlement records today.[9]

Settlement by birth

The general rule holds that a legitimate child's settlement at birth follows that of its father until it is eight years old: 'but after that age it may acquire another settlement'.[10] There is also case law which indicates that children could achieve emancipation before the age of eight and the legal situation remained ambiguous (*Rex v Macclesfield; Rex v Witten cum Twambrokes*).[11] However, Little Dorrit acquired her father's settlement at birth, although a question arises over the place of her birth. Did that affect her settlement? In fact, the legal issues surrounding birth in prison only concern the settlement of an illegitimate child.[12] This writer has been unable as yet to find any case law concerning a mother giving birth in prison who, as here, was not actually a prisoner. There are cases concerned with giving birth in a House of Correction (*Suckley v Whitborn*)[13] and in the County Gaol (*Elsing v The County of Hertfordshire*).[14] For legitimate children where the father possesses a settlement, the place of birth is irrelevant and the child acquires the family settlement at birth (*Coxwell v Shillingford*).[15] Amy's father could only have acquired a settlement in the prison parish (St George) under one of the heads of settlement. This is improbable in his destitute state and after an Act of 1814, even that bare possibility is removed.[16] Thus, her place of settlement at birth is that possessed by her father. As a result, if faced with any request for relief from Amy before her marriage, parish officials would not be interested in obtaining a copy of her birth record from the local parish ledgers; rather they would concern themselves with tracing her father's settlement.

William Dorrit's settlement

William Dorrit's life provides much that is of interest to a poor law lawyer and a great deal that allows us to reconstruct a settlement narrative. We do not know much of his history, however Dickens tells us that he was a 'gentleman'.[17] His ostentatious pretensions to respectability whilst detained in the Marshalsea are a mixture of arrogance, denial and pathetic inadequacy; classical petit bourgeois behaviour in a crisis. The social facade that he requires his family to maintain remains resolutely middle class throughout the many events of the novel; from dire poverty to great wealth William maintains the right to 'his' place in society. William Dorrit's place of settlement as the novel opens is untraceable from the details provided by the author. The Dorrit family moved into the Marshalsea Prison *en masse*, Little Dorrit's birth there indicates the degree of destitution into which the family had fallen.

At the moment he was imprisoned, however, William Dorrit's settlement became relevant to his wife and small children. Although as a prisoner he could not be removed, the rest of the family are vulnerable for: '[a] wife [and children] ought to be sent to the place where her husband was last legally settled'.[18] The application of this rule required separation, removal and parish relief for the Dorrit family and thus the only alternative to the workhouse was keeping the family together in prison.[19] In this manner, the plot mirrors the realities of the Dorrits' poor law vulnerabilities under settlement rules. Hhowever, at some point during his 23 years in prison, William Dorrit's settlement changes. He is informed that he is: 'heir-at-law to a large fortune'.[20] More significantly for our purpose, under common law doctrine possession of an estate confers a settlement.

Settlement by estate

Settlement by estate is defined by Blackstone as: 'such interest as the tenant has in lands, tenements or hereditaments'.[21] The nature of this property is not expressly defined; the principle seems to be that the party should not be removed from 'his' freehold but is entitled to the care of 'his' property (*Ryslip v Harrow*).[22] Nolan comments in 1805 that: '[a]n estate to which the party is entitled by descent will always confer settlement, without regard either to the annual or total value of the interest' (*Rex v Great Farringdon*).[23] There are complex legal discussions concerning proofs of title, for settlement by both inherited and acquired estates, these were unlikely to have affected William Dorrit's possession of a settlement in Dorset.[24]

Separation from family

For Amy, the date of her father's settlement by this inherited estate has significance for establishing her settlement before marriage. Nolan states that where a father's settlement changed after the birth of a child, then as long as the child is part of the family the child takes the new settlement.[25] If that child is emancipated and has acquired a settlement in their own right then any settlement the father subsequently acquired is not transferable to him/her (*Rex v Witten cum Twambrokes*).[26] However, a child who remains with her parents beyond 21 years old in an unbroken continuation derives her settlement from her father.[27] By the same token, if a child separates from her parents during her minority and that separation continues after she reaches the age of discretion, she does not follow her father's settlement (*Rex v Roach*).[28] In Amy's case, this is a matter that would have exercised the ingenuity of the overseers or their representatives, as they seek to resolve the legal issues. Amy Dorrit is 22 as the novel opens. She lives in a separate room in a different part of the prison and is working for Mrs Clennam. The question of her settlement in law at this point hinges upon three matters: when did her father acquire his new settlement as inheritor (date unknown); is she separated from her family at that date; and has she acquired a settlement in her own right? The writer cannot establish the answer to the first question and the last question requires a consideration of settlement by hiring (see p. 127). What follows will consider the matter of separation; if not separated from her family, then Amy may possess her father's settlement in Dorset.

Is Amy emancipated? As the story opens she is not married neither does she appear to have acquired a settlement in her own right. To be legally emancipated she must be actually separated from her family. To make matters more complex, Nolan considers that every separation did not in fact amount to emancipation in law.[29] Thus, in a case where a son left home occasionally to assist in the harvest, he was deemed to remain part of his family (*Rex v Sowerby*).[30] It appears that even where a parent gives a master or others legal control over his child: 'provided he reserves to himself so much of the parental rights as are consistent with it ... he [the child] is not emancipated'.[31] These parental rights could include arranging to wash the child's clothes or receiving their wages. The final proofs of emancipation are concerned with a child returning to the family home before the age of 21 without having achieved a settlement in their own right. The terms of the 1834 Act did not alter this legal position. In these circumstances, such is the level of dependency upon Amy by the whole Dorrit family it seems unlikely that she would be considered as emancipated for settlement purposes. As she is 22, single and certainly considers herself to be part of the family, it seems likely that this minor settlement rule would not have prevented her acquiring her father's settlement in Dorset. That is, unless she had acquired a settlement by other means.

Settlement by hiring and service

This head of settlement might have changed Amy's legal position by giving her a settlement in a London parish and thus either prevented her from acquiring her father's Dorset settlement or superseded it. The rules for settlement by hiring and service derive originally from the terms of a statute of 1691.[32] These require a bona fide contract for one year's service, joined with 'residence as such' for 40 days. In addition, the sections of an Act of 1696–97 add a requirement that: 'such person shall continue and abide in the same service for the space of one whole year'.[33] There are four subordinate heads to this method of gaining a settlement: who is capable of gaining a settlement by hiring and service; the contract of hiring; the year's service; the residence and place in which the settlement is gained.[34] Without going into the extraordinary detail of this head of settlement, it is possible to say that Amy's employment with Mrs Clennam and Flora did not qualify for settlement *per se*. More persuasively, if there are times in the hiring when the servant is left to her own devices and the mistress could not exercise any degree of authority over her, then the service is short of a year by the:

> sum total of these exceptions. Whether these reservations are made of particular seasons or days, or even hours of the day, the servant gains no settlement under a contract infected with this exception.[35]

This was further clarified per Foster J, in *Rex v Wroughton*: 'A right of control and authority, at least so far as relates to the general discipline and government of the servant, must reside in the master at all times during the continuance of the service'.[36]

In conclusion it appears by applying these precedents that Amy gains no settlement through her employment with Mrs Clennam and later with Flora; neither of these women exercises a sufficient level of control over her life. The detailed information required by the courts under this head of settlement has ensured that hirings and thus the working patterns of the labouring classes are found in great detail within the poor law records. An overseer seeking such information would be very aware of what was needed and point his or her questions to that end. This head of settlement, the chief method by which the labouring poor were able to acquire a new settlement, was abolished from 14 August 1834.[37] This leaves one final method by which the heroine of Dickens' novel may acquire a new settlement: that she become Mrs Clennam.

Settlement by marriage

Nolan summarises the legal position as:

> Wherever a woman intermarries with a man who has obtained a known settlement, it is communicated to her, although she has never been where it is gained (*St Giles v Eversley*).[38] And every succeeding settlement that he acquires is in like manner transferred to her immediately.[39]

With Amy's marriage to Arthur her settlement became that of her husband. Therefore, to establish her legal settlement after marriage, it is necessary to ascertain his.

Arthur Clennam's settlement

At the time the novel opens, Arthur Clennam is described as: 'a grave dark man of forty';[40] this places his birth date at around 1785. Arthur tells his friends, the Meagles, that he left England to join his father in China to work in the family business: 'shipped away before I was of age',[41] probably in 1805. He remained: 'more than twenty years in China',[42] and returned to England after his father's death in order to dissolve his financial relationship with the family concern. (The legal significance of these events will be discussed below.) Subsequently, Arthur forms a business partnership with Daniel Doyce, engineer, inventor and joint proprietor of the works and office in Bleeding Heart Yard off Hatton Garden. This dateline, with its geographical and narrative detail, is of vital importance to an overseer's settlement investigation.

It is unclear from the novel the precise nature of the legal estate held by Doyce and then jointly with Clennam after they became partners. In addition, Clennam is described as lodging in Covent Garden upon his return to

London; a room and landing are described, but no further details are provided in the novel.[43] Later, with Daniel Doyce: '[T]he two partners shared a portion of a roomy house in one of the grave old-fashioned City streets, lying not far from the Bank of England, by London Wall.'[44] There, Arthur has a separate sitting room. As we shall see (p. 131), the question of settlement could hinge upon such trivia. Although all these locations are fairly geographically close in London, many are in different parishes.[45] It would be of concern to each potential settlement parish to establish that some other named parish would carry the burden of the couple and any children produced by this young wife. It will be clear by this point to those familiar with the novel, that this writer has moved outside the literary integrity of Dickens' narrative to achieve this legal reconstruction. This couple, with their self-reliance and many friends, are unlikely to approach the overseers for aid. However, here they stand for the many families with young children whose parents, faced with misfortune, fall into destitution. As a result, this left parent(s) and children likely to be a burden upon the rates for a considerable period.

A further settlement issue surrounds the question of Arthur's birth: born out of wedlock, in legal terms he is a bastard. The novel reveals that his father was 'involved' with a young woman trained as a singer. Once Mrs Clennam, Arthur's 'mother', discovers the child's existence, she confronts her husband's mistress and demands the child:

> Give him to me. He shall believe himself to be my son, and he shall be believed by everyone to be my son ... to save your child from being a beggar, you shall swear never to see or communicate with either of them more.[46]

This narrative constitutes more than gossip; it has legal significance in establishing Arthur's settlement. In a further reference to the lack of status connected with illegitimacy Mrs Clennam continues: 'I devoted myself to reclaim the otherwise predestined and lost boy; to give him the reputation of an honest origin'.[47] The novel reveals that the story of his birth is to remain a secret from Arthur. However, as this topic was of great concern to parish overseers it will be reconstructed below.

Settlement by birth

As we have seen, at birth a child takes his or her father's settlement; but this rule does not apply to illegitimate children. Dickens' draft notes for *Little Dorrit* state that Arthur's father's legal relationship with Arthur's mother was to be that: 'he was already married, in a false name: – or as good as married'.[48] However, under the terms of Hardwicke's Act 1753, informal 'common law' marriages were not valid;[49] plus, of course, he already had a wife. Arthur's settlement by birth therefore follows the legal 'rules' for illegitimate children. Such children born before 1834 are settled where they are born. This is the legal explanation for the attitude of poor law authorities towards the arrival of unmarried pregnant women in their parishes; a view brutally articulated by Dalton in 1742:

> Illegitimate children are considered the children of no-one; or as it is sometimes termed, to cut off all idea and hope of peculiar relationships, the child of the people ... There exists no privity of blood between it and the reputed parents, through which it can lay claim to their settlement and it is settled in the place of its birth ... [as] ... lawful children are whose parents have none.[50]

The few exceptions to this rule would not have affected Arthur's legal position at his birth c. 1785 as they concern the mother's removal by fraud or birth in an institution. The proofs required by the settlement inquiry before the Justices include evidence where Arthur was born. This is difficult to ascertain from the text and could be equally difficult for the overseers. However, those officials have a financial interest in doing so and would ask some very personal questions to get hold of the necessary information. Hence, fascinating life-style material for social historians can be found in the records of these particular settlement examinations before Justices. Clare reveals their level of public humiliation.

It is evident that the doctrinal rules of settlement applied to illegitimate children are harsh. This is especially so where the mother gives birth outside her settlement parish and subsequently both mother and baby are removed to that parish. In such circumstances, the child is then likely to be returned to her birth parish at a tender age, as in Wordsworths' poem 'Alice Fell', discussed earlier. This is a likely outcome where the mother's parish wishes to avoid financial liabilities; after all, the child is not their legal and hence financial responsibility. Dalton states that such a pauper child remained with its mother until it was seven years old, then: 'it is to be sent to the place of its birth to be provided for the mother or reputed father not being able'.[51] This legal position explains the very real nature of the threat hanging over Arthur's biological mother had she kept her son and become destitute. Her settlement may not be the place where she gave birth. As a result, Mrs Clennam has the upper hand. The terms of the 1834 Act change the legal position of illegitimate children born after that date to take their mother's settlement.[52] As the Act does not operate retrospectively, Arthur Clennam's birth settlement as an illegitimate child possibly (see p. 135) remains the parish in which he was born; unless he subsequently acquired one by other means.

This presents further difficulties. As Arthur spent all his adult life abroad he could not have acquired a settlement in his own right until his return to England. There, his interests in the family's (commercial) business do not satisfy any settlement requirement as being neither in land nor property.

Once in England, the novel provides no evidence of other methods by which Arthur could acquire a settlement: serving a parish office or being hired and he was too old to be apprenticed. Consequently, the only possible methods left to acquire a settlement are by renting a tenement or by possession of an estate. The latter is the more promising, but renting will be considered first.

Settlement by renting a tenement and paying parish rates

Under the terms of the 1662 Act any person could acquire a settlement by residing in a property with a yearly value of ten pounds. Subsequent case law established that for freehold or copyhold interests the yearly value of the tenement was immaterial.[53] In 1805 the legal position was such that part of a house qualified as a 'tenement': thus renting a fifth and sixth floor unfurnished with one door and one staircase conferred settlement (*Rex v St. George's, Hanover Square*).[54] In the novel, Arthur shares a portion of a house with Daniel Doyce, and until 1819 (see p. 132) such a tenancy could have granted Arthur settlement in that parish, provided that the value of the moiety occupied by him was ten pounds per year.[55] Although the terms of the 1662 Act appear to state that settlement by renting is acquired by qualifying tenements in which persons: 'could come to dwell', by 1805 it is established law that the ability to pay ten pounds per annum is the foundation of the settlement; it is irrelevant whether a pauper has rented for occupation or profit.[56] Thus it was held that a watermill (*Evelyn v Rentcomb*)[57] and a windmill (*Rex v Butley*),[58] neither with living accommodation, are tenements that confer a settlement. It is therefore possible that Arthur's financial interest in the engineering works in Bleeding Heart Yard gave him a settlement in that parish.[59] In the unlikely event that his interest is restricted to the machinery in the works then he could not acquire a settlement.[60] Such complex life circumstances led to disputes between parishes where a pauper potentially held two settlement-conferring tenements. However, earlier case law states that if an individual holds different kinds of tenements in different parishes, the settlement question is resolved by establishing where the party is the lawful occupier at a yearly rental of ten pounds, for a residence of 40 days (*Reg. v Inhabitants of West Ardsley*).[61]

In 1819 and 1825 this legal position is partially amended by statute.[62] After 1826 a tenement to be rented must consist of a separate and distinct dwelling house or building, or of land, or of both.[63] A close reading of the novel reveals that Arthur acquired his interests in house and business around 1826–27 and thus would have been caught by the provisions of these two Acts. The requirements of these two statutes, read in conjunction with the terms of the 1662 Act, ensure that to establish a settlement, Arthur must prove a number of factors. These are: he has *bona fide* rented a tenement consisting of a separate and distinct dwelling house or building: 'in such parish, at and for the sum of ten pounds per year at the least, for the term of one whole year at the least'.[64] There was great legal difficulty about the definition of 'separate and distinct', but there seems little doubt that the terms of the statutes of 1819 and 1825 would have reduced Arthur's claims to acquiring a settlement by his shared residence at London Wall. Two later cases serve to illustrate this position. In 1836 it was decided that an occupier of the middle floor of a house divided into three tenements, who used the outer entrance, but who could reach all his rooms without interfering with the other entrances except for one room, occupied a 'separate and distinct' dwelling house within the meaning of the terms of the 1825 Act (*Rex v Great and Little Unsworth*).[65] Another case concerns the renting and occupation of the ground floor of a house consisting of a shop and two rooms. Entrance was by back and front doors that, along with a passage, were shared with the tenant of the first floor rooms. Both tenants had keys to the doors and shared responsibility for cleaning the passage. On these facts, it was held that this was not a separate and distinct dwelling house and the tenant did not acquire a settlement.[66] In spite of this decision, throughout this period it remains possible to add up the value of commercial and domestic renting to a sum of ten pounds per annum to acquire a settlement. However, the properties must be in the same parish, the residence be separate and distinct, but not the commercially rented land (*Reg. v Inhabitants of West Ardsley*).[67] If Arthur's residence did not qualify financially, but was in the same parish as Bleeding Heart Yard where the engineering works were situated, then he could have acquired a settlement in that parish.

To acquire a settlement after 1831, Arthur and Amy (married in 1827) would need, in addition to all the above, to have occupied a tenement for one year.[68] After 1834 additional requirements were added; that the pauper had been assessed and paid one year's parish poor rate.[69] All the above continue to require residence in the parish for 40 days under the terms of the 1662 Act. The arrival of Arthur in England in 1825 and his particular pattern of residence with Doyce render his settlement by renting unlikely, subject to the possibilities discussed above.

Settlement by estate

The unanswered legal question in the novel, one which concerns this manner of acquiring a settlement, is the precise nature of Arthur and Doyce's financial interests in Bleeding Heart Yard. A positive answer could establish Arthur's settlement in Hatton Garden in the City of London. In support of this proposition, the novel explains that Arthur bought a partnership in the business. As such, it is worth considering the possibility that Arthur Clennam possesses a settlement on the basis of holding an estate in the property consisting of the engineering works in Bleeding Heart Yard. This chapter has considered settlement by estate in the context of William Dorrit, Amy's father. An accepted method of acquiring such an estate was by purchase;[70]

such an estate conferred settlement.[71] Arthur Clennam bought his partnership in 1826 and, if the engineering works potentially conferred a settlement
upon him, then it would only be if he resided: '40 days in the parish in
which his estate lies, and while he is in possession'.[72] Otherwise: 'it makes
no difference whether he resides on his own estate, or at other persons, or in
an alehouse' (*Rex v St Nyott's*).[73] Thus, the proofs are that the party has a
vested interest in possession in lands or tenements situated within the parish
where he claims settlement and that the 40 days residence requirement is
satisfied. If he satisfies these legal requirements, then Arthur possesses a settlement in the City of London, acquired sometime between 1826 and 1827
(the overseers will need to establish the exact date). The terms of the 1834
Act made some minor changes to settlement by estate, but these are unlikely
to have affected Arthur's settlement status.

These heads of the law of settlement and removal possess many more
complexities than have been discussed above. As such, it must have been a
challenge to those sent to enquire into a problem of this nature; the variety
of enquiries settlement required was enormous However, in populous city
parishes some of these overseers would be specialists. It is hardly surprising
that lawyers' fees now seem disproportionate to the individual amounts of
relief being requested and paid to pauper families. Many historians have
considered that this was due to a fear of future parochial liabilities. Perhaps
it was also because lawyers, then as now, charged large fees and, as happens
in legal actions today, a parish may have embarked upon the inquiry and
spent so much money on legal consultations and advice that they became
'locked into' the process. There are other reasons. Some vestries disliked
neighbouring parishes, some were close parishes and some may have liked a
fight. Richard Gough wrote of the first of eight settlement cases that the
parish of Myddle disputed before 1700: 'This was the first contest that we
had and thus wee lost it; but thanks be to God wee never lost any afterwards'.[74] A small parish faced with a family of paupers whose father or
widowed mother share a complex life history similar to Arthur Clennam
would have found themselves with a large bill, not only for legal advice but
also for specialist enquiries and searches to be made.

The overseers' settlement inquiry: objectifying the poor

Following the novel, it seems unlikely that Arthur Clennam and his family
would have sought parish relief. However, if they sought aid then they
entered a well-established legal process of inquiry and enforcement with
formal requirements. The overseers of the parish would immediately enquire
into Arthur's settlement status to establish whether Arthur qualified for settlement available under the various current heads. If he was not settled, the
parish possess legal discretion to grant the family relief on a temporary basis.
However, if a parish wishes to avoid setting up a legal presumption that

Arthur Clennam possesses a settlement where he claims relief, officials would need to begin the formal settlement inquiry. This involves an examination of Arthur's personal history by warrant, under oath before two Justices at the Petty Sessions. If the parish then wishes to remove the family, a decision to initiate removal may only be taken upon the grounds that the said persons are 'chargeable' (receiving poor relief). More importantly, parish officials must establish a specific named parish against which to bring their action, with proofs sufficient to avoid or defeat a potential appeal against that judgement.

Meanwhile, Arthur, like any other poor person, still has the opportunity to produce suitable evidence to show he possesses a settlement where he claims poor relief. If he is unable to do so, this might (at the discretion of parish officials until 1865) lead to him again being brought before two Justices under warrant at the Sessions and examined under oath. If the officials establish a settlement elsewhere to the satisfaction of the court, a writ for removal to that parish, containing the names and ages of the entire family, will be issued. Thus any pauper involved in this formal legal process faces at least two court appearances before Justices, a daunting prospect for any individual, let alone one who is destitute. If a Removal Order is issued, the pauper and family are liable to immediate removal and together will be sent to Arthur's now legally established settlement parish. The receiving parish may appeal against this decision to the Quarter Sessions within 30 days, either upon the grounds that the pauper possesses no legal settlement in their parish or that there is a procedural fault in the removal process. The pauper and family remain in that parish until the legal issues raised in the appeal are settled. These matters could be, and often were, litigated to the highest level; this might take years with the 'objects' of the action, the pauper and family, relieved in the receiving parish. If the receiving parish wins its appeal, then the paupers are returned to the originating parish, which is at liberty to restart the process, but only if it can establish an alternative settlement parish. If no settlement can be proved then it is deemed to be where the pauper was born. If that cannot be ascertained then the originating parish is liable to maintain the family.

These procedures govern all settlement actions and concern the non-settled poor; they are not available against settled, irremovable or unsettled paupers and the Irish and Scots are subject to different legal rules (see Chapter 8). Whatever local motives govern officials' actions in monitoring new arrivals in their parish their potential for action is always circumscribed by these expensive formal legal processes. It is not surprising that they pay casual poor to go away, that they sometimes drive people out, even dump pregnant women outside the parish boundaries; even though some of these actions leave them personally liable to prosecution and they must account for others to the vestry. This is a legal system and operates because it is a legal requirement to maintain the settled poor when destitute. Without that requirement there would not have been a poor law 'system'. Despite that right to relief Clare is a witness to the reluctance and unpleasantness with which officials could carry out their legal duties. In addition, historians have reconstructed sufficient bad behaviour by parish officials to indicate that without the legal rights, duties and obligations protected by settlement, many places would not have relieved the poor and the social history of England would have been very different. This will be considered in Chapter 8; how to reconstruct a poor law system without the right to relief was introduced into Ireland with catastrophic consequences.

However, the legal right to relief existed and the remainder of the chapter will revisit settlement entitlement in a mirror image of the above discussions in order to reconstruct a contemporary inquiry. The following approach is the one that officials adopted in all settlement cases in order to establish the most recent possible settlement. As each new settlement acquired destroys that previously held, enquiries follow a linear method, but moving backwards in time. In this context, if Arthur has not acquired a settlement in the parish where he seeks aid, then the issue of his interest in the property in Bleeding Heart Yard will be investigated and the partnership details considered. If they qualify, provided that Arthur has lived in that parish for 40 days then he possesses a settlement in that parish. If not, then the inquiry will consider his tenancy at London Wall. If that is in the same parish as the engineering works of Bleeding Heart Yard and that qualifies as above, then his settlement there is confirmed. If not then all the problems of establishing separate and distinct dwelling houses become a live legal issue. It may be that none of the above establishes a settlement.

In that case, as there is no evidence that Arthur has acquired a settlement under the other heads of settlement since his return to England, then he possesses his father's settlement in the City of London, near Thames St.[75] Had the fact of Arthur's illegitimacy emerged, then the question of 'bastardy' might become a live issue. However, it is a principle of poor law not to enquire into the nature of the legitimacy of a child unless called into question: 'for the law does not presume that the parents have lived in a state of concubinage criminal in them and productive of penal disability to their innocent offspring'.[76] It appears that it lies with an objecting parish to raise such an argument at appeal at Quarter Sessions. Establishing that settlement requires an examination of a copy of the relevant parish register showing Arthur's birth or christening, with evidence of his identity (*Rex v Creech*).[77] However, in situations where parents acknowledge the pauper as their lawful child, as in Arthur's case, that would have been sufficient (*Rex v Bucklebury*).[78] If this is the case, then this confirms that he possesses a settlement in the City of London, in the parish where he and his father lived so unhappily. In the unlikely situation that 'bastardy' is successfully raised and not subjected to the legal challenge above and all the other proofs have failed, then Arthur possesses a settlement in the parish where he was born. Amy's settlement is not a factor; upon marriage she acquired her husband's settlement.

Although this reconstruction reveals some of the complexities of settlement law, there are other doctrinal aspects not covered as they are not relevant to Amy and Arthur's settlement inquiry. Chief amongst these are derivative settlement, settlement by apprenticeship and the later legal status of irremovability. Nevertheless, this reconstruction demonstrates the potential for costs in spiralling litigation should a parish appeal against a Removal Order and it reveals some of the legal niceties that made such litigation likely; plus there is potential for parish expense by officials who travel on behalf of the ratepayers to investigate settlement claims. In summary, this account offers a brief taste of a repealed branch of the common law in order to illuminate the powerful and immediate impact of that law upon those who were subject to its operation; that is, all those who were vulnerable to poverty. The choice of questions by overseers and Justices was directed by legal and not social considerations, but nevertheless this left a pauper standing in court exposed to public gaze as just another piece of the evidence.[79] This must have been very clear to those paupers who were subjected to this legal process, as so many were. The settlement entitlement guaranteed and protected the right to relief; but this work does not seek to minimise the corollary to that right, the requirement for some to become the object of this legal ritual.

Notes

1 J.H. Baker, 'Why the History of English Law has not been Finished', 59 *The Cambridge Law Journal*, March, 2000, 62–84, at 67.
2 There is a six-hour film in two parts, directed by Christine Edzard, 1987; and a BBC television series, 2008, of *Little Dorrit*.
3 Dickens began his writing career as a law reporter at Doctor Commons: David Sugarman, 'Law and Legal Institutions', *Oxford Reader's Companion to Dickens*, Oxford: Oxford University Press, 1999; Christopher Hibbert, *The Making of Charles Dickens*, London: Longman, 1967; Peter Ackroyd, *Dickens*, London: Minerva Press, 1990.
4 Michael Nolan, *A Treatise of the Laws for the Relief and Settlement of the Poor*, 2 vols, 2nd edn, London: A. Strahan, 1805, reprint, New York and London: Garland Publishing Inc., 1978, vol. I, p. 174.
5 As was then the norm, prisoners' families could live in a debtors' prison with the prisoner. They and other visitors were able to enter and leave at will except at night, when the prison was 'locked down'.
6 Charles Dickens, *Little Dorrit*, London: Penguin Books Ltd, 1998, pp. 15, 68.
7 Trey Philpott, *A Companion to Little Dorrit*, London: Croom Helm, 2003. This author has adopted Philpott's dating scheme. For a slightly different set of dates, see chapter 'Mysteries of the Dickensian Year', in: John Sutherland, *Is Heathcliffe a Murderer?* Oxford: Oxford University Press, 1996.
8 *Little Dorrit*, p. xxii.
9 J.S. Taylor, *Poverty, Migration, and Settlement in the Industrial Revolution; Sojourners' Narratives*, Palo Alto, CA: The Society for the Promotion of Science and Scholarship, 1989.
10 Michael Dalton, *The Country Justice*, London: London: Henry Lintot, 1742, p. 184.

11 A child could be emancipated at seven years old: *Rex v Macclesfield*, Burr. S.C. 458. Another case held that children could gain a settlement in their own right at seven years and 40 days: *Rex v Witten cum Twambrokes*, 3 Term Rep. 353, 2 Bott. 53.
12 Nolan, *Treatise*, vol. I, p. 176.
13 *Suckley v Whitborn*, 2 Bulstr. 358, 2 Bott. 2.
14 *Elsing v The County of Hertfordshire*, 1 Sess. Cas. 99.
15 *Coxwell v Shillingford*, 2 Bott. 23.
16 S. 4, 54 Geo. III *c.* 170 (1814).
17 *Little Dorrit*, p. 68.
18 Dalton, *Country Justice*, 1742, p. 178.
19 Amy's mother died in the country: *Little Dorrit*, p. 74. That left the young Dorrits liable to removal by operation of law to their father's place of settlement, placed in a workhouse or 'farmed' to someone who was paid by the parish.
20 Ibid., p. 396.
21 1 *Blackstone Commentaries*, 103 cited in: Nolan, *Treatise*, vol. II, p. 59.
22 *Ryslip v Harrow*, Salk 524.
23 *Rex v Great Farringdon*, 6 Term rep. 679: Nolan, *Treatise*, vol. II, p. 63.
24 Nolan, *Treatise*, vol. II., pp. 93–96.
25 Ibid., vol. I, p. 166.
26 *Rex v Witten cum Twambrokes*, 3 Term Rep. 353, 2 Bott. 53.
27 Nolan, *Treatise*, vol. I, p. 169. This is derivative settlement.
28 *Rex v Roach*, 6 Term Rep. 247, 2 Bott 57.
29 Nolan, *Treatise*, vol. I, p. 170.
30 *Rex v Sowerby*, 2 East. 176.
31 Nolan, *Treatise*, vol. I, p. 171.
32 3 W & M *c.* 11 (1691).
33 8 & 9 Will. III *c.* 30 (1696–97).
34 Nolan, *Treatise*, vol. I, p. 184. Amy's legal situation is further complicated by the possibility that her lodgings are in a different parish from her employer, Mrs Clennam.
35 Ibid., p. 210.
36 *Rex v Wroughton*, Burr. S.C. 280.
37 Section 64, Poor Law Amendment Act 1834. This also states that service completed before that date qualified a servant for settlement and that the Act did not operate retrospectively.
38 *St Giles v Eversley*, 2 Sess. Cas. 116, 2 Bott. 81.
39 Nolan, *Treatise*, vol. I, p. 152.
40 *Little Dorrit*, p. 30.
41 Ibid., p. 33; when: 'I was twenty': Ibid., p. 58.
42 Ibid., p. 33.
43 Ibid., p. 166.
44 Ibid., p. 299.
45 London contained 109 parishes by the nineteenth century; each legally responsible for maintaining their settled paupers.
46 *Little Dorrit*, p. 741.
47 Ibid., p. 742.
48 Ibid., p. 831.
49 26 Geo. II *c.* 32. The Marriage Act 1753. See also: Rebecca Probert, 'The Impact of the Marriage Act of 1753: Was it Really "A Most Cruel Law for the Fair Sex"?', *Eighteenth Century Studies*, 38, 2, 2005, 47–62; — , 'The Judicial Interpretation of Lord Hardwicke's Act of 1753', *Journal of Legal History*, 23, 2002, 129–51.
50 Dalton, *Country Justice*, 1742, p. 174.
51 Nolan, *Treatise*, vol. I, p. 174.

52   Section 71, Poor Law Amendment Act 1834 states: 'every child born a "bastard" after this Act shall have and follow the settlement of the mother of such a child until the child shall attain the age of 16, or shall acquire a settlement in its own right'.

53   Nolan considered that the true construction of the meaning was that lawful possession of a tenement of that value conferred settlement, even when the occupier was exempt from paying rent: Nolan, *Treatise*, vol. II, pp. 15, 17–18.

54   *Rex v St. George's, Hanover Square*, Burr. S.C. 692; and in *Rex v Whitechapel*, 2 Bott 100.

55   Nolan, *Treatise*, vol. II, p. 37.

56   Ibid.

57   *Evelyn v Rentcomb*, 2 Bott 96.

58   *Rex v Butley*, Burr. S.C. 107; *Rex v Knighton*, 2 Term Rep. 48.

59   *Little Dorrit*, pp. 138–39.

60   A contract for the use of machinery affixed to a tenement was not considered to be 'within the statute': Nolan, *Treatise*, vol. II, p. 26.

61   Ibid., p. 33; also: *Reg. v Inhabitants of West Ardsley* (1863) 32 L.J.M.C. 255. A partnership in land rented for coal mining plus a tenement rented for five pounds, ten shillings per annum failed only because the tenancy in the land ended early in the year and the total rents failed to reach ten pounds in a qualifying year.

62   59 Geo. III *c.* 50 (1819); 6 Geo. IV *c.* 57 (1825).

63   As a result of this provision, small terraced houses were built in the North of England with an extra front door to the basement to make a separate 'dwelling house'. Their purpose was to encourage the immigration of weavers and factory workers. There is an excellent example of this in Leigh, Lancashire, opposite the Cricket Club.

64   Cox, E.W., *The Practice of Poor Removals*, London: J. Crockford, 1848, p. 84.

65   *Rex v Great and Little Unsworth* (1836) 5 L.J.M.C. 139.

66   *Reg. v Inhabitants of Elswick* (1860) 30 L.J.M.C. 66.

67   *Reg. v Inhabitants of West Ardsley* (1863) 32 L.J.M.C. 255.

68   Sections1 and 2, Poor Relief Settlement Act 1831.

69   Section 66, Poor Law Amendment Act 1834.

70   *Littleton*, s. 12; cited in: Nolan, *Treatise*, vol. II, pp. 62–63.

71   There were exceptions such as where, after 25 March 1723: 'such purchase does not amount to the sum of thirty pounds bona fide paid'. The terms of the 1772 Act only concerned estates purchased under that value and an equitable interest could confer settlement subject to the same rules as a legal estate. 9 Geo. I *c.* 7 s. 5 (1722); Nolan, *Treatise*, vol. II, pp. 62–63, 74.

72   Nolan, *Treatise*, vol. II, pp. 62–63, 92.

73   *Rex v St Nyott's*, Burr. S.C. 132.

74   Richard Gough, *The History of Myddle*, David Hey (ed.), London: Penguin Books, 1981, p. 252.

75   *Little Dorrit*, pp. 43, 848, n. 6 and 849 n. 7.

76   Nolan, *Treatise*, vol. I, p. 172.

77   *Rex v Creech*, Burr. S.C. 765.

78   *Rex v Bucklebury*, 1 Term Rep. 164.

79   See: Michel Foucault, *Discipline and Punish*, New York: Pantheon, 1977.

Chapter 7

Lived experience: poor law administration

'How much is conveyed in those two short words The Parish!'[1]

This chapter reconstructs poor law administration within its legal context from the perspective of those who implemented, paid for and administered the system: local vestries, ratepayers, officials, Justices and poor law guardians. As we have seen in Chapter 3 settlement and the legal right to relief provided both the overarching legal framework and the explanation why each autonomous parish relieved its settled poor. What follows illustrates how differences and variations in local practices, adapting to social, economic and other pressures unique to each place, still fall within that legal framework. This chapter will consider parochial legal autonomy, with a brief case study of the operation of Tranmere Township on the Wirral. This is followed by consideration of the establishment and operation of the Wirral Poor Law Union and concludes with a reconstruction of the successful resistance of the ports of Chester and Liverpool to the imposition of the terms of the 1834 Act. These local studies serve as exemplars of law in action, they are not 'typical' of local practice but demonstrate the larger common law framework that both permitted and was built upon the principle of local autonomy. It is this long-standing self-funding character of a rights-based poor law legal system embedded within the localities that provides an explanation for the noticeable divergence between American and English welfare systems and rebuts tenBroek's assertions that the 1601 Act is purely negative.

The parish and its officials

It is evident that the parish has been at the legal heart of the administration of English poor law from its origins. The presumption of parochial responsibility, codified and understood from the 1601 Act, both in the giving of aid and the collection of revenue to sustain that aid, survived the reforms of 1834. The poor law unions set up after 1834 were created by combining groups of parishes; thus unions are grafted administratively upon pre-existing parochial structures that held legal responsibility to maintain their settled poor. In consequence, in spite of reforms each parish remained financially responsible for its settled poor with legal discretion and autonomy in removal decisions until 1865. As the new poor law operated under the legal authority of the 1601 Act, poor relief remained underpinned by the legal rights of the settled poor, with local administrative and funding mechanisms remaining under the supervision of the Justices. The 1601 codification as we have seen in Chapter 3 was also achieved through adapting pre-existing structures, both legal and ecclesiastical within a context of local control, local knowledge and local institutions. In short, from inception until 1865 and beyond, the parish remained the legal and financial hub of the poor law system. That legal parish consisted of its ratepayers, those liable to be levied for the poor rate. From among this number meeting as a vestry, individuals were appointed or elected to initially unpaid administrative posts in order to carry out the duties and obligations laid upon the parish under statute.[2] For the relief of poverty these officials included both churchwardens and overseers of the poor who also set and collected the poor rate. This was done once a year on the basis of the previous year's costs taking into account any assets and money in hand, any still to be collected and any shortfall in the accounts; in other words, this was demand-led local funding, an uncapped and financially open system, invulnerable to government financial restrictions.

These local vestry administrative structures comprised small country parishes, townships and large urban parishes and boroughs. Although their legal responsibilities were the same the tasks required greater dedication by large towns and cities where administrative responsibilities before 1834 could include almshouses, workhouses, schools, asylum and even the management of commons.[3] The terms of the 1601 Act left the matter of how to assess the apportioning of rates open, resulting in much legal debate with the judicial view favouring ability to pay; the argument was finally resolved in favour of the value of land and property.[4] In summary, parochial responsibility and autonomy in poor relief matters is a well-established legal entity supported by legislation and evidenced in practitioners' texts.[5] However, the reformist impetus discussed earlier, combined with the escalating costs of parish rates rising by 500 per cent between c. 1770 and 1819,[6] produced a Select Committee on the Workings of the Poor Laws which met in 1817 to discuss methods of reducing the poor rate, presided over by the Right Honourable William Sturges Bourne.[7] This did not reach agreement, but the chair introduced two Acts in 1818 and 1819 whose terms regulated the procedure of some vestry meetings, authorising the creation of Select Vestries.[8] These consisted of an elected parish committee, a salaried overseer and plural voting in proportion to the amount of rates paid by individuals. This experiment was not universally applauded and was in some decline by 1834.[9] Nevertheless as we shall see below, one Select Vestry, that of Liverpool, successfully repelled the Poor Law Commission.

In its ecclesiastical form the parish already held administrative responsibilities before the Reformation, new ones were acquired by the emerging civil parish. In summary, each parish appointed four principal officers, the churchwarden, the constable, the surveyor of highways and the overseer of the poor.[10] All were unpaid, service was compulsory subject to legal exemptions,[11] officers were often appointed in rotation amongst all parishioners but differing practices were followed in many parishes.[12] Eastwood notes that although magistrates often used their position to urge common policies upon parishes, vestry management of the poor was conducted without any serious outside interference.[13] The only legal 'control' of a vestry's poor relief policy was consequential to the right of settled paupers to poor relief, supported at common law by the legal system. The other duties of vestries, road and bridge repairs, nuisance removal, etc., were not subject to the same priority. Some duties were transferred from manorial functions, some vestry functions were carried out by municipal corporations in larger towns, but the pattern of poor relief prevailed everywhere and the duties were the same. Ratepayers were obliged to meet annually and elect parish officials, annual rates were to be set and policy decisions made so other meetings were necessary.

Eastwood suggests that the 1834 Act emasculated the vestries.[14] In fact, vestries' activities increased after 1834 and continued to do so. There is evidence on a national scale of the continuing power of local autonomy as railway companies were forced to pay large sums in poor rates to vestries.[15] Record offices all over England and Wales bear testimony to the sustained efforts of thousands of local vestries from the sixteenth to the twentieth century in actively dealing with the problems of the poor. Whatever the personal motives and individual methods of those participants, poverty was relieved, taxes were raised and local people occupied themselves with their local responsibilities within a framework of legal obligations enforced by the common law courts. Chief amongst these, the office of overseer of the poor was established under the terms of the 1597 Act, when churchwardens were ordered to act as overseers, some legal writers suggest the role dates from much earlier.[16] Under the legal authority of the 1601 Act, the overseer set and collected the poor rate each year and had a legal duty to submit accounts and the proposed poor rate annually to the Justices of the Peace for signature. For a brief period after the Reformation the Justices were given responsibility for electing two, three or four overseers; this duty was abandoned in 1601.[17] After that date overseers are chosen by their peers and the choice confirmed by the Justices.

As has been fully discussed, parish officers, churchwardens and overseers were under a statutory obligation to relieve and support their poor.[18] Justices possessed legal authority to order officials to relieve any person in need where parish officials improperly refused such relief. Overseers and churchwardens who held poor relief functions were bound under s. 2 of the 1601 Act to meet at least once a month in the parish church after Sunday service to decide future actions. Their responsibilities included setting children and those who had no means to maintain themselves to work and to provide for the old, impotent and blind.[19] Overseers were thus the first line of defence for any parish against unwelcome arrivals, a constant preoccupation of vestries and of modern poor law historians. In that context, in 1764 Burn wrote critically of these officials, believing Justices should have greater powers to curb their excesses:

> Their whole idea is to maintain their poor as cheap as possibly they can at all events; not to lay out twopence in prospect of any future good, but only to serve the present necessity ... to move heaven and earth if any dispute happens about a settlement and in that particular to invert the general rule and stick at no expense; to pull down cottages; to drive out as many inhabitants and admit as few as they possibly can, that is to depopulate the parish in order to lessen the poor rate.[20]

Although overseers were subject to supervision by the Justices and could be indicted for manslaughter if a destitute inhabitant died of starvation, they also possessed the right to insist that the Justices sign their accounts. They were also subject to legal sanctions if they mishandled parish funds, but the position was usually unpaid and unpopular and much latitude seems to have been extended to the recalcitrant. Sir D.A. Lewin notes in the 1828 edition of his poor law text that superior courts are reluctant to prosecute poor law officials in respect of their administration of poor relief, because the officials: 'might be in low circumstances', and therefore a prosecution might cause them to incur: 'expense and inconvenience'.[21] In *R v Meredith* (1803) by a majority of 5:1, it was held that officials could not be indicted for failing to pay poor relief unless it had been ordered by the Justices, except in an emergency where there had been no time to obtain a Justice's Order.[22] Nevertheless, by 1857 George Oke's *Magisterial Synopsis* lists eight pages of offences for which overseers may be prosecuted.[23] This reflected the overseers' important and proactive role in poor relief and settlement, but they operated with the support or at least connivance of their fellow ratepayers. Every parish and township in England kept monthly and, later, weekly records of the activities of overseers, their accounts, the poor rate and any matters a vestry thought significant. Much of this material survives today and reveals local preoccupations and the individuality of place and membership. Nevertheless, together these form a surprisingly consensual administrative machine covering England and Wales, for whilst each component retained a high degree of operative autonomy, all were bound, regulated by and operated within the overarching legal framework.

It was the responsibility of the overseers to initiate removal in a legal process discussed in the previous chapter. However, their duties did not end with obtaining the Removal Order; they must arrange for paupers to be safely conveyed, initially at the cost of the settlement parish, to the place required to receive and provide for them, directly into the hands of the parish officers.[24]

Parish records reveal payments for Justices' warrants and for legal advice in the overseers' accounts.[25] Moreover, if parish officials acted from malice or corrupt motives a pauper could act by motion for a criminal information against them (*Rex v Angell*).[26] Overseers continued to be appointed after 1834 and the overseer remained the person with authority and responsibility for the making, collection and recovery of the poor rate. His or, occasionally, her 'official' duties for the payment of out-relief were transferred to the boards of guardians after 1834 but local records indicate that overseers continued to act much as before in many parishes. We have seen in Chapter 3 how out-relief payments continued into the twentieth century and that overseers retained discretion and legal authority for removal decisions until 1865. They retained poor law functions after this date, recognised in Article 3 of the General Order of 18 December 1882: 'An overseer may admit a casual pauper into a casual ward in cases of sudden and urgent necessity'.[27] The office of overseer of the poor was finally abolished in the Rating and Valuation Act 1925 when rating powers and duties were transferred to public authorities.[28]

The role of the Justices of the Peace in poor law matters provides evidence not only of the legal nature of poor law, but the manner in which the common law framework was held together and enforced in even the smallest hamlet in England and Wales.[29] The Justices were not solely parish officials, their activities mediated and harmonised parish administration and national legislation for they served the County as well as the parish. In summary, much of the English legal system in action was built upon these gentlemen amateur judges who held a pivotal role in local administration.[30] Thus Justices operated in two arenas. The first in their judicial and administrative functions, which extended across the County, working collectively at Quarter and Petty Sessions from the nineteenth century. The second as individuals who held potentially conflicting positions. The first of these was their legal obligation to grant Relief Orders to the settled poor; the second was that as ratepayers, with a personal, financial and social interest in matters concerning the parishes in which they lived. These men oversaw many parish poor law duties including the binding of apprentices and ordering relief for the poor and impotent. A single Justice acting alone could fine a drunkard on the spot, give a gambler a month's hard labour and order a parish to relieve a pauper.[31] Initially only those with some legal training were named: 'of the *quorum*', later this term applied to all.[32] Personal standing and financial substance were a prerequisite and a qualification for enrolment as a member of the magistracy.[33]

In summary, although operating and selected from within the localities, magistrates also represented central 'control'. Special Petty Sessions were held twice a year in each locality, comprising two to five Justices. At Quarter Sessions for the County, their public duties included setting a county rate to pay for the building and repair of bridges and roads, to defray the costs of trials, to maintain law and order and to pay for the erection and maintenance of prisons and asylums. However, both here and at the parish level Justices operated largely autonomously; although unsalaried and not usually legally trained considerable social status attached to the position. The level of local power they held increasingly attracted criticism that reached a crescendo by the 1830s, especially the perceived tendency of the Justices to 'make law' in the localities.[34] As they were individualistic and unsupervised in any formal sense Justices were vulnerable to such critiques; in consequence the absorption of Justices into the reformed poor law as *ex officio* poor law guardians represented an attempt to reduce their power whilst providing continuity.[35] Nassau Senior saw a role for Justices in the new poor law, but in restricting their position from judges to administrators. This has led some commentators to suggest that after 1834 they lost much of their supervisory power over the poor law.[36] So far as local vestry activity is concerned, the records of Tranmere and elsewhere reveal this not to be so; in addition as *ex officio* members of their local boards of guardians, when active they became the most influential members due to their social prestige.[37]

As has been emphasised throughout this work, Justices possessed legal authority prior to 1834 to order relief.[38] In this they could overrule an overseer or parish refusal; this legal procedure provided the enforcement mechanism for a settled pauper's right. What is more, where parish discretion and a settled pauper's rights conflicted, in law the pauper's right was the greater, leading some contemporaries to allege that Justices were too generous in this process.[39] However, they retained jurisdiction for Relief Orders until 1834, and a residue beyond that date. Justices could be prosecuted for misdeeds, but had some immunity if they acted in good faith.[40] However, the superior courts were quick to punish any abuse of summary jurisdiction. A successful action against a Justice for wilful or malicious injury entitled the victor to double costs; some protection for Justices was therefore introduced in the terms of the Justices' Protection Act 1848.[41] In conclusion, Justices occupied a central position in poor law administration and their activities were regulated and delineated by law.

Lived experience: Tranmere Vestry in action

This section reconstructs some poor law vestry functions based around a study of the records of the Tranmere Vestry.[42] What follows is drawn from a larger archival research project that reconstructs local poor law history within its legal context.[43] In brief, Tranmere Township was originally part of the large ecclesiastical Parish of Bebington on the Wirral in Cheshire, for poor law functions the township is based upon its legal existence as a medieval manor, although the manorial court was abolished in the 1830s. Tranmere is situated on what was the main route between Chester and Liverpool along the banks of the River Mersey where it possessed a ferry across the Mersey that ceased operations in 1897.[44] Until the early nineteenth century Tranmere was a medium-sized village and an associated fishing village in Lower Tranmere. William Laird bought land in Birkenhead and Tranmere in 1821 and by 1856 had moved his shipbuilding yard to Tranmere where, in 1851, a leather tannery was already established as a major industry.[45] Additionally, the Chester–Birkenhead Railway opened in 1840, passing through the township, increasing trade and industry and facilitating the access of an increasing labour force.[46]

In consequence of the above, the population of Tranmere expanded by a factor of three between 1821 and 1841, however, that of neighbouring Birkenhead increased by a factor of 41.[47] Thus Birkenhead developed into a large town run by an elected governing body, whilst Tranmere was administered by a vestry composed of its ratepayers. In 1843 one individual possessed half the land in Tranmere, the remainder was in the hands of over 100 proprietors.[48] By the 1860s extensive speculative building covered the township with rows of terraced houses, the streets following the plan of the medieval land holdings, the open fields and townfield strips.[49] Eventually Tranmere became absorbed into and incorporated within the township and Borough of Birkenhead.[50] This administrative development is a reflection that from the nineteenth century Tranmere began to take its social character from neighbouring Birkenhead and Liverpool. Parts of the township, in common with those neighbours, suffered public health problems. These are evident within Dr Robertson's 1847 publication of a study of conditions in Birkenhead and Tranmere; they are as grim as any of the period. He depicts some of the worst streets in his report and thus provides an eyewitness account of the lives of some of the poorest Tranmere residents:

> A house on the Old Chester Road, which being on the lower part of a decline, was subject to all the effects of liquid filth and night soil, which ran down to, and at times surrounded the house, and entered the very sitting room for two years; after coming here the family had no health, as it was termed, all were attacked by fever.[51]

This lack of clean water supply in Tranmere caused many problems, the contamination of the water supplies by seepage from privies, middens, tanneries, slaughterhouses and the like led to supplies as in Back Chester Street where:

> [T]he (water) is so charged with filthy impurities, as literally to stink, turns white when boiled, and, if kept in the house all night, becomes insufferably offensive and useless.[52]

Thus by the mid-nineteenth century Tranmere is no longer the manorial village, whose earliest recorded overseer, John Gleave, was appointed in 1614. By the 1820s Tranmere Township's social and economic structure included pockets of desperate poverty and therefore the vestry established the practice of employing a professional assistant overseer;[53] nominating a junior and senior overseer from the ratepayers, the junior being appointed senior the following year.[54] Tranmere used a poorhouse sanctioned by the vestry in a memorandum of 1817 signed by the overseers and eight ratepayers: 'Be it remembered that the inhabitants of the township of Tranmere hath this day agreed to enter the poor of the said township into a workhouse that shall become troublesome to the said township.'[55] In the 1790s, Tranmere vestry records the presence of a woman ratepayer, Elisabeth Briscoe, who served as overseer in 1795–96.[56] By 1800 her signature has disappeared, and she appears to have been the only active woman vestry member until 7 December 1855 when a packed vestry meeting records the attendance of Elisabeth Roper, Elisabeth Matthews and Elisabeth Doyle.[57]

Tranmere Vestry concerned itself with many local matters: mole catching; the militia stationed at the local barracks and the support of their families;[58] travellers with passes; the disorder at the annual Whitsuntide Wakes with crowds of 40,000 by the 1850s;[59] disagreements over township boundaries; disagreements between overseers; settlement enquiries; visits to Sessions and a myriad of other matters. However, one dominant factor behind every entry in every ledger is the poor relief function. Rates are set every year, the poor accounts laid out in great detail as the underlying legal purposes reveal themselves on every page as understood by those who took part in the vestry, the clerks who wrote the entries and the reader today. Those participating understood that they were fulfilling a formal legal obligation and do so precisely and in detail. In addition, a measure of the financial interest vestry meetings held for participants may be seen in the regular attendance of the Reverend Fielden, Rector of Bebington. Nathaniel Hawthorne says of one incumbent in 1853: '[T]he Rector, enjoying a thousand pounds a year and his nothing-to-do, while a curate does the real duty on a stipend of eighty pounds'.[60] Fielden was not a Tranmere resident and therefore not a ratepayer, his regular attendance is a reflection of both his financial interests in the township and his *ex officio* position as senior magistrate at Petty Sessions in Birkenhead. Although the vestry had a legal obligation to maintain its settled poor, it also retained a residual legal discretion concerning the amount and type of aid and in denying or granting aid to non settled or casual poor within the township. In Tranmere, changing and growing during the nineteenth century, with large numbers of poor passing thorough to and from Liverpool, Chester and beyond, that exercise of 'discretion' had serious financial implications. The other duties of vestries, road and bridge repairs, nuisance removal, etc., were not subject to the same urgency.

After 1834, Tranmere became part of the Wirral Poor Law Union, based upon the old Hundred of Wirral, Cheshire. That area was largely agricultural, except for the Commercial District including Tranmere Township, where the poor law costs rapidly increased as the population expanded with the developing port nearby in Wallasey (Seacombe) and growing industry. Thus Birkenhead, Tranmere and Seacombe acted jointly and, after a Petty Sessions court was established in Birkenhead in 1832, they found it necessary to consult the Justices twice a week on poor law matters.[61] The average three year costs of the poor rate for Tranmere 1834–36 were £499, the highest in the Wirral Union. The comparable costs for the agricultural townships were much lower, ranging between £47 and £105.[62] These Commercial Districts welcomed the new poor law, unlike the agricultural townships and parishes, whose protests were led by the Reverend Joshua King, Rector of Woodchurch on the Wirral (see below).[63] By the 1840s the workhouse, built at Clatterbridge in the heart of the agricultural district, was both too distant and too small to accommodate all the Union's poor. The guardians of the Commercial District sent only a small proportion of their poor to Clatterbridge workhouse after 1841 and held separate meetings from 1848. With the expansion of the shipbuilding industry and the influx of the Irish (see Chapter 8) out-relief was paid to paupers as the vestry exercised its legal discretion. As we have seen in Chapter 3, the Poor Law Commission, later Board, was unable to prevent such local payments.[64] The extent of non-compliance on the Wirral caused the Poor Law Board to initiate discussions to separate the Commercial District from the remainder of the Union and eventually in the 1850s they decided to do so, subdividing the Wirral Union to create the Birkenhead Union.[65]

Tranmere ratepayers opposed this; they did not wish to be included in the new union as they had just committed the township to a necessary sewerage scheme and a town water works and were not willing to contribute to the costs of building a large new workhouse. They also wanted to increase parish representation on the board of guardians. The Wirral guardians rejected this claim. They pointed out that Mr Waring Perrey, member for Tranmere, had attended only two board meetings in five months and that Tranmere alone objected.[66] The township books do not record this issue, but the vestry was left with its share of the costs of the Birkenhead workhouse, which was built in the centre of Tranmere, on Church Road, in 1864–65.[67] Perrey was, however, assiduous in his attendance at vestry meetings, an indication of where his financial interests lay.[68]

There is a wealth of surviving material concerning the Tranmere Vestry and its operation. This section will concentrate upon examples which reveal how the vestry operated and whose interests it represented. The former concerns a meeting chaired by the Reverend Fielden, as noted not a Tranmere resident but an *ex officio* member, on 17 November 1836, to agree the appointment of a paid collector to assist the overseers.[69] The minutes provide evidence both of the legal framework and local interest within which the vestry operates as they state that the meeting is for the: 'Owners of Property and Ratepayers of the Township of Tranmere'. These comprised two distinct groups, non-resident property owners and the tenants and owner occupiers who pay the poor rates. This distinction allowed proprietors as interested parties to attend the meeting in an example of parish autonomy in operation. The second example concerns the next vestry meeting on 18 May 1837, which is differentiated as: 'a Public

Meeting of the Ratepayers'.[70] This is a formal meeting to agree the poor rate accounts, a legal responsibility of the ratepayers; non-resident landowners are not invited for they lack the necessary legal status. It is evident that membership of the vestry was of great importance to ratepayers in order to protect their financial interests and perhaps their social position. It was also a legal duty that always found some willing participants. However, it cannot always have been a pleasure, especially for those appointed as vestry officials and the records of the Tranmere Township reveal the problems faced by overseers and those who challenged their actions.

One such occurred in 1857, concerning the financial accounts of the salaried assistant overseer, Mr Jones. The implication of the inquiry initiated by Mr Cumming (junior overseer and non-salaried ratepayer) was that the assistant overseer was inflating tradesmen's accounts for unstated reasons. The greatest difficulty faced by Cumming was the politics of vestry life. The first action recorded in the dispute was a motion at the annual vestry meeting in March by Mr Cholmley Woodward (a trouble-maker originally from Liverpool whom we shall meet again later) who moved to censure Cumming for his alleged failures to perform certain duties.[71] This was countered by an amendment expressing complete support for Cumming, which was passed on a show of hands: 'by an immense majority'. By April, Cumming is senior overseer and the vestry has set up an 'Investigation Committee' to look into Cumming's charges. Accounts from 1856–57 were inspected but Jones was not available at the final hearing having consulted a solicitor, Richard Holden of Liverpool, who advised him not to attend. Intermixed with the financial allegations are various settlement and removal issues; specifically that Jones had not consulted the vestry in removing paupers, had failed to act to remove and had negligently failed to appeal a Removal Order from Holcombe in Lancashire. This neglect left the vestry responsible for maintaining the pauper family.[72] The Committee declined to express any opinion, referring the matter back to the vestry. By October, Jones was refusing to collect Government Taxes and the minutes record a decision to call a public meeting of the ratepayers to arrange tax collection and consider Jones' conduct.[73] The outcome of this matter is that after hearing from Jones, the report is not accepted by the vestry but it is entered in the vestry Minute Book, a precaution by the vestry as such matters potentially attach legal responsibilities and liabilities. The only visible consequences available to us today are that Cumming does not serve a parish office again. In his evidence in August Cumming stated: 'that he had not only received no assistance from the late Overseer or Assistant Overseer but that every obstacle was thrown in his path in the course of his enquiries'.[74]

This example demonstrates the complexity and pitfalls of active vestry membership and that conservative impulse familiar to anyone who has served on a committee. We can only guess at the personal motives of the parties, much more is concealed than revealed by the minutes. However, there are legal explanations; the vestry is legally responsible for the poor law accounts, it is legally accountable to ratepayers for expenditure; hence the annual poor rate account meeting is solely for ratepayers. Similarly, overseers are legally liable for misconduct, for their accounts and for removing paupers and this must be reported to the vestry and its ratepayers. What is fascinating is that if Jones was incompetent in not removing non settled poor and in not appealing Removal Orders, it is evident from the written record that the vestry declined to act. This was within their legal discretion, only they possessed the legal authority to question the overseer's removal decisions and they chose not to act: parochial legal autonomy in action. Reliable paid overseers are hard to find in Tranmere and Jones had reason to be wary. The minutes of a meeting six years earlier on 12 August 1851, reveal that his predecessor, Mr Thomas Dawkins, was committed to the Castle at Chester as a defaulter: 'in due payment of Government Taxes in the sum of £166 7s 8d'.[75] He had, however, paid over the local rate collections regularly, the overseers having checked twice a week, an unusual occurrence indicating their concerns about Dawkins' financial status.

In spite of the many frustrations involved, record offices all over England and Wales bear testimony to the sustained efforts of the members of thousands of local vestries from the sixteenth to the late nineteenth century, actively dealing with local matters. Whatever the motives and individual methods of those participating, poverty was relieved, taxes raised and local people occupied themselves with local responsibilities within a framework of legal and financial obligations which were supported and enforced by the courts. Recognition of this legal framework explains not only what vestries did, but also why ratepayers so doggedly continued to participate in local vestry activity.

Lived experience: administering the Wirral Poor Law Union

As we have seen, local vestry activity continued after 1834. Some of their responsibilities were modified as parishes were grouped together administratively into Poor Law Unions, accountable to a new central bureaucratic organisation, the Poor Law Commission. The union records generated after 1834 acquired another dimension, the formality of a standardised national bureaucracy. Detailed as these records are, they conceal the motives and passions of those who were responsible locally for administering the system, the poor law guardians who were elected from every vestry in the union. This section briefly reconstructs another aspect of poor law administration; the political 'resistance' of some of the participants.

In the early days, gentry and aristocracy played a prominent role in local boards of guardians, many not elected but as *ex officio* members by virtue of their positions as Justices of the Peace. After the initial start-up excitement, buying land and deciding the size of the workhouse, membership tended to fall away, leaving a few of the guardians to run affairs and local political preoccupations to emerge.[76] For the Wirral Union, the first meeting of the guardians was held in the Magistrates Room at Birkenhead.[77] An Assistant Commissioner, Richard Digby Neave, took the chair until a chairman was elected. The records indicate that he explained the object of the union to those present whose names are recorded. Rules were accepted, salaried officials appointed and further meetings agreed. In common with other areas nationally of mixed characteristics, agricultural and urban, it was decided to divide the union into two parts for poor relief. As discussed earlier, this comprised a smaller but more populous Lower Division (the Commercial District, including Tranmere) and an Upper Division that comprised the majority, agricultural townships. There is much detail but little clue in these minutes to the passions and issues that exercised the guardians. However, six of the agricultural townships in the Upper Division gave evidence to the Royal Commission of 1832–34.[78] They report that in their townships there is little provision for employing the poor except for limited light gardening work; they possess no workhouses and they claim that overseers are rigorous in the examination of the status of those poor to ensure that only the genuinely destitute are relieved. This is achieved by giving payments in kind, in money and in paying cottage rents.[79] These local farmers, unlike those in the South of England, felt that there was no particular link between the diminution of agricultural capital and poor relief payments.[80] There had not been as sharp a rise in the poor rate as in the South of England and the costs in the agricultural parts of Wirral had never been so heavy that overseers had stopped allowances to the able-bodied. There was thus little sympathy from this part of the union for expenditure on a workhouse. Poor relief was a more immediate problem in the Commercial District, including Tranmere Township where population and poor rate costs expanded together.[81] Thus broadly speaking, the Commercial District 'welcomed' the new Poor Law.

In the agricultural district where distress was not severe, there was opposition to the new poor law led by Joshua King, appointed Rector of Woodchurch in 1821. Previously Rector of St Matthews, Bethnal Green, London, King had played a leading part in the opposition to Joseph Merceron who controlled that parish's open vestry from 1787, indulging in jobbery and profiteering. King began the revolt against Merceron in 1809 when appointed Rector, triumphing in 1816 when he gave evidence before the House of Commons and Merceron was successfully indicted and tried in the Court of Kings Bench.[82] Thus King, Wirral poor law guardian and Tory not afraid of a fight, developed connections with the south-west Lancashire Anti-Poor Law Association.[83] His opposition to the new poor is displayed in a letter to the *Chester Courant* in 1836:

> We (the Wirral Guardians) have now reached that stage in the business when it will be necessary in compliance with the mandates of an arbitrary and despotic government, either to put your hands into your own

pockets, or to obtrude them forcibly into the pockets of others ... wherewith to build a workhouse which is not wanted.[84]

King argued against the new law on humanitarian, religious and financial grounds. His opposition compares with that of many clergy in the North of England, but he was not as successful in winning support as, say, Richard Oastler in Huddersfield. This was probably due to the lack of an active local Chartist organisation and little support for the Ten Hours (Factory) Movement in the largely agricultural area. The minutes of the Wirral poor law guardians reveal nothing of this.

The membership of the Wirral board of guardians largely reflected the rural nature of the union, with some gentry and merchants reflecting the interests of the Commercial District. However, a few regular attendees soon dominated proceedings as average attendance was less than 10. The *Chester Chronicle* comments on 14 June 1839 that: 'under the guidance of two or three squires and parsons' the union had been turned into: 'a regular politico-religious manufactory of Tory petitions'. Not an accurate reflection of the membership as Whig squires, magistrates attending *ex officio,* were also working members of the board of guardians. These included Sir Charles Stanley of Ness, Sir Thomas Stanley of Great Sutton (chairman of the guardians 1836 and 1837) and Richard Congreve of Burton (chairman 1839, 1840 and 1841). The comment does reflect the activities of King, of Fielden (magistrate and Rector of Bebington and chairman 1838) and of the Reverend James Mainwaring of Bromborough (chairman from 1843–50). This membership indicates a deeply politicised and divided group in these early years whose only available course of resistance was to write letters and 'argue', temperately recorded in meetings. The new poor law conferred no power upon these 'administrators' to amend their roles and procedures; poor law guardians were locked into a bureaucratic system without rights, only duties and obligations.

Thus there was political 'resistance', but what of the poor in this? One problem with this 'top-down' historical reconstruction is that it appears to suggest that local Tory resistance, including that of clergy, was motivated by political and not humanitarian concerns and that these concerns did not extend to the poor in the house. However, this is an inaccurate reflection of personal engagement by some, as the following example drawn from the 1850s illustrates. Read from a legal perspective it reveals that this 'system' provided little protection for the poor. It further demonstrates that, in this new poor law order of regulations and centralised bureaucratic control, there was a developing mindset whose priority was that the right forms were filled, the reports were correct and all reflected the smooth running of the union. Unfortunately few participants appeared willing to go behind surface conformity, an important subject but one beyond the remit of this work. However, outside the workhouse walls attempts were made to hold the union to account. In 1859 William Kingdon sent a selection of cuttings from the

Liverpool Mercury to the Poor Law Board in London.[85] Their existence reveals public concern about the treatment of the poor in the Wirral workhouse. They report the case of Thomas Fell aged ten, an inmate of the Wirral Union workhouse who had been beaten with a cat of four tails at the workhouse for fouling his bed and refusing food. It was alleged that as a result of the beating the boy died. The allegations continued; that the workhouse surgeon refused to give a certificate for the boy's death; that the coroner had not been informed and, finally, that the certificate had been secretly issued later. The Clerk of the Union replying to the Poor Law Boards questions states that an inquiry into Fell's death had been 'forced' by the Reverend Tattersall of Oxton who was allowed to examine the boy independently. Tattersall, according to the Clerk, was satisfied that the boy had not been made to work too hard; neither had he been threatened. He continues:

> The guardians desire to base their public conduct on the foundation of a Christian feeling, enlarged humanity and not least, on properly regulated deference to a public feeling. The Wirral Guardians stand in the highest class of those which are marked for special approbation by the public officers of the Government.[86]

No action was taken against the workhouse staff and significantly perhaps, the Board of Guardian *Minute Book* does not record the fate of Thomas Fell or any evidence of a workhouse inquiry.

There are legal sanctions available against workhouse staff for neglect of the poor but no successful actions appear in those Minutes. What they do record are many disputes amongst the staff, many complaints against them too but largely by other staff. The major legal preoccupation carried out and certified by Wirral guardians is the recording of 'official' (such as staffing) matters, those that involve expenditure and reporting a smooth-running institution back to London; thereby ensuring the surface proprieties are followed. However, the paupers do not 'run' smoothly and in 1860, a year after Thomas Fell's death, a series of deaths are reported in the *Minutes* in a paragraph entitled: 'Inquiry into deaths in Workhouse'. This concerned the high numbers of deaths in December, January and February:

> It appears that all the deaths were due to natural causes. 12 infants born with delicate constitutions, or admitted into the workhouse in a very destitute condition and unhealthy state died soon afterwards from atrophy [starvation] or convulsions. Eight persons aged 62 (average), Infirmity, Paralysis, Dysentery or Fever, and six Scrofula, Diarrhoea and Hydrocephalia.[87]

The Report concludes that: 'It is unanimously resolved that ... No deaths were caused by neglect, a want of care or bad management.' However, Dr Forest is directed to be more 'particular' in future in recording the death of a patient in the workhouse; no other comment is recorded. This is the nature of poor law as public law, a journey travelled for the settled pauper from the right to relief to the right to have his or her cause of death recorded to the satisfaction of the bureaucrats in London.

Lived experience: successful resistance in Chester and Liverpool

This final section concerns the legal rights of vestries and the nature of legal local autonomy. It has long been 'understood' that implementation of the terms of the 1834 Act was eventually effected across England and Wales despite initial resistance, with local riots and ongoing political debates in Parliament and in the press.[88] This statement should not be taken at face value as, in fact, a number of localities were able to resist the implementation of the Act by using unreformed legal rules concerning Local Act Incorporations. Although some places resisted in other ways, even forcefully like Huddersfield, they eventually succumbed. There were, nevertheless, legal exceptions; comprising those places that had set up their own workhouses under the authority of Private Acts. These continued to operate outside the terms of the Act after 1834. Although they were subject to inspection from the central bureaucracy in London, they remained free of the minutiae of financial and other controls that were eventually to standardise poor relief in England and Wales. One such example was Liverpool, initially as a Select Vestry and responsible for the largest workhouse in Britain;[89] another was the Chester Incorporation, relieving its poor under the legal authority of a Private Act.[90]

Chester is an ancient city situated on the River Dee in Cheshire; it was founded by the Romans and much of Roman Chester still survives. In the Victorian era it lay close to industrialising areas but was not part of them. Moreover, it did not benefit from the canal and turnpike revolutions although it possessed some minor industrialisation.[91] It had once been a busy port, but as the River Dee gradually silted up, so the wharves and docks were moved downriver to Parkgate on the Wirral Peninsular and by 1830 that port too was completely eclipsed by Liverpool, 17 miles away. Thus, Chester suffered stagnation. However, after the arrival of the railway in 1840 it became more prosperous. In spite of its current charm, in the nineteenth century Chester contained some appalling slum housing in its courts.[92] The Chester Incorporation was formed in 1761 when Chester obtained a Local Act of Parliament. The impetus for this costly and complex procedure came from Chester's particular parish make-up. Although Chester is a small city, it contains nine separate parishes, including the extra-parochial cathedral chapter. Each with their separate vestries, administered the poor law for their settled poor, raised a poor rate and appointed officials. Before the Local Act, Chester parishes built individual workhouses, some under the authority of the terms of the Parish

Workhouse Act 1723. After Incorporation, Chester used a workhouse built by Chester Town Council, completed by October 1759.[93] It is particularly significant that the members of all the vestries together formed a small, tightly knit community. These men were also members of the Town Council and of the closely knit Chester Guilds. As a result, the Town Council and local vestry members were connected socially by their local duties. This enabled the group to be both in a position to see the need for a Local Act and to have the means to carry out the necessary expensive and complex processes to obtain the required legislation. That is to say, they shared mutual interests and met regularly in different settings. In addition, as vestry ratepayers they possessed the legal authority to raise a rate to fund the procedure.

Those who obtained the new Act ensured that guardians elected from each parish managed the Incorporation and its workhouse.[94] This resulted in the Chester Incorporation having 74 elected guardians. This is an extraordinary number for a single institution in a small city, but it reflected the inclusive nature of its membership and the large number of parishes the City contains. In addition, Chester Town Council, the mayor, the recorder and the aldermen were *ex officio* members. The Incorporation possessed sole power to raise a poor rate, in proportion to the number of paupers from each parish who were maintained within the workhouse. This innovation was far from the poor law norm as technically it took rating, the fundamental basis of local autonomy, away from the vestries. However, as all vestries had representation on the board, rates remained under vestry control. This unorthodox situation reflects the unity of purpose and trust of the membership of the new Chester Incorporation board of guardians and the mutuality of those who ran the City administration. As a result, it was clearly of great interest to all the ratepayers of the City to have representation on the board of guardians and this explains the unusually large membership. The poor rate continued to be collected by the overseers of each parish and the guardians had the right of appointing and removing officials and fixing their salaries. Paupers were only to be relieved in the Incorporation's workhouse. They could be provided with employment there or hired out to harvest or to perform other work.[95] In addition, the guardians had the power to search for the poor in the city and compel them to enter the workhouse; a medieval and customary survival neither envisaged nor contained in the terms of the 1834 Act. Unlike other Local Acts, Chester guardians could contract for the maintenance of the poor of any of the parishes in the neighbourhood, a process known as 'farming' the poor. The Chester Incorporation was governed under the terns of the Act from 1762 until 1869, for as we shall see below, until then the guardians refused to surrender their Act to the Commission.

The social composition of the guardians in Chester was mixed, but the majority were merchants and craftsmen, with retail shopkeepers and innkeepers in the majority. Unlike the surrounding areas, particularly the Wirral Poor Law Union, the clergy did not take a significant role in the administration of poor relief. Perhaps the fact that Chester is a cathedral city, with a bishop in residence sitting in the centre of a spider's web of many parishes, ensured that the clergy had more interest in ecclesiastical politics than secular matters.[96] In order to administer the Chester Incorporation, the guardians held a weekly 'court' to hear applications for relief and a monthly 'court' that made policy decisions. M.A. Handley notes that, in common with the practice in many later poor law unions, the Chester guardians appear most preoccupied with finishing meetings quickly and keeping down relief costs.[97] As a result, in 1858 when Dr Bedford, a new reforming guardian, accused the master of the workhouse of: 'having provided meat for the inmates that was unfit for human food', he received little support. The *Chester Chronicle* in 1858 reported that: '[The] governor of the board told the doctor that he was decidedly disorderly.'[98] Bedford's attempts at reform subjected him to much ridicule and abuse from the other guardians, eventually leading to his being forcibly ejected from meetings and thereafter excluded. He complained of this to the Poor Law Board in London but, as the Board possessed no legal authority over a Private Act Incorporation, they were unable to interfere.[99]

The Chester guardians had shown an interest in the 1834 Act from its introduction as a bill, mainly to oppose its passing.[100] That Act set out precisely the manner in which a Private Act Incorporation may be brought under its new administration; s. 32 states that an Incorporation may be dissolved by: 'a Majority of not less than Two Thirds of the Guardians of such Union shall so concur therein'. This was something the first Assistant Poor Law Commissioner for the area, Richard Digby Neave, was never able to achieve. Moreover, in 1837 it was established that the Commissioners could not force Local Act Incorporations to comply with the new Act (*R v Poor Law Commissioners, ex parte St Pancras*).[101] In fact, no changes were made in the administration of the poor law in Chester as a result of the 1834 Act.[102] At his first meeting with the Chester guardians, in an attempt to bring the Incorporation under the control of the Commission, Neave suggested that if Chester agreed to adopt the new Act he would ensure that the new union comprised all the townships within seven miles. If not, he threatened to detach all those parishes that had contracted (lucratively for Chester) to put their poor in the Incorporation's workhouse.[103] Two-thirds of the guardians agreed in an informal vote put at this first meeting, but after reflection they decided not to comply. They wrote to the Commission to enquire if the new union would run under the Local Act.[104] Their concern was that they held the workhouse under a beneficial lease and did not wish the considerable expense of buying it from the town council, as required under the terms of the 1834 Act. In spite of their initial support for Neave's plan this issue proved a stumbling block. As a result, the necessary formal agreement required to impose the terms of the Act was not given; the guardian's opposition to change continued. They rejected an amended plan suggested by Neave and resisted persistent attempts to bully and cajole them into surrendering the Act.

The Poor Law Board continued these attempts until the 1860s by which time the Chester workhouse was seriously overcrowded, the problem exacerbated by agricultural labourers in Cheshire who were thrown out of work by the cattle plague. Driven by destitution, they flooded into the city to seek employment and by April 1869 there were 400 inmates in the workhouse.[105] At long last, the Incorporation Management Committee recommended building a new workhouse as the old building was so overcrowded. The financial difficulties this presented to the City drove the guardians to surrender the Incorporation to the Poor Law Board. They formally dissolved the Chester Incorporation, relinquishing their control to central authority. A subsequent rearrangement of the neighbouring Great Boughton Poor Law Union was achieved to incorporate some of its townships into the new Chester Poor Law Union. This action finally brought Chester into compliance with the terms of the 1834 Poor Law Amendment Act.

Liverpool presented a very different picture to Chester in the nineteenth century as today and yet it resembles Chester after 1834 in its initial retention of some legal autonomy in poor relief administration.[106] It too was (and still is) a port, albeit on the River Mersey. However, Liverpool became a port on a massive and very successful commercial scale. In addition, the City of Liverpool is composed of one large parish, unlike Chester's nine, and therefore a single vestry was responsible for the administration of poor relief.[107] This large and populous city contained social and public health problems dwarfing those of Chester. As a consequence, in poor law terms Liverpool was a pathological case. Its workhouse, at one point the largest in Britain, was built on Brownlow Hill in 1772 and later much extended to hold over 5,000 pauper inmates by the end of the nineteenth century; compared with Chester's workhouse, overcrowded when 400 paupers were in residence.[108] Both cities attracted poor Irish immigrants, but as we shall see in the next chapter, Liverpool did so during the Irish famine on an almost unimaginable scale.

This is not the place to reconstruct Liverpool's long poor law history and its complex local administrative and legal structures, including Town Council, borough courts and port moot. To be specific, the origin of Liverpool's successful resistance lay in a vestry decision in 1733 to set up a parish committee that became over time a standing committee dealing with all poor law matters on behalf of the ratepayers of Liverpool. In consequence, when Liverpool elected its first Select Vestry in 1821 under the authority of the terms of the Sturges Bourne Acts 1818 and 1819, some elements of the old parish committee remained; with new title and statutory powers but pursuing largely the same objects as before.[109] However, the vestry minutes reveal that the Select Vestry made strenuous efforts to reduce relief payments, investigate abuses and stop some of the rather corrupt practices that had previously become institutionalised within the operation of the system.[110] It is noticeable that every matter concerning the relief of poverty in Liverpool was on a vast scale; even the social composition of the Select

Vestry was grander than that of the Chester guardians. Unlike Chester, with its Incorporation run largely by tradesmen of the 'middling' sort, the Select Vestry was composed of extremely wealthy merchants and professional men, including many lawyers.[111] The ratepayers elected these members in a system where votes were proportional to the amount of poor rate paid. The Vestry was divided into five boards; one sat every weekday except Tuesday, a secretary attended each. All applicants for relief were interviewed, with the Irish treated particularly severely. The Select Vestry built up a large staff and paid a high salary for professional managers for its institutions including the workhouse.[112] Thus, in 1869 Liverpool paid the master of the workhouse, then with 3,500 inmates, a salary of £350. By comparison, the Wirral Poor Law Union 15 miles away with an average of 200 inmates paid the master £50 per annum. In 1849 the Select Vestry employed 187 officers (64 full time), including 94 teachers in the Industrial Schools.

The workhouse was run on strictly regulated lines and a formal uniform issued.[113] In 1814 it cost about a pound a week to keep a family in the workhouse, a similar cost to Chester. However, the scale of the workhouse operation in Liverpool meant that the annual costs for the Liverpool workhouse were much higher.[114] As a result, the records of the Select Vestry of Liverpool also reveal preoccupations with parish economy. The Chester Incorporation failed to divide paupers into classes and apply a labour test to those receiving out-relief payments.[115] The Select Vestry, by way of contrast, applied a rigorous labour test to paupers, requiring those in receipt of relief to work both in the workhouse and elsewhere. After 1834, as with other Select Vestries, Liverpool was initially permitted to retain its own administrative system. However, unlike Chester, Select Vestries were expected to run their poor relief administration in conformity with the regulations of the central authority. The first mention of this control appears in the *Liverpool Vestry Minutes* in 1836. It records an Order from the Commission read out in a Vestry meeting, for a revaluation of the county rate and to appoint a constable to deal with illegitimacy.[116] The Order is explicit that these matters are to be taken out of the Vestry's hands. In response, the *Vestry Minutes* note that the Poor Law Commission asked for and received full information regarding the management of the parish.[117] As a consequence, and perhaps as a sign of their growing resistance, the Vestry records that they will make no changes until they know if the Commission: 'have any plans of their own to suggest or enforce'.[118] Interestingly, the minutes conclude by noting that the Parish is in good financial shape, all debt has been paid off and more than £5,000 is held in their bankers' hands. The act of specifically recording such an extraordinarily large sum outside the annual accounts may be understood today as the Vestry's attempt to demonstrate the efficiency of their poor law administration to the Commission.

It is noticeable that the Select Vestry minutes are carefully nuanced and anodyne, for as later developments reveal, they followed a 'wait and see' tactic with the central authority. The Select Vestry's dislike of the imposition of the 1834

Act reveals itself in the minutes taken at a meeting held 5 April 1836. Here, Mr Cholmley Woodward, who we met in Tranmere, introduced a perverse motion utterly out of sympathy with the attitude of the majority. He suggested a petition to Parliament for the repeal of the Sturges Bourne Acts so that Liverpool would come under the authority of the 1834 Act. This was roundly defeated on the grounds that: 'the affairs of this Parish have been well and economically administered under the Act'.[119] In fact, the Sturges Bourne Acts did not prove to be a legal barrier to the Commission, but the sheer scale of Liverpool's poor relief responsibilities, combined with its nature as a single parish, may have encouraged the Poor Law Commission to delay implementing the terms of the Act. Finally, despite conciliatory overtures by the Select Vestry, on 11 March 1841 Mr Mott, Assistant Commissioner, formally notified them that the Poor Law would be introduced into Liverpool: 'immediately after Easter'.[120] The Select Vestry was dissolved and replaced by elected poor law guardians.

Liverpool ratepayers were not prepared to accept this and took action to resist the Commission and recover their control over poor law administration in the city. Whatever the Commission ordered, a Select Vestry constitutes the elected portion of a parish vestry that possesses the legal powers, authority and autonomy of any other vestry. In that capacity, as legally so entitled, on 6 March 1841 (in anticipation of the Commission's Order) the Select Vestry petitioned the overseers and churchwardens of the parish to call a vestry meeting: 'to take into consideration the propriety of adopting such measures as may prevent the introduction of this Act into the Parish'.[121] At that meeting, duly called in the correct legally authorised manner, ratepayers discussed their objections to the imposition of the terms of the 1834 Act. Subsequently, although this is, of course, not in the Select Vestry minutes, for this was a decision taken in a full parish meeting, the ratepayers agreed a course of resistance. They used their legal authority to raise money and initiate an application to Parliament for a Local Act. Their intention was to place themselves into the legal position occupied by Chester and operate the poor law under a Local Act Incorporation, taking the administration of poor relief in Liverpool away from the control of the Commission. In November 1841, the ratepayers called and held another Special General Vestry meeting to seek further support for that Private Act to restore Liverpool's local autonomy in poor law administration.[122] This action was successful, aided by continuing Tory parliamentary opposition to the new poor law.[123] As a result, in July 1842, an: 'Act for the administration of the laws relating to the poor in the Parish of Liverpool, in the county of Lancaster' was passed and elections were held to appoint 21 new Select Vestrymen.[124]

This marked the end of the new poor law's sway in Liverpool. The Select Vestry, even when replaced by poor law guardians, retained residual legal powers as elected representatives of a parish vestry. By acting in this legally authorised manner, no person or body outside this group of parish ratepayers possessed the right to challenge their decision. What the vestry also possessed was virtually unanimous agreement to restore local poor law autonomy within a wealthy city where men of influence took an active role in local adminis-tration. Thus, Liverpool successfully challenged and overcame central bureaucracy. The Poor Law Commission made no serious attempt to reverse this for no legal remedy was available to them. Moreover, once the famine devastated the labouring classes in Ireland, sending them to and through England mostly via Liverpool (see Chapter 8) the Poor Law Commission, later Board, appeared to lose all interest in assimilating Liverpool back into the national system.

In fact, of all forms of resistance to the new poor law, only this legal challenge was successful, available under s. 34 of the 1834 Act. Conse-quently, Chester a small city with a small problem passively resisted the implementation of the 1834 Act for 35 years. Liverpool, a very wealthy city with the good fortune to consist of a single parish, retained legal autonomy under the continuing authority of the 1601 Act. Liverpool's vestry, in a city of wealthy, powerful and independent-minded lawyers raised a large amount of money to use law to defeat law. The sheer cleverness and elegant simpli-city of this approach remains apparent today. Liverpool and its lawyers demonstrate law in action and another aspect of those legal rights, duties and obligations that remained at the heart of poor law.

Notes

1 The opening sentence of Charles Dickens, *Sketches By Boz*, first published in book form in 1836, London: Chapman & Hall, 1913, p.1.
2 David Eastwood, *Governing Rural England. Tradition and Transformation in Local Govern-ment 1780–1840*, Oxford: Clarendon Press, 1994.
3 For a survey of an urban vestry's duties see: Eddie Hoare, *The Work of the Edmonton Vestry 1739–48 and 1782–98*, London: Edmonton Hundred Historical Society, 1968.
4 Paul Slack, *Poverty and Policy in Tudor and Stuart England*, London: Longman, 1988, p. 127; E. Cannan, *History of Local Rates in England*, 2nd edn, London: P.S. King and Co., 1912.
5 H.J. Hodgson, *Steer's Parish Law, Being a Digest of the Law Relating to the Civil and Ecclesiastical Government of the Parishes, Friendly Societies etc. and the Relief, Settlement and Removal of the Poor*, 3rd edn, London: Stevens and Norton, 1857.
6 Total poor rates levied in England and Wales in 1758 were a little over £2m; in 1802 £5.3m; by the desperate years of 1818–19 the total was more than £10m: R.C. Richardson and T.B. James (eds), *Urban Experience*, Manchester: Manchester University Press, 1983, pp. 152–53.
7 *First Report of the House of Lords Committee on the Poor Laws*, 10 July 1817; *Second Report of the House of Lords Committee on the Poor Laws*, 28 April 1818; *Third Report of the House of Lords Committee on the Poor Laws*, 26 May 1818.
8 The Acts did not apply to the operation and powers of vestries governed by Local Acts or established custom or to close vestries: 58 Geo. III. *c.* 69 (1818) and 59 Geo. III *c.* 12 (1819).
9 S. and B. Webb, *English Local Government, Vol. I, The Parish and the County*, 1906 reprint, London: Frank Cass and Co., 1963, pp. 162–63.
10 Until the late sixteenth century it was the constable who was responsible for the sup-pression of beggars and after the Act of 1601 remained the principle parish official responsible for the removal of vagrants: W.E. Tate, *The Parish Chest. A Study of the Records*

of Parochial Administration in England, 3rd edn, Cambridge: Cambridge University Press, 1969, p. 185.

11   The following were exempt: attorneys, practising barristers, revenue officers, justices of the peace, aldermen of the City of London, members of the Royal College of Physicians, dissenting ministers, apothecaries, practising members of the Royal College of Surgeons, non-commissioned officers and men of the militia and yeomen of the guard, officers of the army, navy or marines, on full or half pay: Francis Const (ed.), *Decisions of the Court of King's Bench, upon the Law relating to the Poor*, 2 vols, London: Butterworth, 1807, vol. I, p. 9.

12   Webb, *Parish and the County*, pp. 16–18.

13   Eastwood, *Governing Rural England*, p. 32.

14   Ibid., p. 41.

15   R.W. Kostal, *Law and English Railway Capitalism 1825–1875*, Oxford: Clarendon Press, 1998.

16   One view was that the origin of the overseer lay in the office of collector of all local taxes made under by law or parish ordinance, first recorded in a decision of 1371, *Year Books, 44 Edw. III ff*. 18 & 19: Joshua Toulmin Smith, *The Parish, Its Powers and Obligations at Law*, 2nd edn, London: I. Sweet, 1857, pp. 178–82. Another dated the establishment of the office of overseer at 1551: W. C. Maude, *The Poor Law Handbook*, London: Poor Law Officers' Journal, 1903, p. 182.

17   For example, in the parish of Eaton Socon, Bedfordshire two collectors were chosen from 1591–97 and three overseers from *c*. 1617–1872: F.G. Emmison, 'The Relief of the Poor at Eaton Socon, 1706–1834', *The Bedfordshire Historical Record Society*, vol. 15, 1933, 1–98, at 86.

18   Michael Nolan, *A Treatise of the Laws for the Relief and Settlement of the Poor*, 2 vols, 2nd edn, London: A. Strahan, 1805, reprint, New York and London: Garland Publishing Inc., 1978, vol. II, p. 226.

19   This was established under the terms of the Act of 1552. Its enforcement mechanism collapsed with the Reformation, but overseers still continued to be appointed: Eleanor Trotter, *Seventeenth Century Life in the Country Parish*, Cambridge: Cambridge University Press, 1919, p. 74.

20   Richard Burn, *History of the Poor Laws with Observations*, London: Woodfall and Strachan, 1764, pp. 211–12, 286–87.

21   Sir D.A. Lewin, *A Summary of the Laws Relating to the Governance and Maintenance of the Poor*, London: A. Strahan, 1828, 200 n.

22   *R v Meredith* (1803) 168 E.R. 676.

23   George C. Oke, *The Magisterial Synopsis. A Practical Guide for Magistrates, Their Clerks, Attornies and Constables*, London, Butterworths, 1858, pp. 442–50.

24   Nolan, *Treatise*, vol. II, p. 157.

25   The accounts for the parish of Ullesthorpe in 1766 reveal payments of one to three shillings for warrants, and sums from ten shillings and sixpence to one guinea and more for legal advice and for pleading: Hugh Goodacre, 'Ullesthorpe Overseers' Accounts', *Transactions of the Leicestershire Archaeological Society*, XVIII, 1934, 150–55.

26   *Rex v Angell* Hardw. 124.

27   W.C. Maude, *The Poor Law Handbook*, London: Poor Law Officers' Journal, 1903, p. 103.

28   These comprised the councils of county boroughs, non-county boroughs, urban districts and rural districts: John C. Clarke, *Social Administration including the Poor Laws*, 2nd edn, London: Sir Isaac Pitman and Sons, 1935, p. 65.

29   For a legal history of justices see: Lorie Charlesworth, 'Justices of the Peace' (English Common Law), Stanley M. Katz (ed.) *Oxford International Encyclopaedia of Legal History*, New York: Oxford University Press, 2009.

30   Alan Harding, *A Social History of English Law*, London: Penguin Books, 1966, p. 260: G.E. Mingay, *The Gentry. The Rise and Fall of a Ruling Class*, London: Longman, 1976, p. 124; Brian Abel-Smith and Robert Stevens, *Lawyers and the Courts, A Sociological Study of the English Legal System 1750–1965*, London: Heinemann, 1967, p. 13.

31 Harding, *Social History*, p. 260.

32 Trotter, *Seventeenth Century Life*, pp. 203–9.

33 C.H.E. Zangerl, 'The Social Composition of the County Magistracy in England and Wales 1831–87', *The Journal of British Studies*, 40, 1971; A. H. Manchester, *A Modern Legal History of England and Wales 1750–1950*, London: Butterworths, 1980, p. 76.

34 Manchester, *Modern Legal*, p. 76.

35 Harding, *Social History*, p. 269.

36 William C. Lubenow, *The Politics of Government Growth*, Newton Abbott: David & Charles, 1971, p. 59.

37 Ibid.

38 3 Will. and Mary *c.* 11 s. 11 (1691).

39 Ross Cranston, *Legal Foundations of the Welfare State*, London: Weidenfeld & Nicolson, 1985, p. 31.

40 Manchester, *Modern Legal*, p. 78.

41 Ibid.

42 These records are currently held in the archives of the Wirral Museum, Birkenhead; they run in series from 1783 to 1897, with some (now missing) earlier accounts.

43 Lorie Charlesworth, 'Poor Law on the Wirral, The Guardian's Version', *Cheshire History*, 36, 1997–98, 70–81; — , 'Tranmere Township in the Nineteenth Century; An Introduction to the Operation of the Tranmere Vestry', *Cheshire History*, 40, 2000–2001, 40–55.

44 W.R.S. McIntyre, *Birkenhead Yesterday and Today*, Birkenhead: Philip Son and Nephew, 1948, pp. 60, 91.

45 Ibid., p. 43.

46 A. Redford, *Labour Migration in England, 1800–1850*, Manchester, University of Manchester Press, 1926, p. 141.

47 The census returns for the populations of Tranmere and Birkenhead are respectively:
1821 Tranmere, 825: Birkenhead, 200
1831 Tranmere, 1,168: Birkenhead, 2,569
1841 Tranmere, 2,554: Birkenhead, 8,223
1851 Tranmere, 6,519: Birkenhead, 24,285
1861 Tranmere, 9,918: Birkenhead, 35,929.

48 J.E. Allison, *Sidelights on Tranmere*, Birkenhead: Countyvise Ltd., 1976, p. 84.

49 Ibid., p. 36.

50 The Charter of Incorporation was granted on 13 August 1877. McIntyre, *Birkenhead*, pp. 81–82.

51 Ibid., p. 69.

52 Ibid., pp. 111–13.

53 Tranmere eventually paid a number of salaries out of the rates for officials to assist ratepayers. The constable received £40 p.a. in 1837; the salaried overseer received £40 in 1836; £100 in 1857; £200 in 1862.

54 *Tranmere Township Overseers Minute Book 1850–97*, Wirral Museum, Birkenhead (hereafter WM) BC VI 385, CR/C7745.

55 *Tranmere Township Overseers of the Poor Town Book*, 1783–1827 17 May 1817: (WM) BC VI 387; CR/C 7745.

56 Ibid.

57 *Tranmere Township Overseers Minute Book, 1850–97* (WM) BC VI 385.

58 The barracks survived as part of the premises of Forizo Ltd, on Church Road, Higher Tranmere until demolition in 2008.

59 For the extent of the problem and Tranmere Vestry's response see entries in: *Tranmere Township Overseers Minute Book, 1850–59*, 23 May 1850; 25 March 1851; 12 August 1851: (WM) 1BC VI 385, CR/C7745.

60 8 August 1853: Nathaniel Hawthorne, *The English Notebooks*, Steward Randall (ed.), Oxford: Oxford University Press, 1941, pp. 19–21.

61 'Birkenhead Overseers to the Poor Law Commission', 11 September 1834: National Archives, Kew, London (hereafter NA) M.H. 12/1200.

62 M.A. Handley, 'Local Administration of the Poor Law in the Great Boughton and Wirral Unions, and the Chester Local Act Incorporation 1838–71', 1969–70, unpublished thesis, University of Bangor, p. 305. Michael D. Handley, 'Poor Law Administration in the Chester Local Act incorporation, 1831–71', *Transactions of the Historic Society of Lancashire and Cheshire*, 156, 2007, 169–92.

63 Ibid., pp. 306–11.

64 The neighbouring township of Birkenhead relieved thousands of casual paupers from Ireland in the 1840s and lost a relieving officer in the cholera epidemic. From 1848, with the vestry's consent, accounts of their meetings are reported in the *Liverpool Mail* and the *Chester Courant*.

65 'Union Clerk to the Poor Law Board', 15 June 1860: (NA) M.H.12/1210; see also: Dr J.B. Yeoman, *Some Poor History of the Wirrall Union*, Birkenhead: Birkenhead Libraries, 1965.

66 Ibid., p. 322.

67 Now St. Catherine's Hospital, with the central administrative building and porter's lodge still intact, unlike the Wirral Poor Law Union (Clatterbridge Hospital) where all the workhouse buildings have recently been demolished. The Royal Commission for Historical Monuments possesses a set of photographs taken in 1992.

68 Mr Waring Perrey was one of the founder members of the 'Historic Society of Lancashire and Cheshire', Allison, *Sidelights*, p. 92.

69 *Tranmere Township Overseers Poor Rate Accounts, 1827–38*; 'Minutes of Township and Vestry Meetings, 1831–38', 17 November 1836: (WM) BC VI 387.

70 Ibid., 18 May 1837.

71 *Tranmere Township Overseers Minute Book, 1850–97*, 26 March 1857: (WM) BC VI 385.

72 Ibid., 30 April 1857.

73 Ibid., 28 October 1857.

74 Ibid., 22 May 1857.

75 Ibid., 12 August 1851.

76 Anne Digby, *Pauper Palaces*, London: Routledge and Kegan Paul, 1978, p.16.

77 'Minutes of the Board of Guardians, vol. 1', 17 May 1836: Chester Record Office (hereafter CRO) LGW 1/1.

78 *Royal Commission on the Administration of the Poor Laws*, PP 1832–34, Appendix, 1834, XXVII-XXXIX.

79 *Commission on the Administration of the Poor Laws*, PP, 1834, XXXV, Appendix B, Part. I.

80 Ibid., Appendix A, Part 1.

81 Average poor relief costs for 3 years (1834/5/6):-Commercial District townships: Birkenhead £321; Tranmere £499; Seacombe £127. Agricultural townships: Eastham £97; Great Sutton £105; Little Sutton £100; Childer Thornton £47; Whitby £83; Great Neston £475. (The population of this township reflects the presence of a colliery.) 'Birkenhead Overseers to Poor Law Commission', 11 September 1834: (NA) M.H. 12/1210.

82 Webbs, *Parish and the County*, pp. 84–90.

83 M.E. Rose, 'The Anti-Poor Law Agitation in the North of England', *Northern History*, vol. I, 1966, 70–91, at 74.

84 *Chester Courant*, 14 June 1836.

85 *Liverpool Mercury*, 14 December 1859.

86 ' Union Clerk to Poor Law Board', 21 December 1859: (NA) M.H.12/1209.

87 'Minutes of the Board of Guardians, vol. 8', 22 February 1860: (CRO) LGW 1/7.

88 Nicholas C. Edsall, *The Anti-Poor Law Movement*, Manchester: Manchester University Press, 1971; John Knott, *Popular Opposition to the New Poor Law*, London: Croom Helm,

1986; M.E. Rose, 'The Anti Poor Law Movement in the North of England', *Northern History*, I, 1966, 70–91.

89 Select vestries were set up under the terms of the the Sturges Bourne Acts 1818 and 1819 (58 Geo. III. *c*. 69), (59 Geo III. *c*. 12). Even after this was authorised three-quarters (15,635) of all parishes remained unreformed: Webb, *The Parish and the County*, p. 164.

90 For a full account see: Lorie Charlesworth, 'Poor Law in the City: A Comparative Legal Analysis of the Effect of the 1834 Poor Law Amendment Act upon the Administration of Poor Relief in the Ports of Liverpool and Chester', in Andrew Lewis (ed.), *Law in the City: Proceedings of the Seventeenth British Legal History Conference 2005*, Dublin: Four Courts Press, 2007.

91 John Herson, 'Victorian Chester: A City of Change and Ambiguity', in R. Swift (ed.) *Victorian Chester*, Liverpool: Liverpool University Press, 1996, p. 14.

92 Courts are small blind alleys off streets. Often entered though narrow entrances with housing on at least two sides, usually back to back. Such housing was multiple-occupancy, squalid, unsanitary and caused public health disasters. Those in Tranmere are long demolished.

93 Chris Lewis, 'Building Chester's First Workhouse', *Cheshire History*, 38, 1998–99, 50–54 at 52.

94 Handley, 'Local Administration'.

95 Mothers of bastard children, even if not chargeable, could be punished, not only by hard labour and the wearing of a badge, but also by public whipping. In reality, they were paid 2 shillings a week and not punished as the terms of the Local Act stipulated; *Royal Commission on the Administration of the Poor Laws*, PP, 1834, XXXV, Appendix B, Part I.

96 For a contemporary account of ecclesiastical preoccupations published between 1855–67 see: Anthony Trollope's *Barchester Chronicles*.

97 Handley, 'Local Administration', p. 69.

98 *Chester Chronicle*, 29 May 1858.

99 'Dr Bedford to the Poor Law Board', 30 June 1858; 15 July 1858; 30 October 1858; 8 March 1859; 24 March 1859: (NA) MH 12/904.

100 George Harrison, a plumber and the mayor, was reported as stating: 'I shall use my best exertions to prevent aged people from going to the workhouse. I must have the certificate of a surgeon first, before that I allow that an old man's wife be taken from him'; *Chester Courant*, 28 October 1834.

101 *R v Poor Law Commissioners (ex parte St Pancras* (1837)) 6 AD & El 1, 144. This case states that the Poor Law Commissioners have no authority to force the guardians of a parish where a Local Act is in force to elect a board of guardians under the terms of the 1834 Act.

102 The Poor Law Commissioners were not allowed to alter the boundaries of local administrations without their consent, in those parishes where a Local Act was in force: M.A. Crowther, *The Workhouse System 1834–1929*, London: Batsford, 1981, p. 45.

103 *Chester Courant*, 19 April 1836.

104 'Chairman of the Incorporation and Other Guardians to the Poor Law Commission', 21 May 1836: (NA) MH.

105 'Reverend George Salt to the Poor Law Board', 7 April 1869: (NA) MH 12/906.

106 A minor poor law connection between the two cities is that the *Liverpool Vestry Minutes* of 1724 record that a small rent was received for two houses in Forrest Street, Chester, which had been devised for the benefit of the Liverpool poor by Mr Bird: W.L. Blease, 'The Poor Law in Liverpool 1681–1838', *Transactions of the Historic Society of Lancashire and Cheshire*, 61, 1909, 97–182, at 101.

107 Liverpool was originally a part of the parish of Walton-on-the-Hill; it became a separate parish in 1699: George Chandler, *Liverpool*, London: B. T. Batsford, Ltd, 1957, p. 97.

108   The scale of the problem of poverty in Liverpool was enormous. Vestry minutes of 1813 reveal that there were 1,300 paupers in the workhouse, 8,000 receiving relief on the streets and one inhabitant in ten received relief in one form or another. By the 1830s the workhouse housed more than 1,500 people and was the largest in Britain; Ibid., pp. 128, 146–47.

109   Ibid., p. 114.

110   Extravagance on the part of the churchwardens included inflated payment of salaries, expenditure on wine and spirits, the non-collection of rates and so on; Blease 'The Poor Law', pp. 160–61.

111   Much of the mercantile wealth of Liverpool at this time came from the slave trade into the hands of these 'professional men.'

112   In recognition of the scale of the problems of poor relief in the city, Liverpool had a tradition of paid officials. The first was Edward Crane, overseer who, in 1724, was allowed 15 pounds: 'for his trouble'; Blease, 'The Poor Law', p. 108. This practice was later authorised by the terms of the Sturges Bourne Acts.

113   Blease notes that from the time the Select Vestry was established, the records were better kept, minutes more formal and always signed by the chairman: Blease, 'The Poor Law', p. 159.

114   The annual cost of the workhouse in 1834 was £15,638, 25 March 1834: Henry Peet (ed.), *Liverpool Vestry Books 1681–1834*, Liverpool: Liverpool University Press, 1915, vol. II, p. 339. In 1857–58 workhouse costs were £120,121: PP 1857–58, XLIX, Part I, p. 309.

115   'Annual Report of the Select Vestry for 1834', *Liverpool Parish Records* (LRO), 355 Par 1/ 4/3/.

116   21 April 1835; Peet, *Liverpool Vestry*, p. 346.

117   Ibid., p. 347.

118   Ibid.

119   Peet, *Liverpool Vestry*, p. 350.

120   Ibid., 11 March 1841.

121   Ibid., 6 March 1841.

122   Ibid., 4 November 1841, p. 365.

123   'Summary of the Church Accounts … Expenses incurred in applying for Local Act, £350. 0s. 10d', 29 March 1842: Ibid., p. 366.

124   5 & 6 Vict. *c* .88, 30 June 1842: Ibid., p. 367.

Chapter 8

Developments and transformation over time: dichotomising the poor

Curtis[1]

In the rear view mirror,
broad smile; I park when
he walks by. He backtracks

once I'm out: *Do you car*
need washed? lawn? Been
workin' all day, jus' $6 more

for rent I got 2 kids
they ma left me with
Anyone ask I tell them all

'bout Curtis Mayhew
I won't lie
I been inside for

armed robbery I was very
nervous I'm fine
now doin' right

jus' the landlord
won't wait kids don't
eat but I put a roof

over they heads one
room I'm not wild I'm
tryin' hard for the kids

There's a moment our eyes meet
before I stop believing
the bone-thin man before me

who has no children, no room—
who will come back each week
now that I go inside

for the six dollars to hand him
off the porch, like a penance
for living on White Street.

Thus far, this reconstruction of the juristic foundations of poor law has concentrated upon the law of settlement and removal, the legal right of the settled poor to relief and the rights duties and legal obligations of the parish; those 'forgotten' elements of the title. In short, in considering how law is experienced by participants in the poor law 'system' the work has focused upon those who possessed such rights and obligations. This chapter will reconstruct the legal position of the marginalised and excluded, for the right to relief did not protect all equally. In its juristic nature, poor relief epitomises Norrie's legal antinomy:[2] visible at the margins of society and law where poor people are stigmatised, excluded and some criminalised. The most unfortunate of these individuals are 'lawfully' redefined outside the poor law system although not left to starve. This chapter will closely examine some of those outsiders concentrating upon vagrants and the Irish (in England and Ireland). The importance of the right to relief is underlined by a brief discussion concerning the poor law system imposed upon Ireland in 1838, one that specifically excluded a legal right to relief.

There were other 'groups' marginalised under the poor law and the reader might wonder why they are not receiving equal treatment. There are a number of reasons for this; for some, their legal status within poor law has been considered throughout the work. The second is that many academic issues raised by legal 'marginalisation' require critical and theoretical consideration outside the immediate remit of this work and in fact have been the subject of scholarship within many disciplines; for example, moving beyond law and history into cultural and feminist studies. The largest of these marginalised groups is women. However, as discussed for Amy Dorrit, initially women possess all the rights of men under the rules of settlement, they may acquire a settlement in their own right and legitimate daughters, like sons, are born possessing their father's settlement. This alters upon marriage, for then a woman takes her husband's settlement and her previous settlement ceases to exist. This structural subservience is a legal rule absolutely of its time; remembering that women did not have a vote until the late nineteenth century. Moreover, for women, legal 'rules' concerning property, marriage, divorce, custody of children, education, work and inheritance were also structurally unequal by modern values. The past is what it was; women's lesser legal rights reveal how law is created and perpetuated within a contemporary context that is forever contingent. For modern welfare lawyers, however, it is worth emphasising that before marriage the rules of settlement are the same for men and women, rich and poor. In widowhood, once more a woman may acquire a new settlement in her own right; but not pass it to her children who kept their father's settlement, if he possessed one; this specific topic of settlement law has created much legal complexity.[3] It must be emphasised, at a time when most of the population, male or female, did not possess a vote, *all* men and women born in England and Wales possessed a legal settlement somewhere and hence the right to be relieved when destitute.

That still leaves a sub-group who suffered inequalities, abuse and punitive treatment embedded within the administration of poor law; unmarried pregnant women and their children. This has been considered earlier, for example in reconstructing Arthur Clennam's settlement entitlement and in Wordsworth's poem 'Alice Fell'. As noted in those discussions and more fully developed in poor law historians' reconstructions, overseers treated pregnant unmarried women harshly. If the woman was settled, overseers attempted various strategies; one favourite was to 'encourage' her to marry a man settled elsewhere with the legal explanation that the parish would no longer be responsible for a (settled) woman and child (for prior to 1834 a 'bastard' was generally settled where he or she was born). If the mother were non-settled, then before 1834 the prudent overseer might pay the woman to leave the parish, for otherwise the child would become their legal and, hence, financial responsibility. There are many horror stories in the archives, for example of overseers transporting women outside the parish borders to give birth and thus relieve the parish of a financial responsibility. The plot of Dickens' novel *Oliver Twist* echoes another legal point; after the passing of the Poor Relief Act 1814, such children born in the workhouse took their mother's settlement. Hence, the parish beadle and matron of the workhouse search Oliver's (unmarried) mother's clothes for clues to her origins in an attempt to ascertain that place and thus the parish legally responsible for Oliver's maintenance. After 1834 all such children take their mother's settlement, but relief in the union workhouse involved separation of mother and child. There is nothing here to surprise the modern reader; unmarried 'welfare' mothers continue to attract stigma. Under the poor law, legal rights and financial duties attached to settlement provide one explanation for overseer's actions, cultural norms another. The questions this raises concern the nature of those norms, did settlement rules reinforce, create or perpetuate this situation? Such questions may never be answered, but affirm the importance of recognising that the operation of law has direct effect upon both an individual's lived experience and cultural structures.

The final groups are foreigners, the sick and the non-settled poor. The latter have been the subject of most historical reconstructions to date and figure heavily in this work. This is the group who hold certificates, appear in Removal Orders and are the subject of overseers' and hence parochial legal discretion. This is the group a parish may aid or seek to remove, the group who occupied much parish energy. In short, they represent the pathological element of settlement; those whose right to relief was elsewhere and whose over-representation in the legal records perpetuate historians' misunderstanding and hence denial of the right to relief. Foreigners were unsettled; they did not possess a settlement in England and Wales and, as noted earlier, after 1803 must be relieved in any parish where they become destitute.[4] The settled poor who become ill were given aid (medical treatment is too grand a term for contemporary medicine) as a matter of legal entitlement and the new union workhouses had medical officers. Both non-settled and unsettled sick were entitled to medical aid in emergency. That left the settled mentally ill and a whole other group who appear in the records in pejorative terms that are better now described as 'special'. All these are entitled to aid if destitute; members of the last group were sometimes 'farmed' out or sent to a workhouse. The mentally ill were legally differentiated under the poor law and eventually required to be housed in County Asylums, each parish paying for its settled 'lunatics' and a share of the county rate. Peter Bartlett has reconstructed the treatment of the mentally ill under the poor law in a sophisticated socio-legal Foucaultian analysis that illuminates much negativity, some of which remain within current mental health law and in reform proposals.[5]

Dichotomising poverty: the pauper and the vagrant

Criminalising the poor in England is an old tradition.[6] Although centrally led legal methods adopted to control vagrancy date from the fourteenth century, aspects of the later legal administration of poor law share procedures and personnel in a manner that creates a symbiosis between vagrancy and poor law. It is that congruity in administering justice which appears to influence legislation, the treatment of the poor and cultural 'understandings' of poverty, connections that continue today. Some historians argue that, in fact, vagrancy is part of poor law, a suggestion that fails in doctrinal legal terms. However, their operative proximity created an associative antinomy which continues to resonate in modern legal measures surrounding the relief of poverty, in criminal prosecutions of welfare 'cheats' and in policies which emphasise fear of fraudulent claims. However, from a doctrinal perspective these two systems are legally separate, representing two very different types of law, common and criminal, with different rules and consequences.

What follows reconstructs the control of the 'criminal' beggar placed within or perhaps rather 'without' the context of the relief of poverty. Literature, a rich historical source of public opinion, contains many stories about the deceit and cunning of beggars. These range from Chaucer's cynical view of mendicant friars written in the fourteenth century,[7] to Sir Arthur Conan's Doyle's fanciful urban myth about a 'rich' beggar written in the 1890s.[8] These have modern media counterparts discussed by this writer elsewhere.[9]

Admittedly, it is an ahistorical methodology to read the present into the past, but it is equally ahistorical to fail to recognise certain continuities. Thus any reading of the statutes against begging reveals a continuous loathing and fear of beggars. After the devastation caused to the population by the Black Death in the mid-fourteenth century, the localised social structures of society underwent upheaval as survivors moved around for many reasons, including for the poorest, a new money value upon their labour in a decimated population. For others, no doubt, the loosened bonds of society allowed licence.[10] An Ordinance of 1349 instructs that stocks are to be built in every town for the punishment of runaway labourers; the sections of an Act of 1388 order the poor to repair to their birthplace in order to be maintained there. The terms of a later statute, that of 1495, directs that vagabonds and beggars are to be set in those stocks for three days and three nights with a diet of bread and water and for six days for a second offence. Stocks and whipping places were placed in all the parishes of England where they were maintained until well into the nineteenth century and some survive today as historical curiosities.

As much as poor law and vagrancy are legally distinct, this socio-legal reconstruction acknowledges both poor law administration and the measures for the punishment of vagrants involve the legal treatment of the poor by the same officials and the same decision-making bodies. The legal differentiation in the treatment of the two groups is always initiated by the subjective decisions of those officials. Paupers must have sometimes been unjustly branded in all senses vagrant, just as some may have been fortunate to escape that designation. The term vagrant has a technical meaning; a person convicted of a vagrancy offence, much as a 'pauper' is legally defined as a person receiving poor relief. The parish constable had a duty to bring any beggar or destitute person found in the parish before the magistrates and therefore local officials made the initial decision as to the status of that beggar – vagrant or pauper? This process separates the vagrant from the poor law system and places him or her before the criminal law to be punished; that final decision rests with the justices.[11] After punishment, vagrants are returned to their place of birth, thereby avoiding the complexities of settlement. In consequence, a poor person defined as a vagrant by the criminal process is subsequently excluded from the system of settlement examinations; in being subject to an order to return to his or her birthplace there is legal continuity with those earlier provisions concerning the movement of labourers.[12]

In England and Wales, this use of magistrates to enforce provisions against vagrants is an early legal development. From an Act of 1361 justices, who are later to play a significant role in poor relief, are faced on the bench by destitute people in a penal setting with the possibility of ordering their whipping, branding, banishment or hanging. These penal aspects of the treatment of vagrants cannot be over-emphasised.[13] Under the terms of two statutes of 1536 and 1547 vagrancy is designated a felony for repeat offences: some are hanged upon conviction, others severely whipped and sent to gaol.[14] Their number are limited only by the shortage of prisons. Vagrants could be sent for compulsory labour in the bridewells,[15] impressed into military service or exiled under the terms of the 1597 Act.[16] During the sixteenth century there are no clear distinctions drawn between the destitute and those who are deemed to be wilfully so.[17] Nolan echoes that view, although he differentiates between those who beg but are able to work (vagrants) and those who beg because they are unable to maintain themselves through age or bodily infirmity.[18] His view of these earlier statutes is that they make:

> in other respects a wide and proper distinction between rogues and vagabonds, who have recourse to begging in the love of idleness and vice; and beggars who are compelled by decrepitude to glean the necessaries of life from the pity of their fellow creatures.[19]

In consequence of the above, when a poor person is found begging an initial subjective decision is made as to whether that individual is a poor person to be relieved or a vagrant to be punished. More than 20 statutes add details and amend punishments for vagrancy, culminating in the Vagrancy Act 1824, part of the contemporary codification, rationalisation and reform of the criminal law.[20] That Act represents one response to growing concerns about the increase in begging, both in London and elsewhere, recorded by the *Select Committee on Mendicity in the Metropolis* 1815–16. In an opinion still held today, although expressing concern that destitution should not go unrelieved, the Committee is convinced that 'indiscriminate alms-giving' – charity with more heart than head in it – is the real root of the begging evil. Lionel Rose considers the Committee believed that: '[I]f the public were confident that some organised aid were readily available to the genuine unfortunate, impulsive hand-outs would cease and professional beggars would wither away', a perspective shared by some today.[21] It is therefore not surprising that sections of the 1824 Act remain current law, including a division into three incremental classes of offenders based upon numbers of convictions.[22] Other sections of the Act have been superseded or amended by later legislation.[23] The Act is now used mainly for public nuisance offences such as indecent exposure and prior to the introduction of stalking laws there was an attempt to use it for that purpose.[24] Primarily and punitively, magistrates now possess the legal authority and discretion to impose Anti-Social Behaviour Orders (ASBOs) upon persistent beggars, permitting prison sentences for breach of these Orders. Modern definitions of vagrancy retain that lack of precision found, for example, in the terms of an Act of 1598, vagrants are: 'all wandering persons and common labourers, being persons able bodied found loitering and refusing to work ... not having living otherwise to maintain themselves'. Nevertheless, eighteenth and nineteenth century Justices' manuals indicate that members of the bench were expected to be able to make a judgement of such individuals through their own experience.[25] There was a presumption that those who were not part of the respectable poor, who gave no good account of themselves and who looked like vagrants were vagrants.[26] The subtext to this was an assumption that all vagrants were also thieves and rogues who did not deserve, and were therefore not entitled to the parochial protection afforded to the rest of the population under the laws of settlement and removal; the personal right to poor relief.

There is some evidence after 1601 that officials confronted with non-settled paupers used the criminal jurisdiction to prosecute them for vagrancy.[27] This enabled officials to deny certain paupers the right to residence and return them to their birthplace. Terms within the 1662 Act differentiated vagrants from the poor and provided a safety net for that marginal group. Consequently justices required parish officials to accept responsibility for the relief of those who they formerly designated vagrants.[28] The system of certification discussed earlier and parish poor relief itself perhaps reduced the social pressures that had caused many to wander. Nonetheless this did not alter the legal position of those designated as vagrant and this designation remained within the jurisdiction and discretion of the justices. By the nineteenth century, the criminal conviction of a particular type of poor person emphasises the legal division in their status; between the respectable pauper who could seek aid and the poor person convicted of vagrancy who is an individual to be punished. In the *Poor Law Report* 1834, the term 'vagrant' appears in its legal sense; by the 1840s it appears in Parliamentary Reports to include all the casual poor. Eventually, all union workhouses were instructed to build specific segregated accommodation for members of this group. These casual poor, those passing through the union, were initially expected to perform some type of work in return for a night's lodgings. Refusal to perform a task could lead to a criminal conviction for vagrancy and a prison sentence. Some of these casual wards ('spikes') remained in operation for homeless and destitute people until comparatively recently.[29] It is also likely that many vagrants were involved in other crime, vagrancy being a criminal activity by definition, but a legal rule of practice prevented 'vagrant' being recorded for those charged with other crimes before the Quarter Sessions; serving to conceal the destitution of these offenders in those records.

The issue of vagrancy remained a problem for parishes which were required to fund the prosecution of offenders out of the rates. In practice, and so stated within the legal texts, magistrates continue to hold and to exercise wide discretion in their dealings with vagrants. Prior to 1824, the law defined three grades of vagrant offender: Idle and Disorderly; Rogues and Vagabonds; and Incorrigible Rogues.[30] The first group was liable to one month's imprisonment, the second group to imprisonment for up to six months and then to be passed home, the final group was liable to be flogged, imprisoned for up to two years and transported. These definitions continued within the terms of the Vagrancy Act 1824, whose purpose is stated and understood today to be the prevention of a vagrant mode of life.[31] This long association between those

who control vagrancy and those who administer the poor law has surely tainted aspects of the English approach to the relief of poverty. Despite this, from
a legal perspective vagrancy is a separate type of law, vagrants are not entitled
to poor relief; instead they are subject to punishment. Only when genuinely
weak and destitute does the issue of settlement arise and by legal definition a
vagrant is never treated as a pauper. The case law concerning vagrants
demonstrates a fundamental legal presumption of difference, but congruent
legal processes contribute to a social presumption of similarities. In summary,
the vagrant is part of an underclass perceived in legal terms as separate from
other poor, but his or her control and punishment lies in the hands of the
same officials who were responsible for local poor law administration.

By 1834 the legal position of the non-settled destitute individual is still
dependent upon this highly personal decision-making by local officials:
constables, overseers of the poor and the justices of the peace. Behind their
decisions are those made by local ratepayers who pay for poor relief and
criminal prosecutions. The vestry and the Justices share responsibilities
within a complex legal framework. In summary, a vestry has discretion to be
generous with the settled poor but not to deny them aid. In addition vestries
could remove non-settled poor but only subject to formal legal processes and
legal proofs; equally a vestry may decide not to act. Finally, a vestry could
actively seek to prosecute casual poor under the vagrancy laws, or simply pay
beggars a small sum of money to move on. The removal aspects of settlement
law could be punitive for its victims, but always required legal proofs for its
operation. The prosecution for vagrancy was legally a simpler matter; a
beggar merely needs to 'look like' a vagrant. The inter-connectedness of the
operation of these two branches of law leads inexorably to the conclusion that
when a pauper seeks aid he or she risks rather more than a refusal.

There is other evidence of a general social negativity towards the poor and of
the devastation a conviction for vagrancy could bring. Charles Dickens, in his
Christmas story *The Chimes*, published in December 1844, provides a ferocious
indictment of the attitude of many magistrates towards the casual poor,
allowing his creation Will Ferris to passionately articulate the destructive
effect of this often arbitrary designation of 'vagrant' upon the destitute poor.[32]
This, coupled with the nineteenth century extension of the term 'vagrant' to
describe all casual poor in official records, adds to a suspicion that fraud
became attached to claims for aid and appears to have become a cultural *sine
qua non* attached to the poor during this period. This is witnessed by Nathaniel Hawthorne who lived in Rock Park, a mile from Tranmere in the 1850s;
he records meeting an Irish family at the Eastham (Mersey) Ferry on the
Wirral in 1853. They are returning to Ireland in a state of some destitution,
forced to beg upon the road, but they do not beg from the writer who records:

> I am getting to possess some of the English indifference as to beggars and
> poor people; but still when I come face to face with them and have any

intercourse; it seems as if they ought to be the better for me. I wish, instead of sixpence, I had given the poor family ten shillings and denied it to a begging subscriptionist, who has just fleeced me to that amount.[33]

In 1863 Cheshire Quarter Sessions ordered the Chief Constable of the County at the request of the Wirral guardians to assist the relieving officers. Their duties were to consist of searching and examining vagrants [sic] applying for relief and to issue tickets of admission to the workhouse.[34] In addition, although the general tone of the poor law records is pejorative in respect of casual and migrant poor, Wirral Union records indicate that fine social distinctions are being drawn. In response to the Poor Law Board's 'Vagrancy Circular', of November 1868, Wirral guardians amend conditions slightly. They confirm that they have already applied the Circular's provisions that: '[H]onest wayfarers are to be given a night's lodging and are allowed to leave in the morning without performing a task.'[35] How any decision is arrived at as to the honesty or otherwise of an applicant remains conjecture today, but the subjectivity of the process is clear.

It is therefore evident that from the earliest time the dividing line between pauper migrants and vagrants is set by subjective decision-making. Practically, it is difficult now, and perhaps was then, to draw a 'real' distinction between vagrants and any other poor passing through a parish. These might include migrant workers, poor labourers or those reduced to penury by misfortune and all became vulnerable to the designation of 'vagrant' by the Justices. The non-settled poor might slip out of the system of settlement and into the criminal justice system with physical punishments and imprisonment awaiting them. This criminalising of a section of the poor became interconnected with the development of the local administration of poor law after 1662 with the inclusion of vagrancy provisions within the statute; however it is much later, in the 1840s, that some legal commentators began to connect settlement and vagrancy.[36]

Dichotomies of giving: from charity to vagrant

It may appear from the above discussion that the legal response to begging has always consisted of punitive negative measures linked to control. Especially when considered as part of that wider early English social structure that presumes an individual's locality is both socially and geographically fixed. This state of affairs constitutes a cultural norm underpinning the duties and obligations an individual owes to his or her work, family and community. This is the subtext to the wording of the Ordinance of 1349 and of the Vagrancy Act 1824 still partly in force today. However, such accounts require nuancing as the history of begging contains other strands. Just as the act of giving to beggars confers virtue in some cultures, so too it was once encouraged in England and considered a normal part of civilised society as well as an expression of religious values. Poverty itself once held virtue; in the fourteenth century William Langland wrote: 'And much more boldly may a man claim that bliss (of the Kingdom of Heaven) who, though he might have all he could wish for on earth ... yet for the love of God abandons all and lives as a beggar.'[37] Additionally as noted earlier, before the Reformation religious houses provided charitable support for the poor.[38] The effect of the dissolution of the monasteries upon such support was dramatic.[39] For 30 years few new foundations were established and many paupers were evicted from those in existence. A contemporary wrote in 1546: '[T]he pore impotent creatures (had) some relefe of theyr scrappes, where as nowe they have nothyng. Then they had hospitals, and almshouses to be lodged in, but nowe they lye and starve in the stretes.'[40] As noted, the full extent of this loss or the size of local support in this period is only beginning to be revealed, but surviving records indicate much suffering.[41] The dire effects upon the lives of the poor were considerable and Protestants expressed concern. Sir Thomas More in *Utopia* envisages a pension for the aged, Latimer and Ridley advocated the use of the wealth of the church for the benefit of the poor. Almshouses began to be built again in the middle of the sixteenth century but now also in small towns and villages.[42] charities were formed through gifts of land and money to aid the poor and some continue, as we saw in the Liverpool example, fulfilling the same purposes today.

Consequently, there is a continuing tradition of ecclesiastical support for beggars during the sixteenth and seventeenth century. Additionally, in order to maintain their settled poor, parishes licensed them to beg within the boundaries.[43] In this manner, giving to the poor and the act of begging are permitted within local communities, continuing into the nineteenth century as we have seen recorded in Dorothy Wordsworth's *Lakeland Journals*. It is evident that historically the treatment of begging is dichotomised; in short, begging has not been viewed exclusively as a social evil. Giving to beggars is another aspect of our cultural heritage and may still be found in the more positive approach taken by some; by the Rector of Walton in Liverpool and by many organisations and local authorities in assisting and supporting the homeless.

Nonetheless, vagrancy and poor law had separate legal status following different legal authorities, but the two systems ran in parallel. There is evidence of a harsh beginning from the Ordinance of 1349 and that this punitive element is central to the Elizabethan concept of vagrancy which continues to influence the treatment of vagrants to the Vagrancy Act 1824 and beyond. Clive Emsley believes that this Act marks a stricter supervision of the casual poor.[44] If so, this attitude did not long survive, as discussed above, the reforms of 1834 introduced an alternative approach. A destitute individual benefited from the establishment of casual wards and the development of local constabularies who appear to have preferred to pass beggars to the relieving officer rather than process a charge of vagrancy. By way of contrast, after 1834 these measures are extended to all the casual poor and from their perspective such changes appear punitive. By 1865 those who would have been earlier charged and thus designated 'vagrant' were less likely to be so charged and named whilst poor law recipients were more harshly treated than before. Justices might order a poor person to be flogged and sent away, or given aid and sent away, in the exercise of judicial but subjective judgement. Earlier, in the 1840s poor law records reveal that the term vagrant is being used for all the migrant and casual poor in poor law records. A significant section of the poor thus began to acquire quasi-criminal status in the bureaucratic records and perhaps within the bureaucratic mindset.

The Beveridge reforms did not end this dichotomy; s. 41 of the National Assistance Act 1948 contains provisions against those persons who 'wilfully' refuse to maintain themselves. The section was included in the Administration Act 1992 (s. 5), amended by the Jobseekers Act 1995, Schedule 2 Para. 53, which came into force on 7 April 1997. The application Regulations to this Act consist of a modern version of the subjective criteria which led to a prosecution under the 1824 Vagrancy Act;[45] they appear as a list of tasks a claimant must perform to qualify for aid under benefit legislation in 1996 and these continue to appear in various guises.[46] It is no longer need alone which qualifies an individual for relief from poverty, but active proofs that a claimant deserves that aid. All the tasks are bureaucratic measures designed primarily to fulfil the requirements of a box-ticking system rather than to be of value to the claimant. The Regulation and subsequent amendments and changes have more in common with a model of the poor as criminals to be controlled than one of citizens possessing a legal right to relief from poverty.

Standing outside looking in: Irish under the poor law

The Irish, the Scots and foreigners were 'outside' the poor law system as they possessed no settlement in England and Wales; although as casual migrants they could be designated as vagrants.[47] However, the terms of the 1662 Act differentiated the Irish and the Scots from the Welsh and English poor whilst powers contained in the various vagrancy statutes were often used to return them home. This section will concentrate upon the Irish as the movement of Irish seasonal workers had great significance for those who needed their labour in agriculture and elsewhere. In addition, the Irish presented a considerable financial liability for poor relief in those ports affected by their return home, especially those of Chester (Parkgate) and Liverpool, the locations for the following case study. The Irish tended to arrive in boatloads and there were waves of these arrivals during the sixteenth and seventeenth centuries.[48] The Irish travelled in large groups, including entire families and shared what A.L. Beier refers to as: 'flexible relationships',which, he suggests, rendered them threatening to local officials.[49] As a result, local administrative approaches were twofold, either the Irish were bought off with official doles or they were punished as vagrants and returned home. The Irish generally acquired no settlement within England and the pressures that induced their patterns of migration remain largely unchanged.[50] They were stigmatised by the general view of vagrants as respectability was understood to include some intention to remain, Irish migrants rarely had that intention. There were regular sailings from seven designated ports as part of an elaborate system that developed to return Irish 'vagrants' to Ireland.[51] By the nineteenth century the Irish were the largest number numerically, they did work the English disliked because it was dirty, disreputable or otherwise undesirable. In Birkenhead, the Irish specialised in collecting and selling cockles and mussels, or sold sand and rubbing stones.[52]

In poor relief terms, the Irish had a different cultural background; in Ireland the Roman Catholic Church encouraged almsgiving and, with few alternatives available, this rendered begging a normal activity in hard times. As a consequence, seasonal labour migration was a reasonable economic option and numbers remained high. During the 1740s, Irish harvesters arrived from Dublin through Parkgate, then officially designated the port of Chester, and they continued to arrive at the port until 1815 when the River Dee silted up and the traffic moved to the port of Liverpool.[53] A large proportion of those who sailed from Parkgate for Dublin were Irish 'vagrants' who were being sent back under a pass system, each parish paying to pass them through to the port. The numbers are high; from 1750–1800, 25,325 individuals are recorded as passing through in the accounts of the Neston House of Correction, attached to the port of Parkgate.[54] Quarter Sessions' records provide details of individual circumstances within the Removal Orders, thus Hugh Ruewark arrested in January 1758 begging in Middlewich was declared a:

> 'rogue and vagabond' and under the terms of the Poor Law Act 1744 was to be returned to his parish of origin in Kildare. Ruck addressed the magistrate Thomas Swettenham that ... about 15 years ago he was hired for a twelvemonth in the parish of Kilcullen in the County of Kildare, that he served the said twelvemonth ... Since then he hath done no act to give him a legal settlement elsewhere.[55]

The Order states: 'Hugh, Ann his wife and Thomas his child around two years, must be conveyed to Parkgate and thence to Ireland.' Hugh and family were held in the Old Key House of Correction, pending the arrival of a ship to Ireland. In this manner, seasonal workers could use the system to ensure free passage home; there are accounts of Irish begging to ensure that they triggered the vagrancy process.[56] This procedure mirrors the Removal Orders of settlement hearings and demonstrates that the Irish, even when convicted as 'rogues and vagabonds', are subject to a less punitive process than the full rigour of the vagrancy laws. Records of Neston House reveal that it was in fact rarely used for 'Rogues', but for the destitute in need of shelter.[57] This practice ended with the silting of the port.[58]

However, numbers of Irish travelling to England increased in the nineteenth century and by 1816 Parliament's attention was drawn to the increased problem of Irish paupers in Manchester and the seaports and surrounding districts.[59] The terms of an Act of 1819 facilitated the passing of the Irish and of Scottish casuals. This was successful and rather popular with them. Meanwhile, their numbers increased, as did the pressure on the ports. The rules of settlement allowed migrant workers to travel by means of certification, the Irish could not produce such certification, but they found a demand for their services which kept them arriving. The failure of the Irish potato crop in 1821 was followed by famine in 1822 and from this period the numbers of Irish entering England increased dramatically.[60] In addition, Lancashire contained a greater number of Irish settlers than any other county. Records indicate that the Irish immigrants continued to use the pass system to its full and contrived to exploit the system for passage home.[61] After 1822 their legal position became safer as a single magistrate could no longer order the flogging of vagrants, only the bench at Quarter Sessions, whilst transportation to the colonies was abolished. After 1824 the passing of all convicted vagrants under the poor law procedure was abolished, but the Irish could still be sent home under the Sturges Bourne procedure. This led to the anomaly that an Irish vagrant could not be removed across the sea, but an Irish pauper could. The position of the Irish under English poor law was a result of their unsettled status. If they attempted to remain in England they were liable to be examined and dealt with under the rules of settlement and became vulnerable to be returned to Ireland (which might sometimes suit them) unless they either acquired a settlement or the legal status of irremovability.

The legal position occupied by the Irish appears a compromise between the punitive criminal law treatment of vagrants and the right to relief of the settled poor or of others in an emergency. This is apparent in the terms of various statutes that differentiate between the settled poor, the Irish (and Scots) and vagrants. If deemed vagrant, the individual is punished under the criminal law; if Irish, he or she is placed in an administrative system which returns them to Ireland. If a pauper, then the common law question of settlement is raised, poor relief given and the pauper removed if the legal processes so decide. However, access to relief and legal rights at the margins between criminal status and poor law is decided by the subjective judgement of parish officials. Contrariwise, poor law 'rules' concerning the Irish are an aspect of common law settlement, arising because of the unsettled position of the Irish. However, they possess common law rights that they may trigger to be supported and returned home. Their legal position is very different from that of those adjudged vagrant.

These restricted poor law rights possessed by the Irish still surpassed any claim available to them in Ireland. In consequence, during the Irish famine of the 1840s many Irish emigrants made their way to England. In 1847, at the height of the famine influx, the *Chester Chronicle* reports that: 'a great deal of distress prevailed', with: 'more suffering among the lower orders than is generally imagined'.[62] On 14 February 1847 the *Chronicle* reports over 300 destitute Irish are relieved with soup, coal and money from Father Carberry

and his Charity. The newspaper notes these: 'unfortunate and starving creatures were huddled up in large numbers in very confined and filthy dwell-
ings'. The Wirral Poor Law Union record the number of Irish in the casual
wards under the heading, 'Workhouse Vagrants',[63] and in 1849 the Clerk to
the Union wrote to the Poor Law Board in London reporting upon vagrancy,
that: '[T]he Irish poor passed and repassed between Liverpool and Birkenhead preying upon both Unions without detection and claiming support
upon the grounds of destitution.'[64]

The Select Vestry of Liverpool were particularly concerned with the numbers
of Irish poor entering Liverpool, either arriving in a destitute state as migrant
labour, or awaiting their return to Ireland under the vagrancy pass system. In
1824, Select Vestry records reveal that two-thirds of the poor who received
casual relief were Irish.[65] The 1840s brought in huge numbers of destitute
Irish.[66] In 1846, over 280,000 immigrants arrived in Liverpool from Ireland
and less than half sailed on to other countries; in 1847, over 300,000 arrived in
Liverpool and again over half remained behind. Fifty thousand were passengers
on business; the remainder were paupers suffering dire effects from the famine.
The peak arrival in Liverpool was the first four months of 1847 when 144,000
destitute Irish arrived in Liverpool; a contested figure, Christine Kinealey gives
the numbers at 90,000 for the same period.[67] Whichever is correct either constitutes a tidal wave of poverty. There are many deaths recorded amongst these
weakened frail famine survivors but no mass starvations in England; there is,
rather, squalor, sickness and destitution. In short, the legal obligations of the
poor law, with a right to relief legally confirmed for the unsettled poor in
1803,[68] ensures that Liverpool's Select Vestry, the Wirral Poor Law Union, the
Chester Incorporation and charities provide a minimum amount of aid. The
legal story in Ireland is very different.

Poor law without a right to relief: Ireland in the 1840s

The Great Famine of the 1840s left a legacy in Ireland of migration,
depopulation and traumatic folk memory. As such, its continuing political
and cultural implications should not be underestimated. So important are
these perceptions that in 1997 the British Prime Minister, Tony Blair, pub-
licly apologised to the Irish people for Britain's failures during that massive
tragedy. This act of public rhetoric underlines that it is possible to establish a
legal opinion that it was intrinsic to the poor law system imposed in Ireland
under the terms of the Irish Poor Law Act 1838, that widespread distress
would go unrelieved; relief after 1838 was only to be available in a workhouse
with limited accommodation in a financially capped scheme.[69] Worse, even if
this implication was not fully 'understood' by those who initially imposed
that modified version of English poor law upon Ireland, the English Government took no action to alter that legal position once reports of severe distress
and deaths began to be received in London.[70] Contemporaneously, distress on

such a scale could not legally have been left unrelieved in England and Wales where, as we have seen, the legal framework provided administrative and financial structures to alleviate poverty in a rights-based demand-funded welfare system. Moreover, in England and Wales overseers could be indicted for manslaughter if refusal of relief caused the death by starvation of a pauper. However, settlement and its accompanying 'rules' and case law were not introduced into Ireland. Worse, the terms of the Irish Poor Law Act 1838 specifically excluded a right to relief and its operation was grafted upon pre-existing, very different, local administrative structures. Worst of all, once those limited methods were exhausted there was no further legal obligation to relieve distress, save the 'court of public opinion'.

Controversially, there is an Irish politico-cultural school that holds the deaths in Ireland during the famine constitute a deliberate 'genocidal' act by the British Government of the day. Such a perspective appears at first glance to be excessive, counterfactual and ahistorical; the term itself was defined in its modern form by Raphael Lemkin during the Second World War.[71] However, as scholarly contributions to the *Journal of Genocide Research* regularly illustrate, historical reconstructions around definitions of 'genocide' have achieved respectability as a methodological tool to provide meaning and enhance understanding of the past. Notwithstanding their 'historical' interest, such retrospective charges against the past retain immediate political significance. In this context, after the Turkish writer Orhan Pamuk wrote in 2005 of the suffering and massacre of Turkey's Armenian population during the First World War as 'genocide', he was charged with 'insulting Turkishness'. The charge was dropped in 2006 on 'technical grounds' and later that year the writer was awarded the Nobel Prize for Literature. In consequence, Pamuk's retrospective adoption of the term 'genocide' has moved this descriptor beyond dismissal as a literary conceit. This is supported by Bloxham's recent historical reconstruction of these same events as 'genocide'.[72]

It is within this methodological convention that this writer has suggested elsewhere there is a conceptual and doctrinal legal argument to be made for a retrospective charge of genocide against the British Government of the day.[73] This suggestion is grounded within those limited poor law structures deliberately introduced into Ireland. These in turn permitted the British Government and its Irish administration to legally abdicate responsibility for preventing deaths by starvation whilst remaining within what then constituted the law of poor law in Ireland; a counterfactual genocide by 'adoption'.[74] Significantly, genocide may not be an act of war; its definitions do not require a state of war to exist. Article II of the Genocide Convention defines genocide as: any of the following acts committed with intent to destroy, in whole or in part, a national, ethnical, racial or religious group, as such:

(a) Killing members of the group;
(b) Causing serious bodily or mental harm to members of the group;

(c) Deliberately inflicting on the group conditions of life calculated to bring about its physical destruction in whole or in part;

(d) Imposing measures intended to prevent births within the group;

(e) Forcibly transferring children of the group to another group.

From the above it appears that the strongest legal argument might be constructed around section (c); not as a claim that poor law was introduced with the intention to destroy the group, rather suggesting that as the pernicious effects of the operation of that specifically limited version of poor law became clear, no effective action was taken to amend that law. In other words, in the most extreme reading of events the British Government 'adopted' the genocide as a solution to the 'problem' of the Irish.[75]

This is not the place to reconstruct a full analysis of this charge; rather it is that failure of the Irish 'poor law' so-called to relieve famine in Ireland that is significant for this work. The legal explanation for that failure lies in its difference from the poor law in England and Wales, founded upon the continuing legal authority of the 1601 Act with the law of settlement and removal delineating and protecting the legal right to relief. Instead, the Irish Poor Law Act 1838 was imposed without comparable legal and demand-based financial protections for the poor. These factors created the pre-conditions for poor law's failure during the disaster that followed. Kinealey has fully reconstructed these matters, including the British Government's responses to the famine and details of the Irish poor law in operation. She reveals a poor law system operating very differently from that in England and Wales. In short, the Irish poor law is a horrible example of what might have happened in England in times of dearth without poor law's legal rights, duties and obligations. That is why the chapter concludes with this tragic example; for it confirms the importance of the right to relief and underlines the central role of law and legal rights within the operation of poor law in England and Wales.

Notes

1   'Curtis' by Cynthia Hogue was first published in *The Never Wife*, Dubois, PA: Mammoth Press 1999, copyright © by Cynthia Hogue. Used by permission of the author and by permission of Mammoth Press.

2   Alan Norrie, *Crime, Reason and Society*, London: Butterworths, 2001.

3   See: James Burrows, *A Series of the Decisions of the Court of King's Bench upon the Settlement Cases from ... 1732*, 3 vols, London: His Majesty, 1768, p. 124.

4   *R v Eastbourne (Inhabitants) (1803)* 4 East 103; 102 E.R. 769.

5   Peter Bartlett, *The Poor Law of Lunacy*, Leicester: Leicester University Press, 1999.

6   A.L. Beier, *Masterless Men. The Vagrancy Problem in England 1560–1640*, London: Methuen, 1985.

7   In the 'Prologue' Chaucer portrays a friar who uses flattery and charm to obtain alms even from the poor: 'He was the beste beggere in his hoys, ... For thogh a wydwe hadde noght a sho, So plesaunt was his "In principio", Yet wolde he have a ferthyng, er he wente.' (251–55): Geoffrey Chaucer, *The Canterbury Tales*, London: Penguin Popular Classics, 1996, p. 13.

8 Sir Arthur Conan Doyle, 'The Man with the Twisted Lip', republished in *Sherlock Holmes, Short Stories*, 22nd impression, London: Jonathan Cape, 1980, p. 128.

9 Lorie Charlesworth, 'Readings of Begging: The Legal Response to Begging considered in its Modern and Historical Context', *Nottingham Law Journal*, 15, 1, 2006, 1–12.

10 Robert C. Palmer, *English Law in the Age of the Black Death, 1348–1381. A Transformation of Governance and Law*, London and Carolina: University of North Carolina Press, 1993.

11 '[M]agistrates would have to determine in all cases of relief, whether the person asking it in a foreign parish was a vagrant or not': Michael Nolan, *A Treatise of the Laws for the Relief and Settlement of the Poor*, 2 vols, 2nd edn, London: A. Strahan, 1805, reprint, New York and London: Garland Publishing Inc., 1978, vol. I, p. 143.

12 Ian Ward, *Shakespeare and the Legal Imagination*, London: Butterworths, 1999, pp. 120–24.

13 Beier, *Masterless Men*, pp. 160–61.

14 Imprisonment was provided as a penalty under the terms of the statutes of 1383, 1388, 1576 and 1597.

15 In 1553, Edward VI conveyed an old decayed palace, the Bridewell, to the City of London for the: 'safekeeping, punishing and setting to work of idle poor and vagabonds'. Other towns followed suite and the terms of a 1576 Act established houses of correction in all towns: Robert Jutte, *Poverty and Deviance in Early Modern Europe*, Cambridge: Cambridge University Press, 1994, pp. 169–70.

16 After 1608 vagrants could be exiled to Newfoundland, East and West Indies, France, Germany, Spain and the Low Countries. Most were sent to the American Colonies where they were indentured into service.

17 Ivy Pinchbeck and Margaret Hewitt, *Children in English Society*, vol. I, London: Routledge and Kegan Paul, 1969, pp. 94–98.

18 The settlement statutes were not, in Nolan's opinion, concerned with vagrants: Nolan, *Treatise*, vol. I, p. 135.

19 Ibid., p. 137.

20 The Ordinance of Labourers, 23 Ed. III (1349); 2 Rich. II *c.* 6 (1378); 7 Rich. II *c.* 5 (1383); 12 Rich. II (1388); An Act ordering the Irish to be sent back to Ireland, 1 Hen. V *c.* 8, (1413); 11 Hen. VI *c.* 2, (1495); An Act against Vagabonds and Beggars, 22 Hen. VIII *c.* 12 (1530–31); Concerning Punishment of Beggars and Vagabonds, 27 Hen. VIII *c.* 25 (1536); 1 Edw. VI *c.* 3 (1547); 3 & 4 Edw. VI *c.* 16 (1550); 14 Eliz. I *c.* 5 (1572–73); 18 Eliz. I *c.* 3 (1576); 39 Eliz. I *c.* 4 (1597–98); 39 Eliz. I *c.* 40 (1598); 1 Jac. I (1604); 7 Jac. I *c.* 4 (1610); Ordinances against begging in London, (1647 & 1649); 13 Anne *c.* 26 (1714); 13 Geo. II.*c.* 24 (1740); 17 Geo. II *c.* 5 (1744); 32 Geo. III *c.* 45 (1792); The Vagrancy Act repealed all previous statutes then in force: 5 Geo. IV *c.* 83 (1824).

21 Lionel Rose, *'Rogues and Vagabonds: Vagrant Underworld in Britain 1815–1986'*, London: Routledge, 1988, p. 17.

22 Under s. 3 of the Vagrancy Act 1824, on summary conviction an Idle and Disorderly person may be sentenced to one month's imprisonment or 14 days by one magistrate. Hard labour was repealed in 1948 by ss. 1(2) and 83(3) Schedule 10 of the Criminal Justice Act; Rogues and Vagabonds are liable on summary conviction to a maximum of three months' imprisonment; Incorrigible Rogues may be committed to the Crown Court for sentence of up to one year, or an unrestricted hospital order may be made if the requirements of s. 37 of the 1983 Mental Health Act are satisfied.

23 The Criminal Justice Act 1967, s. 91(4), dealt with drunk and disorderly in a public place; The Mental Health Act 1959, s. 136 (now repealed), with mentally disordered persons; The Highways Act 1980, s. 37, with the wilful obstruction of the highway, pavement, etc.

24 *Smith v Chief Superintendent of Woking Police Station* (1983) 76 Cr. App. R. 234.

25 Michael Dalton, *The Country Justice*, London: Henry Lintot, 1742, p. 169.

26 Only a small minority of poor migrants were treated as vagrants, whipped and sent back to their place of birth or last residence with a vagrant's passport: Paul Slack, *Poverty and*

Policy in Tudor and Stuart England, London: Longman, 1988, pp. 91–92; Eden recognised the difficulty. He stated that the vagrancy offences extended under the statute 23 Geo.III *c.* 88: 'are of a very dubious nature, and that it must frequently require nice legal acumen to distinguish whether a person incurs any, and what, penalty, under the vagrant laws': Sir Frederick Morton Eden, *The State of the Poor*, 3 vols, 1797, A.G.L., Rogers (ed.), republished, London: Routledge and Sons Ltd., 1928, vol. I, p. 55.

27   Beier, *Masterless Men*, p. 11.

28   Ibid., p. 173.

29   The Streatham 'spike' in London may be seen in 1968 at the beginning of Antonioni's film *Blow Up*. It was filmed early in the morning with the inmates [played by actors] leaving and was then still operating as a 'casual ward' for the homeless.

30   The first group includes those who neglect their families, are wilful idlers or beg in their parish of settlement; the second group consists of professional beggars, those found outside their parish, those who desert their families or are suspect families'; the third group are recidivists from category two: Lionel Rose, *'Rogues and Vagabonds,'* p. 4.

31   Leon Radzinovicz and Roger Hood, *The Emergence of Penal Policy in Victorian and Edwardian England*, Oxford: Clarendon Paperbacks, 1990, pp. 342–43.

32   Charles Dickens, *Christmas Books*, Oxford: Oxford World Classics, 1988, pp. 174–75.

33   Nathaniel Hawthorne, *The English Notebooks*, Randall Steward (ed.), Oxford: Oxford University Press, 1941, p. 35.

34   M.D. Handley, 'Local Administration of the Poor Law in the Great Boughton and Wirral Unions, and the Chester Local Act Incorporation 1838–71', 1969–70, unpublished thesis, University of Bangor, p. 342.

35   'Wirral Poor Law Union Clerk to the Poor Law Board', 26 December 1868: National Archives, Kew, London (hereafter NA) MH. 12/1212.

36   Lumley states of the 1662 Act: 'This statute was passed with the view of suppressing vagrancy': William Golden Lumley, *A Popular Treatise on the Law of Settlement and Removal*, London: Shaw and Sons, 1842, p. 4. Poynter asserts that from the sixteenth century there is a link in perception between poor law and vagrancy: J.R. Poynter, *Society and Pauperism. English Ideas on Poor Relief 1795–1834*, London: Routledge and Kegan Paul, 1969, p. 2.

37   William Langland, *Piers Ploughman*, London: Penguin Books, 1978, p. 174.

38   Neil S. Rushton, 'Monastic charitable provision in Tudor England', *Continuity and Change*, vol. 16, part 1, May, 2001, 9–44. For examples of that provision at their dissolution in 1535, see: Christopher Haigh, *The Last Days of the Lancashire Monasteries and the Pilgrimage of Grace*, vol. XVII, Third series, Manchester: Chetham Society, 1969, pp. 39, 53–54.

39   Slack, *Poverty and Policy*, p. 81.

40   Ibid., p. 82.

41   Brian Bailey, *Almshouses*, London: Robert Hale, 1988, p. 5.

42   Ibid., p. 90.

43   Slack, *Poverty and Policy*, pp. 118, 123, 126.

44   Clive Emsley, *Crime and Society in England 1750–1900*, 2nd edn, London: Longman, 1996, p. 41.

45   Persons who fail to maintain themselves and their families could be convicted as idle and disorderly persons under s. 3 Vagrancy Act 1824.

46   Section 18 of the Jobseekers Allowance Regulation 1996 lists the steps to be taken by persons actively seeking employment, a pre-condition for the receipt of Jobseekers Allowance, which replaced Unemployment Benefit. The Regulation states that a person seeking this benefit must undertake more than one of these tasks, ('steps' in the text) each week, unless one step is 'all that it is reasonable for that person to do in that week', s.18(1). Interestingly, taking part in an Outward Bound course, s. 18(3) f (i), may be taken into consideration as, more rationally, may the availability of work in the area, s. 18(3) e.

47 For contemporary accounts see: Sir George Nicholls, *A History of the Scotch Poor Law* (1856), reprint, New York: Augustus M. Kelley, 1967; – *A History of the Irish Poor Law* (1856), reprint, New York: Augustus M. Kelley, 1967.

48 Waves of immigration caused by wars and famine were associated by the authorities with Popery and rebellion: Beier, *Masterless Men*, p. 11.

49 Sixteenth century Hibernians [sic] were noted for their 'relaxed' attitude towards incest, bastardy, divorce and adoption: Ibid., p. 62.

50 This was still true of the mid-eighteenth century. By 1796, the united parishes of St Giles and St George, Bloomsbury paid £200 relief for casual poor, comprising: '1,200 poor natives of Ireland': Arthur Redford, *Labour Migration in England, 1800–1850*, 2nd edn, Manchester, Manchester University Press, 1964, pp. 133–34.

51 Bristol, Minehead, Barnstable, Chester, Liverpool, Milford and Workington: Ibid., p. 132.

52 Ibid., p. 154.

53 Geoffrey Place, *The Rise and Fall of Parkgate, Passenger Port for Ireland 1686–1815*, Manchester: Carnegie Publishing Ltd, 1994, p. 174.

54 Ibid., p. 186.

55 Chester Record Office (hereafter CRO) QJF 128–228: Ibid., p. 182. This represents a legal oddity. Settlement law did not run in Ireland, but appears in such cases as a legal fiction used to enable the legal removal of the Irish from England.

56 Ibid., pp. 182–83.

57 Ibid., pp. 183–87.

58 'Irish vagrants. The Magistrates of this county have given notice by circulars that the Dublin packets did not now sail from Parkgate but from Liverpool. Magistrates ... are requested to direct passes in future to Liverpool': *Chester Chronicle*, 28 July 1815.

59 *The First Report on Mendicity in the Metropolis 1815*, 5–9.

60 Redford, *Labour Migration*, p. 140.

61 Lionel Rose, *'Rogues and Vagabonds'*, p. 10.

62 *Chester Chronicle*, 15 January 1847.

63 See: 'Guardian Minute Books, Wirral Poor Law Union', CRO LGW. 1/4.

64 *Second Annual Report of the Poor Law Board*, PP 1849, XXV, p. 101.

65 'Minutes of Vestry.' 1 October 1824: W.L. Blease, 'The Poor Law in Liverpool, 1681–1834', *Transactions of the Historic Society of Lancashire and Cheshire*, 61, 1909, 97–182, at 165.

66 Cecil Woodham-Smith, *The Great Hunger, Ireland 1845–1849*, London: Penguin Books, 1962.

67 Christine Kinealey, *This Great Calamity. The Irish Famine 1845–52*, Dublin: Gill and Macmillan, 1994, p. 332.

68 *R v Eastbourne (Inhabitants) (1803)* 4 East 103; 102 E.R. 769.

69 Kinealey, *This Great Calamity*, pp. 18–30, 106–35.

70 Ibid., pp. 106–35.

71 Daniel Marc Segesser and Myriam Gessler, 'Raphael Lemkin and the International Debate on the Punishment of War Crimes (1919–48)', *Journal of Genocide Research*, 7, 4, 2005, December, 453–68.

72 Donald Bloxham, *The Great Game of Genocide: Imperialism, Nationalism, and the Destruction of the Ottoman Armenians*, Oxford: Oxford University Press, 2007.

73 Lorie Charlesworth, 'Genocide by the Operation of Law? Readings of an English Poor Law in Ireland', paper presented at Experiencing the Law Conference, Institute of Advanced Legal Studies, University of London, December 2006.

74 Convention on the Prevention and Punishment of the Crime of Genocide. Adopted by Resolution 260 (III) A of the UN General Assembly on 9 December 1948. Entry into force: 12 January 1951.

75 Sir George Nicholls, active reformer, 'believer' in theories of political economy, member of the Poor Law Commission and first Poor Law Commissioner for Ireland promoted the Irish Act in its specific terms in order to bringing about the 'social reform' of Irish poverty: Kinealey, *Great Calamity*, p. 180.

Chapter 9

The road to Beveridge: deforming welfare

In considering how a legal right was marginalised, abolished and forgotten, this work began by reconstructing those jurisprudential theories that formed one pre-condition for those proto-modernist legal elements contained within the Poor Law Amendment Act 1834. What follows here is an historical reconstruction of the sources of those administrative reforms set out in the terms of the Act, drawn from a long history of publications and from parliamentary investigation introduced earlier. The final section of the chapter reconstructs how the poor responded to the implementation of the new poor law, factoring in the loss of legal rights. Significantly, despite a history of criticism, settlement was not repealed in 1834 neither was the legal authority of the 1601 Act and the poor continued to be relieved. Poynter and Himmelfarb have reconstructed the reform debate, Himmelfarb taking a stand in favour of the reformers against the 'common law' position as reactionary and paternalist.[1] Poynter reconstructs the breadth of reform literature and indicates its basis in theories of political economy, religion, humanism, jurisprudence, charity and theories of social control. It must be underlined, however, that the most powerful and immediate influences upon reform were the vast increase in the cost of poor relief combined with escalating manifestations of discontent by labourers. Consequently, in responding to contemporary economic problems, discussions by political economists were divorced from a consideration of rights. That considerable history of the legal rights of the poor reconstructed within this work, both in customary and common law, was not a focus of the debate and opponents of reform could not produce a persuasive argument sufficient to counter contemporary accusations of 'antiquated' paternalism.

Parliamentary investigations and reports

During the eighteenth century Parliament introduced various unsuccessful poor law reforms; although Local Acts were passed, few general bills succeeded.[2] The officers of central government played some part in drafting and promoting these measures. From the 1780s Secretaries of State formulated new bills, assisted in their drafting by law officers and judges. Innes believes that this development was partly to draw upon their legal expertise and partly to ensure judicial support in their implementation.[3] Perhaps it was also a reflection of the increased technical detailed provisions these new bills contained. Select Committees did not merely scrutinise bills, they went on investigatory visits and summoned witnesses to testify before them. Significantly, during this period it became increasingly common for Parliament to call for the systematic collection of data before discussions of social policy. For example, in 1751 Parliament used the Quarter Sessions to enquire into relief expenditure on the poor and vagrants.[4] Taken in the context of new jurisprudential theories that provide an intellectual framework for drafting a different form of law, new economic and political theories provide the stimulus for developing the methodology of the government inquiry. Brundage places the moment when poor relief became a serious issue for parliamentary regulation rather than a matter of local concern at c. 1815, the end of the Napoleonic War.[5] Malthusian fears of uncontrolled population growth now appeared persuasive in the context of severe economic depression and increased expressions of violent discontent by both the rural and urban labouring population. As a result, the first of a number of Select Committees was set up to examine poor relief.

Commons Select Committees produced three reports between 1816 and 1819, plus minutes of evidence. The House of Lords set up a Select Committee in 1816 and another in 1831. The evidence in the *Select Committee Reports* depicts chaotic and disorganised poor relief and settlement operation in the localities, like pieces of a jigsaw puzzle jumbled in a box with no picture on the cover. Unsurprisingly as local practices differ greatly, this muddled picture supported a perceived need for that centralised welfare model the reformers eventually achieved. This work has argued that this misrepresents poor law's common law nature, built upon and supporting local autonomy; a legal feature undoubtedly both understood and loathed by reformers. None of the government reports acknowledges the larger legal framework and this obfuscation is repeated in many reconstructions of settlement by historians. The Swing Riots and a general fear of unrest preceded the Royal Commission on the Poor Laws where Edwin Chadwick, formerly secretary to Bentham, was to prove influential. When set up in 1832 it had seven members and 27 Assistant Commissioners whose task was to collect information on the operation of the poor laws. Chadwick was initially appointed an Assistant Commissioner, but joined the Commission in 1833 and he and Nassau Senior proved the most influential members.[6] The Assistants were issued with specific guidelines which appear in the published *Poor Law Report* of 1834. Amongst the matters they examined were the question of magisterial interference and the operation of the vestries, both as examples of the 'evils' of the present law.

After the collection of information was completed Chadwick compiled a series of draft legislative proposals; noting that he desired the reform of local government and Senior was an ardent centralist, the *Report* concluded that

reform and not abolition was required. Senior's personal contempt for popular opinion supporting the rights of the poor may be seen in a letter he wrote
in 1832:

> The riots ... were a practical lesson on the rights of the poor and the
> means of enforcing them. Their wages are not a matter of contract but a
> matter of right, that they depend, not on the value of the labourer's
> service, but on the extent of his wants, or of his expectations ... all these
> monstrous and anarchical doctrines were repeated not only by the rioters
> themselves but by the farmers, the clergy, the magistrates; in short by
> all the ignorant and timid throughout the country.[7]

The *Poor Law Report* produced 'evidence' concerning the operation of settlement and the Commissioners' perception and understanding was that well-
run parishes dealt properly with their poor, but that parochial operation
required improvement.[8] However, the Commission viewed settlement law as
an abuse. Their conclusions, still supported by many historians, were that
the object of settlement is to control mobility; that the methods of obtaining
settlement lead labourers into fraud, deception and all manner of devious-
ness; that settlement discourages people from moving to seek work and
ultimately leads to conflict between overseers and Justices.

One question put to the localities appears frequently in the *Report*: 'Can
you suggest any and what alteration in the settlement laws?' This largely
produced a consensus against settlement by hiring and service.[9] Many who
replied were clergymen from rural areas recounting negative stories, asserting
that rural labourers were afraid to take employment elsewhere and risk losing
their settlement. No systematic examination was undertaken of the legal,
social or economic reasons why the poor valued a settlement, or what loss
would occur to them if this head of settlement was abolished. The poor
appear throughout as a problem to be controlled, not as a group with rights.
The bureaucratic 'official' tone produced by this selection of material dis-
guises the often unsubstantiated, narrow and ill-informed (at least on legal
matters) nature of the opinions collected. This plethora of hard cases pre-
served in the *Report* reads today like a collection of newspaper scare stories. It
is impossible from this distance in time to ascertain how many of these
stories of forced marriages, fraudulent hiring, etc. are occasioned by genuine
attempts to explain what was perceived by many as anachronistic and negative law, or how many were 'tales' told to the important men from London
who were, it was known, collecting evidence concerning poor law reform. A
further incentive to produce a particular reply lies in the likelihood of that
response being cited in a government publication.[10]

Parliamentary investigations and reports continue after 1834; from the perspective of settlement, the *Select Committee Report* of 1847 is of particular interest.[11] Its remit concerns those unforeseen consequences noted in Chapter 3,

of provisions in the Act of 1846 introducing the new form of irremovability after five years' residence.[12] Evidence given by George Lewis, a Poor Law Commissioner, triggered an extended technical legal debate. Nevertheless, Lewis was evasive when confronted with evidence of unions refusing to implement the provisions of the 1846 Act and claimed that he could not remember any matter critical of the Poor Law Commission's operational methodology. Such a response, typical of a bureaucrat before a Parliamentary Select Committee, demonstrates how a protective civil service mentality is already institutionalised in the developing poor law administration. However, this formal methodology of inquiry and response on poor law issues ensured that Parliament remained the only forum for change. The 'impartial' method typifies the positivist nature of the new poor law and forwards its bureaucratic administrative direction. Not everybody accepted this development. Thomas Carlyle, whilst not actually opposed to the new poor law, strenuously deplored:

> [T]he set of ideas, attitudes and values which had given rise to the new poor law, the ethos which made that law appear to be a natural, rational way of coping with the problem of pauperism.[13]

In 1849 the Poor Law Board collected and then published (1850) a *Report* on settlement drafted by its inspectors.[14] The *Report* is largely critical, especially of settlement's perceived purposive tendency to encourage the establishment of close parishes.[15] Other criticisms appeared in print by Sir Edmund Head, a former Poor Law Commissioner (1848), Sir George Nicholls, Secretary to the Poor Law Board (1850), George Goode (1851) and Robert Pashley (1852).[16] Matthew Talbot Baines, President of the Poor Law Board, introduced a bill in 1854 to abolish removal and place the relief costs upon the common fund of the union. However, Irish MPs blocked the bill in order to secure protection from removal for Irish migrants. A Select Committee examined this and other issues and a bill was introduced in 1861 conferring irremovability after three years' continuous residence in a parish. The resulting terms set out within the Act required parishes to contribute to the union common fund on the basis of rateable value rather than relief expenditure. As noted earlier this was unsuccessful. Meanwhile, the implementation of the terms of the Poor Removal Act 1846 had resulted in shifting much of the burden of local poor relief costs from wealthy country landlords to the towns. This in some cases left the poor to relieve the poor. By the 1850s the drift from rural to urban areas was exacerbating this situation and the poor rate fell heaviest upon the poorest parishes.[17]

The Select Committee of 1861, reporting in 1864 stated:

> [A]ny measure for extending the area of rating should (in the opinion of the committee) embrace provision for making the whole cost of the poor in each union chargeable on the common fund of the union.[18]

In common with most evidence concerning settlement presented to Select Committees on settlement law, details published in 1864 appear confused and inconsistent.[19]

Eight of the 30 witnesses who appear before the 1861 Select Committee make responses upon settlement either concerning its general effect or its operation locally. Among those parish officials who gave evidence there is no consensus that settlement is a problem although all agree that appeals are expensive. For example, John Heaver, overseer of the parish of Christchurch, Spitalfields in London states that his parish contains a population of 16,200; that the bulk of that population are employed in manufacture and that nearly 3,000 are maintained wholly or partially from the poor rate. The parish has a poorhouse relieving an average of 360 persons per week with 564 residents last week; no pauper receiving relief out of the house is totally maintained by parochial assistance. The previous year's poor rate raised about £3,000. Heaver states that they had a settlement appeal that year to Hicks Hall and that law expenses generally last year cost between £150 and £200 a year to the vestry clerk; the charges for taking counsels' opinion. Heaver states that the cost of actual removals and appeals against removal amounted to no more than £100 a year. Heaver also gave evidence that his and other London parishes, consisting of Mile End, Bethnal Green, Shoreditch, Bishopsgate and Whitechapel, had their own private arrangements to remove paupers.[20] This is a practice available under parochial autonomy but 'outside' the new poor law regulatory scheme.

Robert Oldershaw Esq., vestry clerk of St Mary Islington, gave evidence concerning his parish with a population almost equal in size to that of Christchurch. At that date there are 407 persons in the house and 48 children in Palmers Green. The parish pays him a (high) salary of £350 as vestry clerk and clerk to the trustees. Significantly it emerges that Oldershaw's duties do not involve him in any regular contact with paupers; he makes decisions about poor relief and attends the trustees at their meetings. He was in fact appointed to consider the questions of law as to settlements. He also reveals that much of the expense incurred by the parish is due to its situation on the High North Road and the parish is therefore responsible for issuing passes for soldiers and sailors en route for Liverpool and the North. Evidence from these very different officials ensures that superficially inconsistent procedures are read as chaotic failure, supporting the reformers' call for the abolition of parish settlement. This constitutes an ideological position; evidence within the *Report* may also be read as a legal system flexible enough to permit operative autonomy that targets local need. These two proximate parishes demonstrate that the general effect of settlement may not be deduced from the particular and that the parliamentary method of inquiry, although it reveals much detail, was flawed if expecting each official to reveal fundamental 'truth' about the operation of the law of settlement and removal.

Contemporary opinions concerning poor law reform

In short, most reformers take the view that the poor are a problem, they deplore the perceived laxity of local control and the weakness and generosity of Justices who are (they argue) too ready to order the relief of paupers. Those opinions considered below wished to reform the old poor law; the final author Joshua Toulmin Smith takes an 'historical' perspective in support of parish autonomy and writes later, in the 1850s, to reform the new poor law. The earliest substantial reconstruction of the operation of the poor laws with a summary of suggestions for reform is that by Richard Burn, lawyer, who published a history of the poor laws in 1764. This text has become accepted as the definitive contemporary poor law account and is the source of much of the Webbs' poor law reconstruction. Burn's *History* takes a common law approach, 'tracing' poor laws directly from the reign of the Saxon kings Edgar and Alfred. The early chapters of his work list 'relevant' statutes in a methodology that was much copied until recently in all law textbooks. It is a practitioner's version of history, an historicist decontextualised narrative, reminiscent in some of its aspects of the Justices manual he authored (first edition, 1757). Burn's value here lies in his lawyerly approach with commentaries on earlier writings advocating reform, considering that: 'Something in the poor laws is wrong; which the wisdom of parliament for ages hath not been able to set right.'[21] However, this does not lead him to reject the relief of poverty, as he cites the seventeenth century opinion of Lord Chief Justice Hale:

> Where there are many very poor, the rich cannot long or safely continue such. Necessity renders men of phlegmatic and dull nature stupid and undisciplinable, and men of more fiery or active constitutions rapacious and desperate.[22]

Burn recounts that Hale perceived the parochial basis of poor relief and hence parochial autonomy (although he did not use the term) as faults in the 'efficient' operation of the law. Hale's reform proposal, one that appears again and again, is that Justices should reorganise parishes into units and set a rate to provide workhouses for the poor.[23] Sir Joshua Childs, writing in 1669, suggested the abolition of settlement law. Child, too, believed the causes of poverty lay: 'in leaving it to the care of every parish to maintain their own poor only'.[24] He understood the settlement entitlement as punitive in intent as he observes from his own experiences in London that removal was: 'a punishment without effect ... because it reforms not the party, nor disposes the minds of others to obedience, which are the true ends of all punishments'.[25] Child's perception was that the problem did not lie in poor law administration but in a weakness in the settlement laws themselves. His solution was the setting up of a central body to receive parish taxes into a common treasury. Burns considers a number of other reform proposals, those of John Carey and Mr Hay

(1735) who propose incorporated workhouses.[26] The latter's suggestions also include reforming settlement upon the basis of one year's residence and making the County the unit of settlement. Hay states that the obligation of each parish to relieve its poor gave it too narrow an interest and that this is: 'the root from which every evil relating to the poor hath sprung; and which must ever grow up, until they are eradicated ... and till they be set on work on a national or at least provincial fund'.[27] All these suggestions share a concern with efficiency in a climate of reform based upon pragmatism not rights; schemes that will provide a practical framework upon which others later map utilitarian and positivist theories (and law). In summary, Burn considers a plethora of reform schemes that provide substantive evidence of public debate lasting more than 150 years.[28] Burn's criticism is that most aim for too much too soon.[29] He does not, as happens later, castigate the activities of the Justices in granting relief; as a lawyer he privileges the Justices as the most suitable body of men to oversee the relief of poverty.[30] More, he does not wish to see settlement reformed, recognising that the legal complexity of its role in relief renders abolition impracticable; his lawyer's perspective provides a prescient explanation for why settlement remained law until 1948.

Sir Frederick Morton Eden's, *The State of the Poor* (1795) has unfortunately not proved as influential in poor law reconstructions as Burn's *History*, perhaps because he was not a lawyer. The factual details of Eden's works are often cited, but not his full reflections on settlement. In short, historians have noted but rejected his conclusions and yet Eden's is the sole contemporary empirical study of how the poor lived under the poor laws. Eden provides a history of settlement and poor law, giving a fuller discussion to reform proposals than Burn; viewing those of Hay and Adam as: 'much too highly coloured'.[31] He agrees with the view of settlement expressed by Howlett:

> Their operation considered in a general view, has been very trifling indeed. How seldom do the young and healthy when single find any difficulty in changing their residence and fixing where they please?[32]

Eden notes moreover, that tradesmen and manufacturers do not concern themselves with the issue of settlement when taking apprentices or employing journeymen. If they had done so then Sheffield, Birmingham and Manchester would have remained villages. Eden 'believes' that poor relief is a right, although lacking a lawyer's knowledge of the legal rules governing relief and settlement; nevertheless he logically deduces the existence of that legal right from the extensive pattern of parochial relief giving. Finally, in travelling England in order to ascertain the state of poor relief he concludes that the evils of settlement are greatly overstated.

Considerable public discussion concerning poor law reform continued in the early nineteenth century. Opinions expressed concerning settlement reflect those writers' political positions, uncluttered by any serious analysis of the law. John Davison in 1820 writes: 'The constant policy of our Courts of Justice has been, to make settlement easily obtained', a view entirely unsubstantiated by the case law.[33] Davison takes a brutal view, that settlement ought to be 'deserved'. He does not deny the hardship that would be caused by reform but saw that as no bad thing, stimulating the poor to greater efforts on their own behalf.[34] Of many similar articles, it is worth picking out one written by Nassau Senior in 1831, which criticises settlement law for its complexity, ambiguity and the expense of litigation; the cure is to allow settlement by birth only.[35] Senior typifies the views of his predecessors in disregarding the legal relationship between the parish and the right to relief. In short, the pattern of publications throughout this period emphasises a view of settlement contributing to the problems of the poor.[36]

Opinions about the operation and effects of settlement law remain as confused and negative after 1834 as before. The escalating costs of poor relief, combined with other social pressures, led most to believe that change was necessary but no one was clear as to what exactly was wrong with the system. This uncertainty left the field free for the ideological purity of the positivist theories of Austin and others to dominate the legislative proposals, but technically settlement remained largely unaltered. After the chaotic results of the attempt to reform settlement in 1846, Head's *Report* to the Select Committee was published in 1848 containing a full discussion of settlement. Head asserts that it was believed that the power of removal was the only check on the: 'false humanity of justices', but that since *R v Eastbourne* any destitute person was entitled to relief.[37] He (mis)construes this decision to conclude that settlement had become irrelevant, a view not shared by the law texts or in the case itself. He further states that without the 'rights' (a rare acknowledgement) that were formerly associated with settlement, that is the repealed right to obtain an Order for relief from a magistrate, settlement appears anachronistic and negative; although he does not underestimate the problems in reforming such complex law.[38] Head's *Report* takes the form of a detached discursive narrative; its tone of problems and solutions has been echoed in many of the writings of modern historians. The legal nature of the rights of the poor, of parishes and of parochial obligation does not appear except to be dismissed in the discussion.

However, Robert Pashley, another lawyer who published on the poor laws in 1852, reveals an alternative perspective. He provides insight into an earlier and more positive view of settlement law even as he attacks that law as outmoded:

> There was once a time, as appears by the Law Reports when judges used to speak of settlement as a thing to be favoured in the law and when they used to consider it not in its real light as a great restriction on natural liberty, but as a peculiar privilege of the poor.[39]

Pashley was critical of the reforms to settlement introduced in 1834 as insufficient and that those repealing hiring and service could not operate retrospectively and had not ended litigation concerning the matter. Instead: '[The reforms] had a great effect in rendering in all cases difficult and in the vast majority of cases impossible, for any adult labourer ever to acquire a settlement at all.'[40] This situation provides another example why lawyers frequently resist reform to complex legal areas, it is impossible to predict the effects of minor adjustments which are often productive of major difficulties. Pashley predicts the development of derivative settlement as a major legal topic, noting correctly that it would lead to increasing difficulties both in law and in practice. In spite of this, in that spirit of legal over-confidence that still causes problems, Pashley desired further reform.

Joshua Toulmin Smith was also unhappy with the *status quo* but from a very different perspective, producing his major work on the parish in the 1850s. This work, written by a lawyer, reflects both his political beliefs and his legal opinion; it is that great rarity, a passionately written book about law.[41] Toulmin Smith has a particular aim in writing his book, he desires to:

> help and strengthen that healthy sense of public duty and individual responsibility, the active existence of which in every neighbourhood is the first essential, and only hope and means, to reaching a high standard of true civilisation, and to the maintaining of a Free State.[42]

Writing some 20 years after the new poor law is introduced; Toulmin Smith speaks positively of the role of the parish, a position at variance with new poor law jurisprudence and contemporary negative accounts of settlement law. He does not separate law from politics and history, taking a common law position to deplore contemporaries who dismiss parish vestries and: 'hold what they are pleased to call "Parish squabbles" as beneath them'.[43] Toulmin Smith emphasises the many duties and obligations still performed by local vestries and castigates the new bureaucratic system which he believed to have oppressed so many on the Continent. No positivist, Smith's work serves as a reminder that not everyone supported the new developments.

By 1854 the chief objections to settlement are that it impedes the movement of the poor, causes them hardship and imposes a heavy cost upon the parish.[44] Toulmin Smith expresses the irony that supporters of the reformed poor law which causes so much grief for the poor should castigate settlement on the grounds of causing misery. For him the greatest evil in the Act is that the reform had made it almost impossible for labourers to acquire a settlement. His view, so sharp with hindsight, is that the abolition of settlement will:

> destroy all neighbourly feeling between those who claim, or may be liable to claim relief and the rest of the community. Sympathy will be

gone. Bitter feelings must grow. A war of classes will be created ... The brand of contamination will be upon all who seek relief. Instead of the eye of neighbours, in his own parish, being upon every man, where his numbers are never great, all will be herded in crowded places away from neighbours; and ... they will be kept in countenance by their numbers, hardened against shame or self-respect, and the few of worse character will deprave the whole.[45]

Radically, Toulmin Smith suggests it should be made easier to obtain a settlement and predicts a national poor rate run by functionaries, where all local interest in the poor would be destroyed and there would be no inducement to care for the welfare of neighbours. His work concludes with a copy of the vestry minutes of Steeple Ashton from the early seventeenth century in order to demonstrate the former depth and breadth of parochial poor law functions; it is an elegy for what has been lost.

1834 and its opponents: localism and rights

Understandably, the poor themselves did not passively accept the implementation of the new poor law. That their opposition was local may be understood as the manifestation of a legal economy grounded in localism. Other threads of protest occupy the larger, public and political sphere, expressing dislike and suspicion of any extension of the powers and influence of central government. For example, in 1834, during the reform debates in Parliament, Poulet Scrope MP objected that:

[The bill] ... was prepared to abrogate, at a word, the legal and ancient title of the poor to existence – a title three hundred years old, as old, as legal, as fully recognised in Acts of Parliament, as the title of the wealthiest of noble to his estate, and founded on still more evident principles of justice and truth.[46]

This position was shared by other MPs, most forcefully by William Cobbett MP who was passionate in his opposition to the bill, provoking numerous personal attack such as that expressed by Colonel Torrens in a letter to *The Times*, 17 June 1834, that Cobbett: 'was the advocate of barbarism – he belonged to another age, to an age that was past, and he (Colonel Torrens) was happy to find him among his opponents'[47]

Poor law historians have reconstructed many aspects of the reform debate. Himmelfarb writes that some of the Tories in Parliament oppose the bill in 1834 on humanitarian grounds, as the proposals would reduce the able-bodied pauper to the status of a prisoner.[48] Generally unsympathetic as her position often appears to be, Himmelfarb makes an interesting point.[49] She suggests that because they were locked into their position opposing the Act in principle, Tories and others missed their chance during debates to miti-gate the rigours of the workhouse system.[50] Himmelfarb characterises their position as paternalist in the pejorative sense, disliking the motives of those who were responsible for administering the old poor law even when (faintly) praising them. Her position ignores or misunderstands the legal dimension and dichotomises her own scholarship; as she intellectually supports the reforms whilst remaining aware that this position is ethically compromised by the coming horrors of the new poor law. This results in transference as she adopts the bizarre position of blaming the opponents for the con-sequences of the reforms they opposed:

> Those of us who deplore the loss of the old moral economy cannot be entirely dismissive of the idea of paternalism that was an integral part of that moral economy. One may question the viability of the paternalist ethic in an industrial age or be suspicious of the motives and interests of those who professed it. But one cannot dispute that such an ethic exis-ted, that large numbers spoke and acted in its name, that it played a considerable part in opposition to the new poor law, and that it was conducive to a more generous, less punitive form of relief than the uti-litarian ethic espoused by most of the reformers.[51]

Poynter reconstructs political opposition from a different perspective; he suggests that the gentry in Parliament, as the 'natural' leaders of society, assume it is their duty to show initiative in poor law matters in their local-ities and therefore hold that it is improper for Parliament to meddle with such local matters.[52] This cannot be a full explanation, as most of the members, reformist and their opponents, belong to that same class. It can be stated that the Tories in Parliament disliked the expansion of central gov-ernment as an infringement of local autonomy and perhaps as a curtailment of their personal interests. However, other groups shared this resentment including some Whigs and Radicals.[53] A number of opponents of the bill occupy an ambiguous position, desiring reform particularly of the allowance system, but disliking other terms it includes.[54] In all this noise, no voice spoke persuasively of the legal rights of the poor. Rather objections centred upon support for parochial institutions, bolstered by arguments grounded in history and the constitution, deploring the proposed destruction of tradi-tional institutions; a theme explored earlier within the reconstruction of contemporary jurisprudence. These political objections, couched in language grounded in a call to defend England's past and traditions were not strong enough to resist the novel dynamic political and juristic momentum.

Linking the support for local autonomy to an emotional appeal based upon the past was and still is, as we have seen with Himmelfarb, understood as reactionary paternalism. Yet its supporters were an odd mixture: Con-servatives (Sibthorpe, Newdegate, Peter Borthwick), Radical Reformers (John

Fielden, John Wakely and John Walter) and Liberals (Crawford).[55] *The Times*, in its campaign against the new poor law, took up the theme of central authority usurping the legitimate power of parochial agencies, portraying the Act as an attack on all forms of local government.[56] Chadwick, sitting at the heart of the new poor law order, dismissed their arguments as: 'despicable rant'.[57] For him, local government represented an irresponsible power structure dominated by local cliques. Neither side referenced that structure of laws and rights which was the foundation of that local autonomy or considered reforms which would have protected the common law rights of the poor.

Protest: enclosure and the Poor Law Amendment Act 1834

The final element in this reconstruction of welfare's forgotten past, concerned with the deformation and forgetting of rights that long protected the poor from starvation, is the reaction of the poor to that loss of legal rights. It must be noted that, although technically the right to relief for the settled poor survives until 1948, from 1834 it is as a legal underpinning and explanation for workhouse relief. For the poor, abolition of the personal right to apply to a Justice for relief must have been shocking. We have seen how historians reconstruct the power and force of the poor's cry of lost rights, even as they fail to acknowledge the legal nature of those rights. For the poor there was also a link between custom, enclosure and the reforms of 1834 that transcends doctrinal legal considerations; for their economic well-being was threatened and their survival as independent labourers curtailed as the workhouse beckoned. In short, the loss for many of the labouring poor of what they well understood as legal rights must have made the reforms all the more galling; changes over which they had no control and in which their voices were not heard. Historians have reconstructed their culture of protest; this section of the chapter will briefly consider the protests concerned with enclosure within that context of lost rights and poor law reform. From this perspective, enclosure of customary lands is an early feature of modernism; unenclosed land was decried by contemporaries as primitive.[58] Modern research has doubted this view as open villages operated by a sophisticated method of agreement, customary law, negotiation and a commonality of interests. Their loss adversely affected the most vulnerable members of English society, those without legal title to or interests in land. The purposive view, sometimes expressed, of the deliberate destruction of these rights as a matter of class oppression may be an over-simplification, but enclosure certainly represented a triumph of economic interests over traditional rights.

Enclosure of land is achieved by Act of Parliament.[59] By this method the ownership of, and rights in, every strip of land in the open fields and meadows and the parish or manorial commons and wastes are taken from the lord and the villagers and abolished. The land is reallocated in proportion to legally proved title, old boundaries ignored, new roads set out, hedges planted, fences erected and new fields set out and allocated to those with a recognised legal claim; enclosure created the modern face of English agriculture. The earliest enclosure Act in 1545 enclosed Hounslow Heath; the next notable Act is that of 1606, enclosing a third of Herefordshire.[60] Between 1700 and 1760, 280 Acts were passed, from 1760–1840, 4,000 enclosures were achieved.[61] Counter-petitions to Parliament objecting to enclosure were rare; they increased overall costs and were rarely successful.[62] There was a legal mechanism to appeal to Quarter Sessions against the Enclosure Commissioners' decision, but no higher appeal. The poor, the landless and small farmers were usually in a difficult legal position, particularly until the second quarter of the nineteenth century, because of the nature of their customary rights.[63] In consequence, the losers are those who eke a marginal living with the benefit of the commons and wastes.[64] G.E. Mingay has noted that one of the problems created by enclosure is that compensation for loss of rights is awarded to the owners of property, the right attaching to the property not the person and thus not to the tenants who use those rights.[65] Allotments of land made for common rights were often rather small and the ability to graze a cow or sheep was lost to smallholders.[66] The outcome of the destruction of rights of common ensured that the poor lost the possibility of eking out their lives by the various shifts traditionally available to them and thus their self-sufficiency. As a result, the poor resisted enclosure, but in traditional ways; a legal option was rarely available to them either because of cost or their lack of legal status. Consequentially, their protests operated at local levels and it is there that J.M. Neeson has found them.[67] These included stubborn non-compliance, procrastination, mischief, rumour, stealing documents from Commissioners, letters to newspapers and local petitions. After enclosure local opposition remained but became more overtly unlawful, including fence-breaking, stealing wood and occasional riots, often unreported in newspapers.[68] Landless families in losing their common rights, suffer the greatest hardship. Enclosure was not always opposed, but opposition was not unusual or atypical, expressing a deep sense of loss, of the theft of the inheritance of the rural poor.[69] The enclosure of manors and the distress this caused forms a backdrop to the introduction of the new poor law.

Historians have reconstructed those protests which greeted the initial efforts to establish the new poor law but invariably their academic explanation is a loss of cultural or customary and not legal rights.[70] Although poor law protests later became enmeshed within the movement for factory reform and Chartism, initially they represented a response to the new poor law as an attack on local rights. As a result, in spite of some massed demonstrations in the North of England, poor law protests remain essentially local; hence their resonance and similarity with enclosure protests.[71] The national battle was waged mainly in print; a section of the press opposed the Act including both local and national publications, ranging from Cobbett's *Political Register* to the *Quarterly Review* and *The Times*.[72] As the aim of this section is to ascertain how far a sense of lost legal rights motivated these protests, it involves a re-reading of historians' conclusions. John Knott, for example, believes that these protests were not individual events but rather a: 'self conscious process guided in almost every instance by a coherent and rational system of beliefs and assumptions'.[73] Unfortunately, he follows a conventional path to reject the legal nature and hence the existence of a right to relief. Following this category error, Knott characterises the poor's system of beliefs as variously: 'customs, values and assumptions' and the right to relief as: 'the moral economy notions of the rights of the poor (which) operated within a framework of paternalism and deference'. For Knott, protest is an expression of a loss of metaphysical and not legal rights based upon: 'this old moral economy notion, that the poor had a right to relief, which was to clash head on with the political economy beliefs embodied in the new poor law'.[74]

In a somewhat different approach, Nicholas Edsall notes that initial protests in the South and West took the form of spontaneous riots, but he too remains unaware of the loss of legal rights.[75] As a result, his account is descriptive rather than analytical, concluding that there was no leadership, no organisation; rather protest consists of panic responses initiated by local 'inefficiency' (sic) in introducing the new system and some mischief-making by opportunists. Edsall's account records that much opposition was focused upon responding to the actions of the Assistant Commission as it imposed the new administrative order upon the localities. He misses the immediacy of the subsequent loss of legal rights to the settled poor as the Poor Law Commissioners move into their towns and villages. In consequence, Edsall reconstructs protest as an ideological core of resistance for Tory opposition who believed that poor relief is an historical right. In this approach there is no awareness that the poor are protesting a very real loss of legal status within the poor law system. In short, Edsall does not factor any loss of legal rights into his discussion of motivation and causes behind the protests, nor does he demonstrate any awareness of that legal dimension.

William Cobbett: speaking for the poor

William Cobbett MP, Radical, sometime 'political' prisoner, polemicist, believer in rights and founder, in 1802, of one of the great popular newspapers, the *Political Register*, declared in Parliament: 'The poor rates were not the property of the rich to be controlled by them. It was not "other people's money" which vestries gave to the poor.'[76] Himmelfarb describes Cobbett as having passion, eccentricity and: 'an inordinate sense of moral righteousness'.[77] Unfortunately, too, Cobbett was rabidly anti-Semitic and in consequence it is difficult to give him his place. Nevertheless, Cobbett wrote extensively on many matters, spoke passionately in Parliament against the

1834 Act, took the historical traditionalist position and fervently believed in the rights of the poor. In *Rural Rides*, published in 1830, he vividly recounts the poverty and the successes of the labouring poor, valuing and respecting those lives in a manner that is not found in any other contemporary commentator. It is in the works of Cobbett that awareness of the legal rights of the poor may be found.

Cobbett's intellectual position on poor law can be found in *A History of the Protestant Revolution* produced in 1827. He traces the rights of the poor to the tithes of pre-Conquest England, arguing that, at the Reformation, the tithes, together with the property of the monasteries, were transferred to the King who parcelled them out to individuals. His opinion is that the poor rates were established to restore to the poor the rights they had lost at the Reformation, a somewhat romantic view of the pragmatic solution to the loss of monastic aid, but closer to the legal picture than many modern accounts. Knott has repeated Cobbett's incorrect suggestion that poor law was a descendant of canon law.[78] However, Cobbett believed in these origins and used them to underline his 'rights' argument, that poor relief is linked to rights in property, stating: 'If you maintain that the poor have no rights to relief, you loosen all the ligaments of property'.[79] In his *Advice to Young Men*, published in 1829, Cobbett states that when the pauper receives relief:

> he receives it not as an alms: he is no mendicant; he begs not; he comes to receive that which the law of the country awards him in lieu of the larger portion assigned him by the law of nature.[80]

It cannot be said that Cobbett understood poor law's legal doctrines and the technical principles of settlement, but he asserted poor law's legal nature in writing of the legal rights of the poor.[81] This is the part of welfare's past that is forgotten, even as historians often cite Cobbett's words. In this 'forgetting', poor law is deformed into 'lesser' rights, and in this manner legal rights pass from cultural and academic memory.

Notes

1 J.R. Poynter, *Society and Pauperism. English Ideas on Poor Relief 1795–1834*, London: Routledge and Kegan Paul, 1969; Gertrude Himmelfarb, *The Idea of Poverty. England in the Early Industrial Age*, London: Faber & Faber, 1984.
2 Joanna Innes, 'Parliament and the Shaping of Eighteenth Century Social Policy', *Transactions of the Royal Historical Society*, 5th series, 40, 1990, 63–92, at 70.
3 Ibid., pp. 78–79.
4 Ibid., p. 86.
5 A. Brundage, *The Making of the New Poor Law*, London: Hutchinson, 1978, p. 8.
6 Ibid., p. 20.
7 'To Lord Brougham', 14 September 1832, cited in: Peter Dunkley, 'Whigs and Paupers: The Reform of the New Poor Laws, 1830–34', *Journal of British Studies*, XX, 1981, 124–49, at 139.

8 S.G. and E.O.A. Checkland (eds), *The Poor Law Report of 1834*, London: Penguin Books, 1974, p. 33.
9 Ibid., p. 244.
10 Ibid., pp. 246–55.
11 *Select Committee to Enquire into the Operation of Settlement and the Poor Removal Act, First Report* and Minutes of Evidence, 1847, PP. 82 XI.I.
12 See Chapter 3.
13 See Thomas Carlyle, *Chartism* (1843) and *Past and Present* (1847). Cited in: Himmelfarb, *Idea of* Poverty, p. 204.
14 *Poor Law Board, Report ... on the Law of Settlement and Removal of the Poor*, p. 1152, XXVII, 1850.
15 M.E. Rose, 'Settlement, Removal and the New Poor Law', in D. Fraser (ed.) *New Poor Law in the Nineteenth Century*, London: Macmillan, 1976, p. 30.
16 Sir Edmund Head, 'Report to the Select Committee on Settlement and Poor Removal', *Edinburgh Review*, LXXXVIII, April, 1848, 451–72; Sir George Nicholls, *Memorandum on Settlement, Removal and Rating*, Nov. 1850, PP. 90, LV, Part 1, 1854; George Coode, *Report on the Law of Settlement and Removal*, HC no. 675 of 1851; Robert Pashley, *Pauperism and Poor Laws*, London: Longman, Brown, Green and Longmans, 1852.
17 Maurice Caplan, 'The New Poor Law and the Struggle for Union Chargeability', *International Review of Social History*, XXIII, 1978, 267–300, at 383.
18 *Select Committee to Consider Poor Relief, Report*, PP 349, 1864, IX; Appendices, PP. 349, 1864, IX.
19 *Select Committee to Consider Poor Relief, Report*, PP. 1864, IX; Appendices, PP 349, 1864, IX.
20 Ibid., p. 33.
21 Richard Burn, *History of the Poor Laws with Observations*, London: H. Woodfall and W. Strachan, 1764, p. 134.
22 Ibid., 135.
23 Ibid., pp. 146–47.
24 Ibid., p. 165.
25 Ibid.
26 Ibid., p. 183.
27 Ibid., pp. 185–86.
28 These include Thomas Alcock's suggestion (1752) of replacing the 1601 Act with a system of maintaining the poor by voluntary charity; the abolition of settlement and making each county a corporation to care for its poor (the Earl of Hillsborough and Sir Richard Lloyd, 1753). Thomas Gilbert's *Plan for the Better Relief and Employment of the Poor*, published in 1781, was another such scheme based upon dividing the county.
29 Burn, *History of the Poor Laws*, p. 203.
30 Ibid., p. 226.
31 Sir Frederick Morton Eden, *The State of the Poor*, 3 vols, 1797, A.G.L. Rogers (ed.), republished, London: Routledge and Sons Ltd, 1928, p. 53.
32 Ibid., p. 54.
33 John Davison, 'Consideration of the Poor Law', *Edinburgh Review*, 33, 1820, 91–108, at 97.
34 Ibid., p. 98.
35 Nassau W. Senior, 'Three Lectures on the Rate of Wages, with a Preface on the Causes of the Present Disturbances', *Edinburgh Review*, 53, 1831, 43–63, at 58.
36 William Day, 'An Inquiry into the Poor Laws and Surplus Labour and Their Mutual Reaction', *Quarterly Review*, 48, 1832, 320–43; C. Wetherall, 'Present State of the Poor Law Question', *Quarterly Review*, 50, 1833, 347–73.
37 *R v Eastbourne (Inhabitants) (1803)* 4 East 103; 102 E.R. 769. The case refers to unsettled individuals.
38 Head, 'Report', p. 456.

39 Pashley, *Pauperism and Poor Laws*, pp. 268–69.
40 Ibid.
41 Joshua Toulmin Smith, *The Parish, its Powers and Obligations at Law*, 2nd edn, London: I. Sweet, 1857, pp. iii, v.
42 Ibid., p. vi.
43 Ibid., pp. 4–5.
44 Ibid., p. 417.
45 Ibid., pp. 423–24.
46 *Hansard,* 3rd, series. 23, 1320–34, 26 May 1834, cited in: A. Brundage, *The Making of the New Poor Law*, London: Hutchinson, 1978, p. 60.
47 Ibid., 62–64.
48 Himmelfarb, *Idea of Poverty*, p. 183.
49 Himmelfarb suggests: 'if we can sympathise with the poor who harbour memories (and illusions) of a more humane "moral economy"': Ibid., p. 188.
50 Ibid., pp. 188–89.
51 Ibid., p. 190.
52 Poynter, *Society and Pauperism*, p. xxi.
53 P.P. Craig, *Administrative Law*, 3rd edn, Oxford: Sweet and Maxwell, 1994, p. 42.
54 William, C. Lubenow, *The Politics of Government Growth*, Newton Abbott: David & Charles, 1971, p. 43.
55 For a discussion of the opponents: Ibid., pp. 42–56.
56 Ibid., p. 45.
57 Ibid., p. 62.
58 Arthur Young, *A General View of the Agriculture of Lincolnshire*, published in 1813, refers to the: 'civilisation of enclosure'. Robert Allen, 'Agriculture during the Industrial Revolution', in R. Floud and D. McCloskey (eds) *Economic History since 1700, Vol. 1, 1700–1860*, 2nd edn, Cambridge: Cambridge University Press, 1984, p. 99.
59 For a full discussion of the legal processes involved, see: Frank Sharman, 'An Introduction to the Enclosure Acts', *The Journal of Legal History*, 10, 1989, 45–70.
60 Ibid., p. 47.
61 Ibid., p. 48.
62 Ibid., p. 53.
63 Andrea C. Loux, 'The Persistence of the Ancient Regime: Custom, Utility, and the Common Law in the Nineteenth Century', *Cornell Law Review*, 79, 1993, 183–218, at 198.
64 E.P. Thompson, *The Making of the English Working Class*, London: Penguin Books, 1982: E.J. Hobsbawm, *Industry and Empire: An Economic History of Britain*, 2nd edn, London: Abacus, 1968; Sharman, 'Introduction'.
65 G.E. Mingay, *Parliamentary Enclosure in England*, London: Longman, 1997, p. 125.
66 Ibid., p. 130.
67 J.M. Neeson, *Commoners: Common Right, Enclosure and Social Change in England, 1700–1820*, Cambridge: Cambridge University Press, 1993, pp. 259–93.
68 Ibid., p. 132.
69 Ibid., p. 291.
70 M.E. Rose, 'The Anti Poor Law Movement in the North of England', *Northern History*, vol. I, 1966, 70–91; Nicholas C. Edsall, *The Anti-Poor Law Movement,* Manchester: Manchester University Press, 1971; John Knott, *Popular Opposition to the New Poor Law*, London: Croom Helm, 1986.
71 Knott, *Popular Opposition*, p. 270.
72 Edsall, *Anti-Poor Law*, p. 25.
73 Knott, *Popular Opposition*, p. ii.
74 Ibid., pp. 7–8, 30, 31, 33–34.
75 Edsall, *Anti-Poor Law*, p. 31.

76 XII 328/9, cited in: Ibid., p. 217.
77 Himmelfarb, *Idea of Poverty*, p. 207.
78 Knott, *Popular Opposition*, p. 13.
79 Cited in: Himmelfarb, *Idea of Poverty*, p. 211.
80 Ibid., p. 218.
81 *Political Register*, 11 June 1835: Ibid., p. 210.

Chapter 10

End thoughts: on the transience of legal memory

Today the workhouse and the [new] poor law are part of Britain's 'heritage', so much so that the National Trust has restored Southwell Poor Law Union, Nottinghamshire, for public enjoyment; it opened (again) in 2002. Fundamental to that heritage, supplying a delicious frisson of vicarious empathy to the paying visitors as they wander through Southwell, are the ghosts of former residents. Their shadows enable visitors to recapture some of the cruelty, social stigma and fear that surrounded the new poor law, a hated cultural norm they still recognise. This is hardly surprising, for that norm survives as powerful folk memory and continues to (negatively) influence aspects of modern welfare provision. It was that norm which influenced a desire for reform leading to the *Beveridge Report* of 1942. This, in turn, produced the modern Welfare State, in revulsion against a poor law whose memory attracts visitors to Southwell to wonder at the cruelty of a prison for the poor. There are other consequences to such powerful memories and this work has discussed the most damning; the forgetting of those positive elements in poor law's and, hence, welfare's legal rights-based past. It is not just historians who have forgotten, modern welfare itself is now disconnected from those original poor law personal rights, duties and obligations protected and enforced under the law of settlement and removal. There was not and may never be a revival of an immediate personal legal right to relief once possessed by the settled poor. This is unsurprising, as this work reveals how that right has been consistently undervalued, marginalised, denied and, finally, forgotten. However, this account does not minimise those subjective elements in the manner and amounts poor relief was given or deny that proving destitution allowed discretion to parish officials; elements today understood as 'conditionality'. However, these negativities do not erase positive elements embedded within an entire legal structure containing enforcement mechanisms and sanctions to protect the right to relief. The nightmare of the Great Famine in Ireland under a poor law without settlement and legal rights illustrates how little relief might have been given to the poor if relief was 'customary' or 'politically negotiated' as so many historians believe.

This study asserts that historians have fallen into legal error in their consensus that there was no legal right to relief; an orthodoxy of denial arrived at by consulting each other and not the law and legal rules. The work has retraced the route by which historians arrived at their legally incorrect conclusions and reconstructed a socio-legal alternative version of poor law history; one that demonstrates the doctrinal existence of the right to relief and provides a technical legal opinion to that effect, fully supported by the relevant legal authorities. That journey included historical reconstructions of various aspects of poor law now factoring in that legal right to relief. Amongst other aspects, this reveals how the right to relief rarely featured in contemporary reformist and anti-reformist literature, parliamentary reports or juristic theorising. However there are three locations where it is consistently in evidence. The first is within legal texts and case law, seldom consulted today and then miscited or misunderstood. The second is within those local records that reveal centuries of uncontested unquestioned relief payments for the destitute settled poor; their significance has been consistently marginalised, misconstrued or undervalued in historical reconstructions. The third and final location is in the words and actions of the poor; fully attested to and reconstructed within numerous poor law histories. Unfortunately, because most historians have taken a position of denial, the poor have not been heard.

As such, for the discipline of history and for scholars who rely on works produced from within that discipline, this work is a revisionist text. Most revisionist where it proposes that social histories of the poor law have compounded error by failing to provide legally accurate accounts of that past; accounts that are subsequently transmitted via legal academics and others to government policy-makers.

The importance of historical reconstructions to current law should not be underestimated. This writer has written positively elsewhere of the extent to which legal scholarship is developing a convention of framing legal analysis and discussions of legal reform within historical reconstructions of law's origins, purposes, methodologies and juristic nature.[1] It is noticeable, however, that for welfare law this has not proved a positive trend as legal scholars follow historians into a poor law without law. This work has reconstructed some explanations for such law-blindness and considers the chief culprit to be that cultural norm now forming one of Southwell's major attractions, the lingering negative influence of reforms introduced in 1834. The writer concludes, therefore, that these reforms were truly pernicious, not just because they devastated the lives of paupers within disciplined 'orderly' union workhouses. Not even as a pauper's personal right to apply to a Justice for relief, except in kind in an emergency, was abolished. It seems that the reforms proved most toxic in their dominance of folk memory and in colouring poor law historical reconstructions with their negativity, a darkness that obscures the memory of poor law's rights, duties and obligations. As scholars we might intellectually reconstruct this transformation as an

204 Welfare's Forgotten Past

expression of modernity; destroying then masking legal memories of a personal [human] right. This state of affairs is hardly acceptable and is equally problematic for North American welfare, where a version of the English poor law system was transplanted into the new colonial British settlements. 'Forgetting' continues as welfare studies published within Britain and the USA specifically reconstruct poor law origins to authenticate their scholarship, but rely upon historians' reconstructions that persistently and incorrectly deny the existence of the legal right to relief.

This book therefore offers a legal framework to assist poor law historians in making sense of surviving records; permitting researchers to see beyond chaos, confusion and local differences to the underlying pervasive legal structure of poor law. Equally for legal scholars, it serves as a reminder that although historical reconstructions enrich our understanding of how law was experienced in the past, it is still a requirement that we test legal conclusions, or conclusions concerning law, with legal techniques. Such is the contribution law may bring to a broader scholarship. This is not simply a matter of interdisciplinary angst for, as this work has argued throughout, a juristic argument exists that suggests 'forgetting' the existence and importance of the legal nature of the right to relief continues to deform understanding of the development of the British welfare system. In summary, poor law's past is a legal past that has been inaccurately reconstructed in accounts containing many and persistent legal errors. These incorrect legal accounts are reproduced to provide an historical foundation within scholarship that seeks answers and solutions to current political and legal problems surrounding poverty and welfare. In consequence, no academic model produced to date contains a poor law reconstruction or analysis based upon those legal rights that were the source of and explanation for the relief of poverty in England and Wales for 350 years. This writer therefore suggests it is timely to listen to those labourers and paupers who spoke of their rights and meant law; we owe it to their current successors in poverty.

Note

1 Lorie Charlesworth, 'On Historical Contextualisation: Some Critical Socio-legal Reflections', *Crimes and Misdemeanors: Exploring Law and Deviance in Historical Perspective*, 1, 1, 2007, 1–40.

Appendix

Table Illustrating the Law of Settlement

Heads of settlement	Origin	Enactments relating to	Whether or not abolished
Hiring and service	Statute	3 W&M *c.* 11 1691 8&9 W. III *c.* 30 1696–97 4&5 W. IV *c.* 76 1834	Abolished 1834
Serving parish office	"	3 W&M *c.* 11 1691 4&5 W. IV *c.* 76 1834	"
Payment and parish rates	"	3 W&M *c.* 11 1691 35 Geo. III *c.* 101 1795 6 Geo. IV *c.* 57 1825	Restricted to payments for a £10 tenement
Apprentice ship	"	3 W&M *c.* 11 1691 31 Geo. II *c.* 11 1757 56 Geo. III *c.* 139 1816 4&5 W. IV *c.* 6 1834	Abolished for sea service and fishermen 1834
Renting a tenement	"	13&14 C. II *c.* 16 1662 6 Geo. IV *c.* 57 1825 1 W.IV *c.* 18 1831 4&5 W.IV *c.* 76 1834	No
Residence for 3 years in the parish	"	39&40 Vict *c.* 61 1876	No
Estate	Common law	9 Geo. I *c.* 7 1722 4&5 W.IV c76 1834	No, restricted in 1722 and 1834
Birth	Common law and statute	13 Geo. III *c.* 82 1773 54 Geo. III *c.* 170 1814 39&40 Vict. *c.* 61 1876	No
Parentage	Common law re legitimate children Statute re illegitimate	4&5 W. IV *c.* 76 1834 39&40 Vict. *c.* 61 1876	No No
Marriage with reference to the wife	Common law	39&40 Vict. *c.* 61 1876	No

Source: F.C. Montague, 'The Law of Settlement and Removal', 1888, Law Quarterly Review at 50.

Bibliography

Abbreviations

CRO: Chester Record Office.
LRO: Liverpool Record Office.
NA: National Archives, Kew, London.
PP: Parliamentary Papers.
WM: Wirral Museum, Birkenhead.

Archival Sources

Tranmere Vestry Book, 1783–1827, WM BC VI 387; WM CR/C 7745.
Tranmere Township Overseers Poor Rate Accounts, 1827–38 and Minutes of Township and Vestry
  Meetings 1831–38, WM BC VI 387.
Tranmere Vestry Minute Book, 1838–1850, WM B/093/1. (BC)
Tranmere Township Minute Book, 1850–97, WM BC VI 385; WM CR/C7745.
Tranmere Township Poor Rate Book, 1836–8, WM BC VI 338; R@7746.
Tranmere Township Overseers Books, 1850–4, WM BC VI 384; C7743.
Public Health Act 1848 (Tranmere) WM BC IV 975.
Chester Quarter Sessions, CRO QJB/QJF series.
Poor Law Commission Papers, Wirral Poor Law Union, NA/MH.12 series.
Wirral Poor Law Union, NA/LGW series.

Chester Chronicle
Chester Courant
The Independent

Printed primary sources and secondary literature

Abel-Smith, Brian and Stevens, Robert, *Lawyers and the Courts, A Sociological Study of the English Legal System 1750–1965*, London: Heinemann, 1967.
Ackroyd, Peter, *Dickens*, London: Minerva Press, 1990.
Adolphus, J., *Observations on the Vagrant Act in Relation to the Liberty of the Subject*, London: John Murray, 1824.
Allen, Robert, 'Agriculture during the Industrial Revolution', in Floud, R. and McCloskey, D. (eds) *Economic History since 1700, Vol. 1, 1700–1860*, 2nd edn, Cambridge: Cambridge University Press, 1984.

Allison, J.E., *Sidelights on Tranmere*, Birkenhead: Countywise Ltd, 1976.

Anderson, Michael, *Family Structure in Nineteenth Century Lancashire*, Cambridge: Cambridge University Press, 1971.

Archer, J.E., 'The Wells-Charlesworth Debate: A Personal Comment on Arson in Norfolk and Suffolk', in Reed, Mick and Wells, Roger (eds) *Class, Conflict and Protest in the English Countryside, 1700–1880*, London: Frank Cass, 1990.

Arthurs, W.K., *Without the Law; Administrative Justice and Legal Pluralism in Nineteenth Century England*, Toronto: University of Toronto Press, 1983.

Aschrott, P.F., *The English Poor Law System Past and Present*, 2nd edn, London: Knight & Co., 1902.

Ashcroft, Richard, 'Lockean Ideas, Poverty and the Development of Liberal Political Theory', in Brewer, J. (ed.) *Early Modern Conceptions of Property*, London: Routledge, 1995.

Ashforth, David, 'Settlement and Removals in Urban Areas, Bradford 1834–71', in Rose, M. E. (ed.) *The Poor and the City*, Leicester: Leicester University Press, 1985.

Ashton. T.S., *An Economic History of Britain: The Eighteenth Century*, London: Methuen, 1966.

Atiyah, P.S., *The Rise and Fall of Freedom of Contract*, Oxford: Clarendon Press, 1979.

——, *Law and Modern Society*, 2nd edn, Oxford: Oxford University Press, 1995.

Ault, W.O., 'Manor Court and Parish Church in Fifteenth Century England: A Study of Village By-Laws', *Speculum, A Journal of Medieval Studies*, XLII, 1, 1967, 53–67.

Austin, John, *The Province of Jurisprudence Determined*, 1832, London: Prometheus Books, 2000.

——, *The Lectures on Jurisprudence or the Philosophy of Positive Law*, 1863, reprint, London: John Murray, 1920.

Bailey, Brian, *Almshouses*, London: Robert Hale, 1988.

Baker, J.H., 'Why the History of English Law has not been Finished', *Cambridge Law Journal*, March, 2000, 62–84.

Banks, Sarah, 'Nineteenth Century Scandal or Twentieth Century Model? A New Look at Open and Close Parishes', *Economic History Review*, 2nd series, ol. XLI, 1988, 51–73.

Barker-Read, Mary, 'The Treatment of the Aged Poor in Five Selected West Kent Parishes from Settlement to Speenhamland', 1989, unpublished thesis, Open University.

Bartlett, Peter, *The Poor Law of Lunacy*, Leicester: Leicester University Press, 1999.

——, 'On Historical Contextualisation: A Lawyer Responds', *Crimes and Misdemeanours*, 1/2 2007, 102–6; http://www.research.plymouth.ac.uk/solon/journal/issue1.2/Debate%20Forum. pdf (accessed 5 June 2009).

Beard, Charles Austin, *The Office of Justice of the Peace in England in its Origin and Development*, New York: Columbia University Press, 1904.

Beaudoin, Steven M., *Poverty in Word History*, London and New York: Routledge, 2007.

Beier, A.L., *Masterless Men. The Vagrancy Problem in England 1560–1640*, London: Methuen, 1985.

Belchem, John, *Popular Radicalism in Nineteenth Century Britain*, London: Macmillan Press, 1996.

Bennett, J.H.E. and Dewhurst, J.C. (eds) 'Quarter Sessions Records, with Other Records of the Justices of the Peace for the County Palatine of Chester 1559–1760', *Record Society of Lancashire and Cheshire*, 1940.

Bentham, Jeremy, *Fragments on Government,* London: 1832.

——, *Of Laws in General*, Hart: H.L.A. (ed.), London: Croom Helm, 1970.

——, *Writings on the Poor Laws*, vol. I, Quinn, Michael (ed.), Oxford: Clarendon Press, 2001.

Berryman, Blanche (ed.), 'Mitcham Settlement Examinations 1784–1814', *Surrey Record Society*, 27, 1973.

Beveridge, William, *Social Insurance and Allied Services*, London: The Macmillan Company, 1942.

Blackstone, William, *Commentaries on the Laws of England*, 4 vols, Oxford: Clarendon Press, 1775.

Blagg, T.M. (ed.), 'Newark Certificates of Settlement 1697–1822', *Thoroton Society Record Service*, XI, 1943.

Blaug, Mark, 'The Myth of the Old Poor Law and the Making of the New', *Journal of Economic History*, XXIII, 2, June, 1963.

——, 'The Poor Law Report Re-examined', *The Journal of Economic History*, XXIV, 1968, 229–45.

Blease, W.L., 'The Poor Law in Liverpool, 1681–1834', *Transactions of the Historic Society of Lancashire and Cheshire*, 61, 1909, 97–182.

Bloxham, Donald, *The Great Game of Genocide: Imperialism, Nationalism, and the Destruction of the Ottoman Armenians*, Oxford: Oxford University Press, 2007.

Borwick, Patrick David Robert, 'An English Provincial Society, North Lancashire 1770–1820', 1994, unpublished thesis, University of Lancaster.

Botelho, Lynn, 'Aged and Impotent: Parish Relief of the Aged Poor in Early Modern Suffolk', in Daunton, Martin (ed.) *Charity, Self Interest and Welfare in the English Past*, London: UCL Press, 1996.

Bott, E., *A Collection of Decisions of the Court of King's Bench on the Poor Laws*, 3rd edn, London: J. Butterworth, 1793.

Boyer, George R., *An Economic History of the English Poor Law 1750–1850*, Cambridge: Cambridge University Press, 1990.

Bretton, R., 'Settlement Certificates and Removal Orders', *Transactions of the Halifax Antiquarian Society*, 1959, 9–26.

Brewer, John and Styles, John (eds), *An Ungovernable People. The English and their Law in the Seventeenth and Eighteenth Century*, London: Routledge, 1980.

Brewer, John and Staves, Susan (ed.), *Early Modern Conceptions of Property*, London: Routledge, 1995.

Brown, Stewart, *The Wapentake of Wirral*, Liverpool: Young, 1907.

Browning, Christopher, *Ordinary Men: Reserve Police Battalion 101 and the Final Solution in Poland*, New York: HarperCollins, 1992.

Brundage, A., 'The Landed Interest and the New Poor Law: A Reappraisal of the Revolution in Government', *English Historical Review*, LXXXVIII, 1972, 27–48.

——, 'The Landed Interest and the New Poor Law: a Reply', *English Historical Review*, XC, 1975, 347–51.

——, *The Making of the New Poor Law*, London: Hutchinson, 1978.

——, *England's 'Prussian Minister'. Edwin Chadwick and the Politics of Government Growth 1832–1854*, Pennsylvania: Pennsylvania State University Press, 1988.

Brundage, James A., 'Legal Aid for the Poor and the Professionalisation of Law in the Middle Ages', *The Journal of Legal History*, 9, 2, 1988, 169–79.

——, *Medieval Canon Law*, London: Longman, 1995.

Burn, Richard, *The History of the Poor Laws with Observations*, London: H. Woodfall and W. Strachan, 1764.

——, *The Justice of the Peace and the Parish Officer*, 16th edn, 4 vols, London: H. Woodfall and W. Strachan, 1788.

Burne, R.V.H., 'The Treatment of the Poor in Eighteenth Century in Chester', *The Journal of the Chester and North Wales Architectural, Archaeological and Historic Society*, 52, 1965, 33–48.

Burnett, John, *Useful Toil: Autobiographies of Working People from the 1820s to the 1920s*, 2nd edn, London: Routledge, 1994.

——, *Idle Hands: The Experience of Unemployment 1790–1990*, London: Routledge, 1994.

Burrow, J.W., *Evolution and Society. A Study in Victorian Social Theory*, Cambridge: Cambridge University Press, 1966.

Burrows, James, *A Series of the Decisions of the Court of King's Bench upon the Settlement Cases from. 1732*, 3 vols, London: His Majesty, 1768.

Bushaway, Bob, *By Rite, Custom, Ceremony and Community in England 1700–1880*, London: Junction Books, 1982.

Butcher, E.E. (ed.), 'Bristol Corporation of the Poor; Selected Records 1696–1834', *Bristol Record Society*, vol. III, 1932.

Caird, James, *English Agriculture in 1850–1*, London: Longman, Brown, Green and Longmans, 1851.

Cannadine, Jane Rosenheim (ed.), *The First Modern Society. Essays in Honour of Lawrence Stone*, Cambridge: Cambridge University Press, 1989.

Cannan, E., *History of Local Rates in England*, 2nd edn, London: P.S. King and Co., 1912.

Caplan, Maurice, 'The New Poor Law and the Struggle for Union Chargeability', *International Review of Social History*, XXIII, 1978, 267–300.

Caunce, Steve, 'Farm Servants and the Development of Capitalism in Early English Agriculture', *Agricultural History Review*, 45, 1997, 45–60.

Chance, W., *Children Under the Poor Law*, London: Swan Sonnenschein and Co., 1897.

Chandler, George, *Liverpool*, London: B. T. Batsford Ltd, 1957.

Charlesworth, Andrew, 'The Development of the English Rural Proletariat and Social Protest, 1700–1850: A Comment', in Reed, Mick and Wells, Roger (eds) *Class, Conflict and Protest in the English Countryside, 1700–1880*, London: Frank Cass, 1990.

Charlesworth, Lorie, 'Consumer Protection in Sale of Goods Agreements; An Ancient Right in Modern Guise', *Liverpool Law Review*, XVI, 2 1994, 167–86.

——, 'Poor Law on the Wirral, The Guardian's Version', *Cheshire History*, 36, 1997–98, 70–81.

——, 'Salutary and Humane Law, A Legal History of the Law of Settlement and Removal, *c*. 1795–1865', 1998, unpublished thesis, University of Manchester.

——, 'A Brief History of English Poor Law', *Journal of Social Security Law*, 2, 1999, 79–92.

——, 'Why is it a Crime to be Poor?', *Liverpool Law Review*, 2/3, 1999, 149–67.

——, 'Tranmere Township in the Nineteenth Century; An Introduction to the Operation of the Tranmere Vestry', *Cheshire History*, 40, 2000–2001, 40–55.

——, 'John Clare's *The Parish*, a Rural Idyll?', *Liverpool Law Review*, 2/3, 2001, 167–78.

——, 'Readings of Begging: The Legal Response to Begging Considered in its Modern and Historical Context', *Nottingham Law Journal*, 15, 1, 2006, 1–12.

——, 'Genocide by the Operation of Law? Readings of an English Poor Law in Ireland'. paper presented at Experiencing the Law Conference, Institute of Advanced Legal Studies, University of London, December 2006.

——, 'On Historical Contextualisation: Some Critical Socio-Legal Reflections', *Crimes and Misdemeanours: Exploring Law and Deviance in Historical Perspective*, 1, 1 2007, 1–40; http://www.research.plymouth.ac.uk/solon/journal/issue%201.1/CharlesworthCandMIssue1.pdf (accessed 5 June 2009).

——, 'Poor Law in the City: A Comparative Legal Analysis of the Effect of the 1834 Poor Law Amendment Act upon the Administration of Poor Relief in the Ports of Liverpool and Chester', in Lewis, Andrew (ed.) *Law in the City: Proceedings of the Seventeenth British Legal History Conference 2005*, Dublin: Four Courts Press, 2007.

——, 'Theory's Betrayal of Legality, is there No Law after Auschwitz? An Historical Reconstruction that Explores how far Juristic Posturing Colludes with Negative Political

Agendas', paper presented at From Human Rights to the Primacy of the Political Con-
ference, University of Lancaster, November 2008.
——, 'Justices of the Peace' (English Common Law), in Katz, Stanley M. (ed.) *Oxford International Encyclopaedia of Legal History,* New York: Oxford University Press, 2009.
——, 'Poor Law', (English Common Law), vol. 4, in Katz, Stanley M. (ed.) *Oxford International Encyclopaedia of Legal History,* New York: Oxford University Press, 2009.
Chaucer, Geoffrey, *The Canterbury Tales,* London: Penguin Popular Classics, 1996.
Checkland, S.G. and Checkland, E.O.A. (eds), *The Poor Law Report of 1834,* London: Penguin Books, 1974.
Chesterman, Michael, *Charities, Trusts and Social Welfare,* London: Weidenfeld & Nicolson, 1979.
Clarke, John C., *Social Administration including the Poor Laws,* 2nd edn, London: Sir Isaac Pitman and Sons, 1935.
Clarke, P., 'Migration in England during the Late Seventeenth Century and Early Eighteenth Century', *Past and Present,* 83, 1979, 57–90.
Clarkson, William, *J.F. Archbold's Summary of the Law Relative to Appeals against Orders of Removal etc ...* , London: Sweet, 1826.
Clay, C.G.A., *Economic Expansion and Social Change: England, 1500–1700,* 2 vols, Cambridge: Cambridge University Press, 1984.
Coats, A.W., 'Economic Thought and Poor Law Policy in the Eighteenth Century', *Economic History Review,* XIII, 1960, 39–51.
Cobbett, William, *A History of the Protestant Revolution in England and Ireland,* publisher William Cobbett, 1827.
——, *Rural Rides,* 1830, Woodcock, George (ed.), London: Penguin Books, 1967.
Cockburn, J.S., 'The North Riding Justices, 1690–1750. A Study in Local Administration', *Yorkshire Archaeological Journal,* 4, 1, 1963, 481–515.
Cocks, R.C.J., *Sir Henry Maine, A Study in Victorian Jurisprudence,* Cambridge: Cambridge University Press, 1988.
Cole, G.D.H. and Cole, Margaret, *The Opinions of William Cobbett,* London: The Cobbett Publishing Company Ltd, 1944.
Cole, G.D.H. and Postgate, Raymond, *The Common People 1746–1946,* 4th edn, London: Routledge, 1965.
Collins, E.J.T., 'Migrant Labour in British Agriculture in the Nineteenth Century', *The Economic History Review,* 2nd series, XXIX, 1976, 38–58.
Colquhoun, P., 'Inquiry into the Poor Laws', *Quarterly Review,* 8, 1812, 319–56.
Conan Doyle, Sir Arthur, 'The Man with the Twisted Lip', republished in *Sherlock Holmes, Short Stories,* 22nd impression, London: Jonathan Cape, 1980.
Const, Francis (ed.), *Decisions of the Court of King's Bench, upon the Law relating to the Poor,* 2 vols, London: Butterworth, 1793.
——, *The Laws Relating to the Poor,* London: Butterworth, 1807.
Coode, George, *Report on the Law of Settlement and Removal,* HC no. 675 of 1851.
Cowherd, Raymond G., *Economists and the English Poor Laws,* Ohio: Ohio University Press, 1977.
Cox, E.W., *The Practice of Poor Removals,* London: J. Crockford, 1848.
Craig, P.P., 'Dicey: Unitary Self-Correcting Democracy and Public Law', *Law Quarterly Review,* 106, 1990, 105–43.
——, *Administrative Law,* 3rd edn, Oxford: Sweet and Maxwell, 1994.
Cranston, Ross, *Legal Foundations of the Welfare State,* London: Weidenfeld & Nicolson, 1985.
Crowther, M.A., *The Workhouse System, 1834–1929,* London: Batsford, 1981.

Dalton, Michael, *The Countrey Justice*, London: The Society of Stationers, 1618; reprint, Norwood, NJ: Walter J. Johnson Inc., 1975.

——, *The Country Justice*, London: Henry Lintot, 1727.

——, *The Country Justice*, London: London: Henry Lintot, 1742.

Daunton, Martin (ed.), *Charity, Self-Interest and Welfare in the English Past*, London: UCL Press, 1996.

Davey, Herbert, *Poor Law Settlement and Removal*, London: Stevens and Sons, 1908.

Davies, C.S., 'The Agricultural History of Cheshire, 1750–1850', 3rd series, vol. X, *Chetham Society Manchester*, 1960.

Davies, Howard and Holcroft, David, *Jurisprudence: Texts and Commentary*, London: Butterworths, 1991.

Davison, John, 'Consideration of the Poor Law', *Edinburgh Review*, 33, 1820, 91–108.

Day, William, 'An Inquiry into the Poor Laws and Surplus Labour, and Their Mutual Reaction', *Quarterly Review*, 48, 1832, 320–43.

Deacon, Alan and Bradshaw, Jonathan, *Reserved for the Poor. The Means Test in British Social Policy*, Oxford: Blackwell, 1983.

Dean, Hartley, *Welfare, Law and Citizenship*, Hertfordshire: Prentice-Hall, 1996.

Dicey, A.V., *A Study of the Law of the Constitution*, London: Macmillan and Co. Ltd, 1885.

Dickens, Charles, *Sketches By Boz*, London: Chapman & Hall, 1913.

——, *Bleak House*, London: Penguin Books, 1994.

——, *Little Dorrit*, London: Penguin Books Ltd, 1998.

——, *Christmas Books*, Oxford: Oxford University Press, 1988.

Digby, Anne, 'The Labour Market and the Continuity of Social Policy after 1834: The Case of the Eastern Counties', *Economic History Review*, XXVIII, 1975, 69–83.

——, *Pauper Palaces*, London: Routledge and Kegan Paul, 1978.

——, *The Poor Law in Nineteenth Century England*, London: The Historical Association, 1989.

Dinwiddy, J.R. 'Early Nineteenth Century Reactions to Benthamism', *Transactions of the Royal Historical Society*, 5th series, vol. 34, 1983, 47–69.

Doupe, M. and Salter, M., 'The Cheshire World View', *King's College Law Journal*, 11, 1, 2000, 49–77.

Dowdell, E.G., *A Hundred Years of Quarter Sessions. The Government of Middlesex from 1660–1760*, Cambridge: Cambridge University Press, 1932.

Duffy, Eamonn, *The Voices of Morebath*, New Haven and London: Yale University Press, 2001.

Duman, Daniel, *The Judicial Bench in England 1727–1875. The Reshaping of a Professional Elite*, London: Royal Historical Society, 1982.

Dumsday, W.H., *The Relieving Officers' Handbook*, London: Haddon, Best and Co., 1902.

Dunkley, Peter, 'The Landed Interest and the New Poor Law: A Critical Note', *English Historical Review*, LXXXVIII, 1973, 836–41.

——, 'The Hungry Forties and the New Poor Law: A Case Study', *The Historical Journal*, XVII, 2, 1974, 329–64.

——, 'Paternalism, the Magistracy and Poor Relief in England, 1795–1834', *International Review of Social History*, XXIV, Part 4, 1979, 371–97.

——, 'Whigs and Paupers: The Reform of the New Poor Laws, 1830–34', *Journal of British Studies*, XX, 1981, 124–49.

Dworkin, R., *Taking Rights Seriously*, Cambridge, MA: Harvard University Press, 1977.

Dyck, Ian, *William Cobbett and Rural Popular Culture*, Cambridge: Cambridge University Press, 1992.

Eastwood, David, *Governing Rural England. Tradition and Transformation in Local Government 1780–1840*, Oxford: Clarendon Press, 1994.

——, *Government and Community in the English Province, 1700–1870*, London: Macmillan and Co., 1997.

Eden, Sir Frederick Morton, *The State of the Poor*, 3 vols, 1797, Rogers, A.G.L. (ed.), London: Routledge and Sons Ltd, 1928.

Editors of The Poor Law Officers' Journal, *The Law Relating to the Relief of the Poor*, 3rd edn, London: Law and Local Government Publications Ltd, 1927.

Edsall, Nicholas C., *The Anti-Poor Law Movement*, Manchester: Manchester University Press, 1971.

Emmison, F.G., 'The Relief of the Poor at Eaton Socon, 1706–1834', *The Bedfordshire Historical Record Society*, 15, 1933, 1–98.

Emsley, Clive, *Crime and Society in England 1750–1900*, 2nd edn, London: Longman, 1996.

Englander, David, *Poverty and Poor Law Reform in Nineteenth Century Britain, 1834–1914*, London: Longman, 1998.

Evans, Eric J., *The Contentious Tithe*, London: Routledge and Kegan Paul, 1976.

Feaver, George, *From Status to Contract: A Biography of Sir Henry Maine 1822–1888*, London: Longman, 1969.

Ferguson, R.B., 'The Horwitz Thesis and Common Law Discourse in England', *Oxford Journal of Legal Studies*, 3, 1983, 34–57.

——, 'Commercial Expectation and the Guarantees of the Law, Sale Transactions in the mid-Nineteenth Century', in Sugarman, D. and Rubin, G.R. (eds) *Law, Economy and Society*, London: Butterworths, 1984.

Finer, S.E., *The Life and Times of Sir Edwin Chadwick*, London: Methuen and Co., 1952.

First Report of the House of Lords Committee on the Poor Laws, printed by and for C. Clement, 10 July 1817.

Fitzpatrick, David, 'The Irish in Britain: Settlers or Transients?', in Buckland, P. and Belchem, J. (eds) *The Irish in British Labour History*, Liverpool: University of Liverpool Centre for Irish Studies, 1993.

Fitzroy Jones, I., 'Aspects of Poor Law Administration, Seventeenth to Nineteenth Centuries from Trull Overseers' Accounts', *The Proceedings of the Somerset Archaeological and Natural History Society*, XCV, 1952, 72–105.

Flinn, M.W., *British Population Growth 1700–1850*, London: Macmillan, 1970.

Foucault, Michel, *Discipline and Punish*, New York: Pantheon, 1977.

Fraser, Derek, *The Evolution of the British Welfare State. A History of Social Policy since the Industrial Revolution*, London: Macmillan, 1976.

——, 'The English Poor Law and The Origins of the British Welfare State', in Mommsen, W.J. (ed.) *The Emergence of the Welfare State in Britain and Germany 1850–1950*, London: Croom Helm, 1981.

Fraser, Derek (ed.), *The New Poor Law in the Nineteenth Century*, London: Macmillan, 1976.

Friedlander, Saul, *Nazi Germany and the Jews, Vol. 1, The Years of Persecution, 1933–1939*, New York: Phoenix, 1997.

Friedman, Lawrence, 'Opening the Time Capsule: A Progress Report on Studies of Courts over Time', *Law and Society Review*, 24, 1990, 229–40.

Gasquet, Abbot, D.D., *Parish Life in Medieval England*, 2nd edn, London: Methuen and Co., 1907.

Gilbert, Thomas, *Plan for the Better Relief and Employment of the Poor*, London: G. Wilkie, 1781.

Gilley, Sheriden, 'English Attitudes to the Irish in England, 1789–1900', in Holmes, Colin (ed.) *Immigrants and Minorities in British Society*, London: Allen & Unwin, 1978.

Gillom, John, *The Overseers of the Poor*, Chicago: University of Chicago Press, 2001.

Gilmore, Grant, *The Death of Contract*, Ohio: Ohio State University Press, 1974.

Glassey, L.J.K., *Politics and the Appointment of Justices of the Peace 1675–1740*, Oxford: Clarendon Press, 1979.

Gleason, J.H., *The Justices of the Peace in England 1558–1640. A Later Eirenarcha*, Oxford: Oxford University Press, 1969.

Glen, Reginald Cunningham, *The General Orders of the Poor Law Commissioners, The Poor Law Board and the Local Government Board*, 11th edn, London: Knight and Co., 1898.

Glen, W. Cunningham, *J.F. Archbold, The Poor Law*, 13th edn, London: Shaw and Sons, 1878.

Goldhagen, Daniel, *Hitler's Willing Executioners; Ordinary Germans and the Holocaust*, New York: Alfred A. Knopf, Inc., 1996.

Goodacre, Hugh, 'Ullesthorpe Overseers' Accounts', *Transactions of the Leicestershire Archaeological Society*, XVIII, 1934, 150–55.

Gordon, Robert W., 'Critical Legal Histories', *Stanford Law Review*, 36, Jan. 1984, 57–125.

Gordon, W.M. and Fergus, T.D., *Legal History in the Making: Proceedings of the Ninth British Legal History Conference, Glasgow*, 1989, London: Hambledon Continuum, 1991.

Gough, Richard, *The History of Myddle*, Hey, David (ed.), London: Penguin Books, 1981.

Gowing, D, 'Migration in Gloucester 1662–1865. A Geographical Evaluation of the Documentary Evidence Related to the Administration of the Law of Settlement and Removal', 1979, unpublished thesis, University of Southampton.

Gray, Irvine, 'Cheltenham Settlement Examinations 1815–26', *Record Section of the Bristol and Gloucestershire Archaeological Society*, vol. VII, 1969.

Griffiths, J.A.G., *The Politics of the Judiciary*, London: Fontana Press, 1991.

Grigg, D.B., 'E.G. Ravenstein on the "Laws of Migration"', *Journal of Historical Geography*, 3, 2, 1977, 41–54.

Gwillim, Sir Henry, *Tithes, A Collection of Acts and Records of Parliament with Reports of Cases*, 4 vols, 2nd edn, London: Butterworth, 1825.

Haigh, Christopher, *The Last Days of the Lancashire Monasteries and the Pilgrimage of Grace*, 3rd series, vol. XVII, Manchester: Chetham Society, 1969.

Hammond, J.L. and Hammond, B., *The Village Labourer, 1760–1832*, 2 vols, 1911, reprint, Stroud: Alan Sutton Publishing Ltd, 1995.

——, *The Bleak Age*, London: Penguin Books, 1947.

Hampson, Ethel, M., 'Settlement and Removal in Cambridgeshire 1662–1834', *Cambridge Historical Journal*, II, 1928, 273–89.

——, *The Treatment of Poverty in Cambridgeshire 1597–1834*, Cambridge: Cambridge University Press, 1934.

Handley, M.A., 'Local Administration of the Poor Law in the Great Boughton and Wirral Unions, and the Chester Local Act Incorporation 1838–71', 1969–70, unpublished thesis, University of Bangor.

——, 'Poor Law Administration in the Chester Local Act incorporation, 1831–71', *Transactions of the Historic Society of Lancashire and Cheshire*, 156, 2007, 169–92.

Harding, Alan, *A Social History of English Law*, London: Penguin Books, 1966.

Harlow, Carol, and Rawlings, Richard, *Law and Administration*, 2nd edn, London: Butterworths, 1997.

Harris, J.R. (ed.), *Liverpool and Merseyside*, London: Frank Cass, 1969.

Harris, J.W., *Property and Justice*, Oxford: Clarendon Press, 1996.

Hart, H.L.A., *The Concept of Law*, Oxford: Oxford University Press, 1961.

Hawthorne, Nathaniel, *The English Notebooks*, Steward Randall (ed.), Oxford: Oxford University Press, 1941.

Hay, D., Rule, J., Linebaugh, P. and Thompson, E.P. (eds), *Albion's Fatal Tree*, London and New York: Allen Lane, 1975.

Head, Sir Edmund, 'Report to the Select Committee on Settlement and Poor Removal', *Edinburgh Review*, LXXXVIII, April 1848, 451–72.

Healey, Jonathan, 'Poverty, Deservingness and Popular Politics: The Contested Relief of Agnes Braithwaite, 1701–6', *Transactions of the Historic Society of Lancashire and Cheshire*, 156, 2007, 131–56.

Hems, Alison, 'Aspects of Poverty and the Poor Laws in Early Modern England', 1985, unpublished thesis, University of Liverpool.

Hennock, E.P., 'Finance and Politics in Urban Local Government 1835–1900', *Historical Journal*, VI, 1963, 212–25.

Herson, John, 'Irish Migration and Settlement in Victorian England, a Small Town Perspective', in Swift, R. and Gilley, Sheriden (eds) *The Irish in Britain 1815–1939*, London: Pinter Publishers, 1989.

——, 'Victorian Chester: A City of Change and Ambiguity', in Swift, R. (ed.) *Victorian Chester*, Liverpool: Liverpool University Press, 1996.

Hibbert, Christopher, *The Making of Charles Dickens*, London: Longman, 1967.

Himmelfarb, Gertrude, *The Idea of Poverty. England in the Early Industrial Age*, London: Faber & Faber, 1984.

Hindle, G.B., *Provision for the Relief of the Poor in Manchester 1754–1826*, Manchester: Manchester University Press, 1975.

Hindle, Steve, *On the Parish? The Micro-Politics of Poor Relief in Rural England c.1550–1750*, Oxford: Clarendon Press, 2000.

Hinton, F.H., 'Notes on the Administration of the Relief of the Poor of Lacock, 1583 to 1834', *The Wiltshire Archaeological & Natural History Magazine*, XLIX, June 1942, 166–218.

Hitchcock, Tim, King, Peter and Sharpe, Pamela (eds), *Chronicling Poverty; The Voices and Strategies of the English Poor, 1640–1840*, London: Macmillan, 1997.

Hoare, Eddie, *The Work of the Edmonton Vestry 1739–48 and 1782–98*, London: Edmonton Hundred Historical Society, 1968.

Hobsbawm, E.J., *Industry and Empire: an Economic History of Britain*, 2nd edn, London: Abacus, 1968.

Hobsbawm, E.J. and Rude, G., *Captain Swing*, New York: Lawrence and Wishart, 1968.

Hodgson, H.J., *Steer's Parish Law, Being a Digest of the Law Relating to the Civil and Ecclesiastical Government of the Parishes, Friendly Societies etc. and the Relief, Settlement and Removal of the Poor*, 3rd edn, London: Stevens and Norton, 1857.

Hoeflich, M.H., 'A Renaissance in Legal History?', *University of Illinois Law Review*, 3, 1984, 507–9.

Hofstadter, Richard, *The Paranoid Style in American Politics and Other Essays*, New York: Knopf, 1965.

Hogue, Cynthia, *The Never Wife*, Dubois, PA: Mammoth Books, 1999.

Holderness, B.A., '"Open" and "Close" Parishes in England in the Eighteenth Centuries', *Agricultural History Review*, 2, 1972, 126–39.

Holdsworth, W.A., *The Handy Book of Parish Law*, 3rd edn, London: George Routledge and Sons, 1872.

——, *A History of English Law*, 17 vols, 1936, London: Sweet and Maxwell, 1971.

Holland, William, *Paupers and Pigkillers The Diary of William Holland A Somerset Parson, 1799–1818*, Ayres, Jane (ed.), Stroud: Allan Sutton Publishing, 1984.

Holmes, Colin (ed.) *Immigrants and Minorities in British Society*, London: Allen & Unwin, 1978.

Horwitz, Morton J., 'The Conservative Tradition in the Writing of American Legal History', *American Journal of Legal History*, 7, 1973, 275–94.

——, 'The Rise of Legal Formalism', *American Journal of Legal History*, 19, 1975, 251–64.

——, *The Transformation of American Law, 1780–1860*, Cambridge, MA: Harvard University Press, 1977.

——, 'Why is Anglo-American Jurisprudence Unhistorical?', *Oxford Journal of Legal Studies*, 17, 4, 1997, 551–86.

Hoskins, W.G., *Provincial England, Essays in Social and Economic History*, London: Macmillan, 1965.

Houlbrooke, *Ralph, Church Courts and the People during the English Reformation 1520–1570*, Oxford: Oxford University Press, 1979.

Howard, J.H., 'Treatment of the Poor in Eighteenth Century Chester', *Journal of the Chester Archaeological Society*, 52, 1965, 33–48.

Howkins, Alun and Verdun, Nicola, 'Adaptable and Sustainable? Male Farm Service and the Agricultural Labour Force in Midland and Southern England, *c.* 1850–1925', *Economic History Review*, 61, 2, 2006, 467–95.

Humphries, Jane, 'Enclosures, Common Rights and Women: The Proletarianisation of Families in the Late Eighteenth and Early Nineteenth Centuries', *The Journal of Economic History*, 1, 1990, 17–42.

Innes, Joanna, 'Parliament and the Shaping of Eighteenth Century Social Policy', *Transactions of the Royal Historical Society*, 5th series, 40, 1990, 63–92.

——, 'The Mixed Economy of Welfare in Early Modern England: Assessments of the Ooptions from Hale to Malthus c.1683–1803', in Daunton, Martin (ed.) *Charity, Self-Interest and Welfare in the English Past*, London, UCL Press, 1996.

Jackson, Betty Lee, 'The Poor Law in Rural Lancashire 1820–50', 1986, unpublished thesis, University of Lancaster.

Jackson, John Archer, *The Irish in Britain*, London: Routledge, 1963.

James, Patricia, *Population Malthus, His Life and Times*, London: Routledge and Kegan Paul, 1979.

Jennings, W. Ivor, *The Poor Law Code*, 2nd edn, London: Charles Knight and Co., 1936.

Jones, Colin, 'Some Recent Trends in the History of Charity', in Daunton, Martin (ed.) *Charity, Self-Interest and Welfare in the English Past*, London: UCL Press, 1996.

Jordon, W.K., *Philanthropy in England 1480–1660*, London: Allen & Unwin, 1959.

——, *The Charities of Rural England 1480–1660*, London: George Allen & Unwin, 1961.

——, *The Social Institutions of Lancaster*, Manchester: Manchester University Press, 1962.

Jutte, Robert, *Poverty and Deviance in Early Modern Europe*, Cambridge: Cambridge University Press, 1994.

Kamenka, E. and Neale, R.S. (eds), *Feudalism, Capitalism and Beyond*, London: Edward Arnold, 1975.

Kelsen, H., 'Plato and Natural Law', *Vanderbilt Law Review*, 1960.

——, *The Pure Theory of Law*, California: California University Press, 1967.

Kelly, J.M., *A Short History of Western Legal Theory*, Oxford: Clarendon Press, 1992.

Kent, J.R., 'Population Mobility and Alms: Poor Migrants in the Midlands during the Early Seventeenth Century', *Local Population Studies*, 27, 1981, 35–51.

Ketchley, C.P., 'Settlement and its Legal Definition', *The Amateur Historian*, 29, 1956, 268–70.

Kidd, Alan J., 'Outcast Manchester: Voluntary Charity, Poor Relief and the Casual Poor 1860–1905', in Roberts, K.W. (ed.) *Class and Culture, Studies in Cultures, Production and Social Policy in Victorian Manchester*, Manchester: Manchester University Press, 1985.

——, 'Historians or Polemicists? How the Webbs Wrote their History of the English Poor Law', *Economic History Review*, 2nd series, XL, 3, 1987, 400–417.

Kinealey, Christine, *This Great Calamity. The Irish Famine 1845–52*, Dublin: Gill and Macmillan, 1994.

King, Steven, *Poverty and Welfare in England 1700–1850*, Manchester: Manchester University Press, 2000.

Kiralfy, Albert, 'The Humble-Jumble: Legal Redress under the Open-Field System', *The Journal of Legal History*, 10, 1989, 2–28.

Knafla, Louise A. and Binnie, Susan, W.S. (eds), *Law, Society and the State: Essays in Modern Legal History*, Toronto: University of Toronto Press, 1995.

Knodel, John E., *Demographic Behaviour in the Past. A Study of Fourteen German Village Populations in the Eighteenth and Nineteenth Centuries*, Cambridge: Cambridge University Press, 1988.

Knott, John, *Popular Opposition to the New Poor Law*, London: Croom Helm, 1986.

Kostal, R.W., *Law and English Railway Capitalism 1825–1875*, Oxford: Clarendon Press, 1998.

Lamb, *Eirenarch*, 2 vols, London: 1630.

Landau, Norma, *The Justices of the Peace 1679–1760*, Berkeley, California: University of California Press, 1984.

——, 'The Laws of Settlement and the Surveillance of Immigration in Eighteenth Century Kent', *Continuity and Change*, 3, 1988, 391–420.

——, 'The Regulation of Immigration, Economic Structures and Definition of the Poor in Eighteenth Century England', *Historical Journal*, 33, 3, 1990, 541–71.

——, 'The Eighteenth-century Context of the Laws of Settlement', *Continuity and Change*, 63, 1991, 417–39.

Langbein, John H., 'Albion's Fatal Flaws', *Past and Present*, 98, 1983, 96–120.

Langland, William, *Piers Ploughman*, London: Penguin Books, 1978.

Lees, Lynn Hollen, *The Solidarities of Strangers. The English Poor Laws and the People, 1700–1948*, Cambridge: Cambridge University Press, 1998.

Leonard, E.M., *The Early History of English Poor Relief*, London: Routledge, 1965.

Levine, Daniel, *Poverty and Society: The Growth of the American Welfare State in International Comparison*, New Brunswick and London: Rutgers University Press, 1988.

Levy, S. Leon, *Nassau W. Senior 1790–1864*, Devon: David & Charles, 1970.

Lewin, Sir D.A., *A Summary of the Laws Relating to the Governance and Maintenance of the Poor*, London: A. Strahan, 1828.

Lewis, Chris, 'Building Chester's First Workhouse', *Cheshire History*, 38, 1998–99, 50–54.

Lewis, R.A., 'William Day and the Poor Law Commissioners', *University of Birmingham History Journal*, XV, 1964, 163–95.

——, *Edwin Chadwick and the Public Health Movement 1832–1854*, London: Longman, 1952.

Lidbetter, E.J., *Handbooks for Public Assistance Officers.Vol. I. Settlement and Removal* London: Law and Local Government Publications Ltd, 1932.

Linebaugh, Peter, 'Marxist Social History and Conservative Legal History: A Reply to Professor Langbein', *New York University Law Review*, 60, 1985, 213–43.

Linebaugh, Peter and Reddiker, Marcus, *The Many-Headed Hydra*, London: Verso, 2000.

Little, David, *Religion, Order and Law, A Study in Pre-Revolutionary England*, Oxford: Blackwell Publishers, 1971.

Lobban, Michael, *The Common Law and English Jurisprudence, 1760–1850*, Oxford: Clarendon Press, 1991.

——, 'Was there a Nineteenth Century "English School of Jurisprudence"?, *Journal of Legal History*, 16, 1995, 34–62.

Longmate, Norman, *The Workhouse*, London: St Martin's Press, 1974.

Loux, Andrea C., 'The Persistence of the Ancient Regime: Custom, Utility, and the Common Law in the Nineteenth Century', *Cornell Law Review*, 79, 1993, 183–218.

Lowe, W.J., *The Irish in Mid-Victorian Lancashire. The Shaping of a Working-Class Community*, New York: Peter Lang Publishers Inc., 1989

Lubenow, William C., *The Politics of Government Growth*, Newton Abbott: David and Charles, 1971.

Lumley, William Golden, *A Popular Treatise on the Law of Settlement and Removal*, London: Shaw and Sons, 1842.

McCleary, G.F., *The Malthusian Population Theory*, London: Faber & Faber, 1953.

MacDonagh, Oliver, *A Pattern of Government Growth 1800–1860. The Passenger Acts and their Enforcement*, London: MacGibbon and Kee, 1969.

——, *Early Victorian Government 1830–1870*, London: Weidenfeld & Nicolson, 1977.

McGregor, O.R., *Social History and Law Reform*, London: Stevens and Sons, 1981.

McIntyre, W.R.S., *Birkenhead Yesterday and Today*, Birkenhead: Philip Son and Nephew, 1948.

Macpherson, C.B., 'Capitalism and the Changing Concept of Property', in Kamenka, E. and Neale, R.S. (eds) *Feudalism, Capitalism and Beyond*, London: Edward Arnold, 1975.

——, *Property. Mainstream and Critical Positions*, Toronto: Wiley Blackwell, 1978.

Maine, Sir Henry Sumner, *Ancient Law*, 10th edn, London: John Murray, 1905.

Maitland, F.W., *Bracton and Azo*, vol. VIII, London: Selden Society, 1884.

Malthus, Thomas Robert, *An Essay on the Principle of Population and a Summary View of the Principles of Population* 1798, Flew, Anthony (ed.), London: Routledge and Sons, 1970.

Manchester, A.H., *A Modern Legal History of England and Wales 1750–1950*, London: Butterworths, 1980.

——, 'An Introduction to Iconographical Studies of Legal History', in Gordon, W.M. and Ferguson, T.D. (eds) *Legal History in the Making, Proceedings of the Ninth British Legal History Conference*, Glasgow: Hambledon Continuum, 1991.

Mandler, Peter, 'The Making of the New Poor Law Redivivus', *Past and Present*, 117, 1984, 131–57.

——, 'Tories and Paupers: Christian Political Economy and the Making of the New Poor Law', *Historical Journal*, 33, 1, 1990, 81–103.

Marchant, Ronald A., *The Church under the Law*, Cambridge: Cambridge University Press, 1969.

Marshall, Dorothy, *The English Poor in the Eighteenth Century; A Study in Social and Administrative History*, London: George Routledge and Sons Ltd, 1926.

Marshall, J.D., *The Old Poor Law, 1795–1834*, London: Macmillan, 1968.

——, 'Nottinghamshire Reformers and the New Poor Law', *Economic History Review*, XII, 1961, 382–96.

Martin, E.W., *Comparative Development in Social Welfare*, London: George Allen & Unwin, 1972.

Maude, W.C., *The Poor Law Handbook*, London: Poor Law Officers' Journal, 1903.

Mayhew, Henry, *London Labour and the London Poor 1851–62*, reprint, London: Frank Cass & Co., 1967.

Melville, R., 'Records of Apprenticeships and Settlements in a Berkshire Village in the Eighteenth Century', *Transactions of the Newbury and District Field Club*, 1954, 32–43.

Midwinter, E.C., *Social Administration in Lancashire 1830–1860*, Manchester: Manchester University Press, 1969.

Mills, D.R., 'The Poor Laws and the Distribution of Population, c.1600–1860, with Special Reference to Lincolnshire', *Transactions of the Institute of British Geographers*, XXVI, 1959, 185–95.

——, 'The Geographical Effects of the Laws of Settlement in Nottinghamshire: An Analysis of Francis Howell's Report, 1848', Mills, D.R. (ed.) *English Rural Communities*, London: Macmillan, 1973.

——, *Lord and Peasants in Nineteenth Century Britain*, London: Croom Helm, 1980.

Milsom, S.F.C., 'An Old Play in Modern Dress', *Yale Law Journal*, 84, 1975, 185–90.

Mingay, G.E., *The Gentry. The Rise and Fall of a Ruling Class*, London: Longman, 1976.

——, *Land and Society in England 1750–1980*, London: Longman, 1994.

——, *Parliamentary Enclosure in England*, London: Longman, 1997.

Minority Report to the Royal Commission on the Poor Law, 1909.

Mollat, Michael, *The Poor in the Middle Ages, An Essay in Social History*, New Haven and London: Yale University Press, 1986.

Montague, F.C., 'The Law of Settlement and Removal', *Law Quarterly Review*, XIII, 1888, 40–51.

Moore, E. Garth, *An Introduction to English Canon Law*, Oxford: Clarendon Press, 1967.

Moore, Peter, 'Waiving History Goodbye. Lawyers' Records and the Scholar', in Knafla, Louise A. and Binnie, Susan W.S. (eds) *Law, Society and the State: Essays in Modern Legal History*, Toronto: University of Toronto Press, 1995.

Morris, Lydia, *Dangerous Classes. The Underclass and Social Citizenship*, London: Routledge, 1994.

Morrison, Kathryn, *The Workhouse. A Study of Poor Law Buildings in England*, Swindon: Royal Commission for Historical Monuments, 1999.

Mortimer, W.W., *The History of the Hundred of Wirral*, Manchester: E. J. Morten, 1847.

Moses, Gary, 'Proletarian Labourers? East Riding Farm Servants', *Agricultural History Review*, 47, 1, 1999, 78–94.

Mullineux, C.E., *Pauper and Poorhouse. A Study of the Administration of the Poor Laws in a Lancashire Parish*, Swinton and Pendlebury: Public Libraries, 1966.

Neale, R.S. (ed.), *History and Class. Essential Readings in Theory and Interpretation*, Oxford: Basil Blackwell, 1984.

Neeson, J.M., *Commoners: Common Right, Enclosure and Social Change in England, 1700–1820*, Cambridge, Cambridge University Press, 1993.

Newbold, Edward, 'The Geography of Poor Relief Expenditure in Late Eighteenth and Early Nineteenth Century Rural Oxfordshire', 1995, unpublished thesis, University of Oxford.

Nicholls, Sir George, *History of the English Poor Law*, vol. 1, 1851, vol. 2, 1860, vol. 3, published posthumously, reissued, London: P.S. King and Son, 1904.

——, *A History of the Irish Poor Law*, 1856, New York: Augustus M. Kelley, 1967.

——, *A History of the Scotch Poor Law*, 1856, New York: Augustus M. Kelley, 1967.

——, *Memorandum on Settlement, Removal and Rating, Nov. 1850, PP, 90, LV, Part 1, 1854*.

Nolan, Michael, *A Treatise of the Laws for the Relief and Settlement of the Poor*, 2 vols, 2nd edn, London: A. Strahan, 1805, reprint, New York and London: Garland Publishing Inc., 1978.

Norrie, Alan, *Crime, Reason and Society*, London: Butterworths, 2001.

North, The Honourable Roger, *A Discourse of the Poor, Shewing the Pernicious Tentency of the Laws now in Force for their Maintenance and Settlement, Etc*, London: 1753.

O'Donnell, Alice, 'The Administration of the Poor Law in Liverpool between 1782–1834', 1993, unpublished thesis, University of Liverpool.

Oke, George C., *The Magisterial Synopsis. A Practical Guide for Magistrates, Their Clerks, Attornies and Constables*, London, Butterworths, 1858.

Osborne, Bertram, *Justices of the Peace 1361–1848*, Dorset: Sedgehill Press, 1960.

Owen, Hugh, *Manual for Overseers, Assistant Overseers, Collectors of Poor Rates and Vestry Clerks*, 7th edn, London: Knight and Co., 1884.

Oxley, G.W., 'The Administration of the Old Poor Law in the West Derby Hundred of Lancashire 1601–1834', 1966, unpublished thesis, University of Liverpool.

——, 'The Relief of the Permanent Poor in South West Lancashire under the Old Poor Law', in Harris, J.R. (ed.) *Liverpool and Merseyside*, London: Frank Cass, 1969.

——, *Poor Relief in England and Wales,1601–1834*, Newton Abbot: David & Charles, 1974.

Page, Francis M., 'The Customary Poor Law of Three Cambridgeshire Manors', *Cambridge Historical Journal*, III, 2, 1930, 125–33.

Palmer, Robert C., *English Law in the Age of the Black Death, 1348–1381. A Transformation of Governance and Law*, London and Carolina: University of North Carolina Press, 1993.

Pashley, Robert, *Pauperism and Poor Laws*, London: Longman, Brown, Green and Longmans, 1852.

Paz-Fuchs, Amir, *Welfare to Work: Conditional Rights in Social Policy*, Oxford: Oxford University Press, 2008.

Peet, Henry (ed.), *Liverpool Vestry Books 1681–1834*, 2 vols, Liverpool: Liverpool University Press, 1912 and 1915.

Pelling, Henry, *A History of British Trade Unionism*, London: Penguin Books, 1963.

Philpott, Trey, *A Companion to Little Dorrit*, London: Croom Helm, 2003.

Pinchbeck, Ivy and Hewitt, Margaret, *Children in English Society, vol. I, Children in English Society. From Tudor Times to the Eighteenth Century*, London: Routledge and Kegan Paul, 1969.

Place, Geoffrey, *The Rise and Fall of Parkgate, Passenger Port for Ireland 1686–1815*, Manchester: Carnegie Publishing Ltd, 1994.

Platt, Colin, *The Parish Churches of Medieval England*, London: Bounty Books, 1996.

Plucknett, Theodore, *A Concise History of the Common Law*, 5th edn, London: Butterworth and Co., 1956.

Poggi, Gianfranco, *The Development of the Modern State*, Stanford, CA: Stanford University Press, 1978.

Poor Law Board, *Report ... on the Law of Settlement and Removal of the Poor*, PP. 1850 [1152] xxvi.

Poor Law Commission, Ninth Annual Report, 1843.

Poor Law Report, PP, 1834, XXIX.

Porter, Roy, *Enlightenment, Britain and the Creation of the Modern World*, London: Penguin Books, 2001.

Pound, John, *Poverty and Vagrancy in Tudor England*, London: Longman, 1971.

Poynter, J.R., *Society and Pauperism. English Ideas on Poor Relief 1795–1834*, London: Routledge and Kegan Paul, 1969.

Probert, Rebecca, 'The Impact of the Marriage Act of 1753: Was it Really "A Most Cruel Law for the Fair Sex"?', *Eighteenth Century Studies*, 38, 2, 2005, 47–62.

——, 'The Judicial Interpretation of Lord Hardwicke's Act of 1753', *Journal of Legal History*, 23, 2002, 129–51.

Proctor, W., 'Poor Law Administration in Preston Union', *Transactions of the Historic Society of Lancashire and Cheshire*, 117, 1965, 145–66.

Pullan, Brian, 'Catholics and the Poor in Early Modern Europe', *Transactions of the Royal Historical Society*, 5th series, 26, 1976, 15–34.

Radzinovicz, Leon and Hood, Roger, *The Emergence of Penal Policy in Victorian and Edwardian England*, Oxford: Oxford University Press, 1990.

Redford, Arthur, *Labour Migration in England, 1800–1850*, Manchester: University of Manchester Press, 1926.

Reed, M. and Wells, R., *Class, Conflict and Protest in the English Countryside, 1700–1880*, London: Frank Cass, 1990.

Report of the Royal Commission on the Poor Laws of 1909, London: Macmillan and Co. Ltd, 1909.

Ribton-Turner, C.J., *History of Vagrants and Vagrancy and Beggars and Begging*, London: Chapman & Hall, 1887.

Richardson, R.C. and James, T.B. (eds), *The Urban Experience. A Sourcebook: English, Scottish and Welsh Towns, 1450–1700*, Manchester: Manchester University Press, 1983.

Richardson, Ruth, *Death, Dissection and the Destitute*, London: Routledge, 1988.

Richardson, S.I., *Edmonton Poor Law Union 1837–1854*, London: Edmonton Hundred Historical Society, 1969.

Roberts, D., *Victorian Origins of the British Welfare State*, New Haven and London: Yale University Press, 1961.

Roberts, D., 'How Cruel was the Victorian Poor Law?' *Historical Journal*, VI, 1963, 97–106.

Roberts, Stephen K., *Recovery and Restoration in an English County. Devon Local Administration 1646–1670*, Exeter: University of Exeter Press, 1985.

Robinson, Eric (ed.), *John Clare's The Parish*, London: Penguin Books, 1985.

Robson, Robert, *The Attourney in Eighteenth Century England*, Cambridge: Cambridge University Press, 1959.

Rodgers, C.P., 'Humanism, History and the Common Law', *Journal of Legal History*, 6, 1985, 129–56.

Rogers, Graham, 'Custom and Common Right: Waste Land Enclosure and Social Change in West Lancashire', *The Agricultural History Review*, 41, 1993, 137–54.

Rose, Lionel, *Rogues and Vagabonds: The Vagrant Underground in Britain 1815–1985*, London: Routledge, 1988.

Rose, M.E., 'The Anti Poor Law Movement in the North of England', *Northern History*, I, 1966, 70–91.

——, *The Relief of Poverty 1834–1914*, London: Macmillan, 1972.

——, 'Settlement, Removal and the New Poor Law', in Fraser, D. (ed.) *New Poor Law in the Nineteenth Century,* London: Macmillan, 1976.

——, *The Poor and the City; The English Poor Law in its Urban Context, 1834–1914*, Leicester: Leicester University Press, 1985.

Rose, M.E.(ed.) *English Poor Law 1780–1930*, Newton Abbot: David & Charles, 1971.

Ross, Alf, *On Law and Justice*, Berkeley, CA: University of California Press, 1959.

Rowbotham, Judith, 'Legislating for Your Own Good – Criminalising Moral Choice. The Modern Echoes of the Victorian Vaccination Acts', *Liverpool Law Review*, 30, 1, 2009,13–33.

Rowe, John, 'The Laws of Settlement in Gulval Parish-1739–1821', *The Royal Cornwall Polytechnic Society Annual Report*, Cornwall, 1953.

Rubin G.R. and Sugarman, D., 'Towards a New History of Law and Material Society in England 1750–1914', in Rubin G.R. and Sugarman, D. (eds) *Law Economy and Society,* London: Butterworths, 1984.

Rubin, Miri, *Charity and Community in Medieval Cambridge*, Cambridge: Cambridge University Press, 1987.

Rule, John, *The Labouring Classes in Early Industrial England 1750–1850*, London: Longman, 1994.

——, *Albion's People. English Society 1714–1815*, London: Longman, 1996.

Rushton, Neil S., 'Monastic Charitable Provision in Tudor England', *Continuity and Change*, 16, 1, May, 2001, 9–44.

Rushton, P., 'The Poor Law, The Parish and the Community in North-East England 1600–1800', *Northern History*, vol. XXV, 1989.

Salmond, Sir John, *Jurisprudence*, 10th edn, London: Sweet and Maxwell, 1947.

Sambrook, James, *William Cobbett*, London: Routledge and Kegan Paul, 1973.

Schofield, Philip, 'Jeremy Bentham and Nineteenth Century English Jurisprudence', *The Journal of Legal History*, 12, 1, 1991, 58–88.

Scott, T. and Starkey, P., *The Middle Ages in the North West*, Oxford: Leopard's Head Press, 1995.

Second Report of the House of Lords Committee on the Poor Laws, printed by and for C. Clement, 28 April 1818.

Segesser, Daniel Marc and Gessler, Myriam, 'Raphael Lemkin and the International Debate on the Punishment of War Crimes (1919–48)', *Journal of Genocide Research*, 7, 4, 2005, 453–68.

Select Committees to consider the Poor Law, Report, 1816, PP 485 IV. 325; Report, Minutes of Evidence, Appendices, 1817, PP 462 VI.I; *Report*, Appendices, 1818, PP 107 VI.

Select Committee of the House Of Lords to Consider the Poor Laws, Report, Minutes of Evidence, Appendices, 1818, PP 400 V.91.

Select Committee to Enquire into the Operation of Settlement and the Poor Removal Act. First Report and Minutes of Evidence, 1847, PP 82 XI.I.

Select Committee to Consider Poor Relief, Report, 1864. Appendices, PP 349, 1864, IX.

Senior, N.W., 'Three Lectures on the Rate of Wages, with a Preface on the Causes of the Present Disturbances', *Edinburgh Review*, 53, 1831, 43–63.

Shape, J.A., *Crime in Early Modern England, 1550–1750*, London: Longman, 1984.

Sharman, Frank, 'An Introduction to the Enclosure Acts', *Journal of Legal History*, 10, 1989, 45–70.

Sharpe, Pamela, 'Poor Children as Apprentices in Colyton, 1598–1830', *Continuity and Change*, 6, 2, 1991, 253–70.

Shaw, J., *The Parochial Lawyer, or, Churchwarden and Overseer's Guide and Assistant*, 3rd edn, London: Sherwood, Gilbert, and Piper, 1831.

Simey, M.B., *Charity Rediscovered; A Study of Philanthropic Effort in Nineteenth Century Liverpool*, originally published as *Charitable Effort in Liverpool in the 19th Century Liverpool*, 1951, Liverpool: Liverpool University Press, 1992.

Simpson, A.W.B., *Leading Cases in the Common Law*, Oxford: Clarendon Press, 1995.

Skocpol, Theda, *Social Policy in the United States: Future Possibilities in Historical Perspective*, Princeton, NJ: Princeton University Press, 1995.

Slack, Paul, *Poverty and Policy in Tudor and Stuart England*, London: Longman, 1988.

——, *The English Poor Law 1531–1782*, London: Palgrave Macmillan, 1990.

Smandych, Russell C., 'William Osgoode, John Graves Simcoe and the Exclusion of the English Poor Law from Upper Canada', in Knafla, Louise A. and Binnie, Susan W.S. (eds) *Law, Society and the State: Essays in Modern Legal History*, Toronto: University of Toronto Press, 1995.

Smith, Adam, *The Wealth of Nations* 1776, London: Penguin, 1977.

Smith, Joshua Toulmin, *The Parish, Its Powers and Obligations at Law*, 2nd edn, London: I. Sweet, 1857.

Smith, K.J.M. and McLaren, J.P.S. 'History's Living Legacy: An Outline of 'Modern' Historiography of the Common Law' *Legal Studies*, 21, 2, 2001, 251–324.

Smith, Richard M. (ed.), *Land, Kinship and Life-Cycle*, Cambridge: Cambridge University Press, 1984.

——, 'Charity, Self-Interest and Welfare: Reflections from Demographic and Family History', in Daunton, Martin (ed.) *Charity, Self-Interest and Welfare in the English Past*, London: UCL Press, 1996.

Snell, K.D.M., 'Agricultural Seasonal Employment, the Standard of Living, and Women's Work in the South and East, 1690–1860', *Economic History Review*, XXXIV, 3, 1981, 407–37.

——, *Annals of the Labouring Poor. Social Change in Agrarian England 1660–1900*, Cambridge: Cambridge University Press, 1985.

——, 'Pauper Settlement and the Right to Poor Relief in England and Wales', *Continuity and Change*, 63, 1991, 375–415.

——, 'Settlement, Poor Law and the Rural Historian; New Approaches and Opportunities', *Rural History*, 32, 1992, 145–72.

Sogner, Solvi, 'Aspects of the Demographic Situation in Seventeen Parishes in Shropshire 1711–60 – An Exercise Based on Parish Registers', *Population Studies*, 17, 1963, 126–46.

Solar, Peter M., 'Poor Relief and English Economic Development before the Industrial Revolution', *Economic History Review*, XLVIII, 1995, 1–22.

Song, B.K., 'The Poor Law and Labour Markets in Oxfordshire, 1750–1870', unpublished thesis, University of Oxford, 1996.

Stein, Peter, *Legal Evolution, The Story of an Idea*, Cambridge: Cambridge University Press, 1980.

Sterett, Susan, 'Constitutionalism and the Common Law-Nineteenth Century Social Welfare in the United States,' *Oxford Journal of Legal Studies*, 17, 1997, 587–610.

Stone, Lawrence, *The Road to Divorce, England 1530–1987*, Oxford: Oxford University Press, 1992.

Storch, Robert D., 'Persistence and Change in Nineteenth Century Popular Culture', in Storch, Robert D. (ed.) *Popular Culture and Custom in Nineteenth Century England*, London: Croom Helm, 1982.

Styles, Philip, 'The Evolution of the Law of Settlement', *Historical Journal*, IX, 1964, 33–63.

Sugarman, D., 'Review of the Transformation of American Law, 1780–1860, *British Journal of Law and Society*, 7, 1980, 297–310.

——, 'Theory and Practice in Law and History: A Prologue to the Study of the Relationship between Law and Economy', in Fryer, B., Hunt, A., McBarnet, D. and Moorhouse, B. (eds) *Law, State and Society*, London: Croom Helm, 1981.

——, 'The Legal Boundaries of Liberty: Dicey, Liberalism and Legal Science, Review', *Modern Law Review*, 46, 1983, 102–6.

——, 'Writing "Law and Society" Histories', *Modern Law Revue*, 55, 1992, 292–308.

——, 'Bourgeois Collectivism, Professional Power and the Boundaries of the State. The Private and Public Life of the Law Society, 1825–1914', *International Journal of the Legal Profession*, 3, 1996, 81–135.

——(ed.), *Law in History: Histories of Law and Society*, 2 vols, New York: New York University Press, 1996.

——, 'Law and Legal Institutions', *Oxford Reader's Companion to Dickens*, Oxford: Oxford University Press, 1999.

Sugarman, D. and Rubin, G.R. (eds), *Law, Economy and Society*, London: Butterworths, 1984.

Sutherland, John, *Is Heathcliffe a Murderer?* Oxford: Oxford University Press, 1996.

Swift, Roger, 'Anti-Irish Violence in Victorian England: Some Perspectives', *Criminal Justice History*, 15, 1994, 127–40.

Swift, Roger and Gilley, Sheridan (eds), *The Irish in the Victorian City*, London: Routledge, 1985.

Tate, W.E., *The English Village Community and the Enclosure Movements*, London: Victor Gollancz Ltd, 1967.

——, *The Parish Chest. A Study of the Records of Parochial Administration in England*, 3rd edn, Cambridge: Cambridge University Press, 1969.

Taylor, Arthur J., *Laissez-faire and State Intervention in Nineteenth Century Britain*, London: Palgrave Macmillan, 1972.

Taylor, J.S., 'The Mythology of the Old Poor Law', *Journal of Economic History*, XXIX, 1969, 292–97.

——, 'The Impact of Pauper Settlement 1691–1834', *Past and Present*, LXIII, 1976, 42–74.

——, *Poverty, Migration, and Settlement in the Industrial Revolution; Sojourners' Narratives*, Palo Alto, CA: The Society for the Promotion of Science and Scholarship, 1989.

——, 'A Different Kind of Speenhamland: Nonresident Relief in the Industrial Revolution', *Journal of British Studies*, 30, 1991, 183–208.

Taylor, Peter, 'Quarter Sessions in Lancashire in the Middle of the Eighteenth Century. The Court in Session and its Records', *Transactions of the Historic Society of Lancashire and Cheshire*, 139, 1990, 68–82.

tenBroek, Jacobus, 'California's Dual System of Family Law: Its Origins, Development and Present Status', Parts 1–2 of 3, *Stanford Law Review*, 16, 1964, 257; 17, 1964, 614.

——, (ed.), *The Law of the Poor*, San Francisco: Chandler Publications, 1966.

tenBroek, J. and Matson, Floyd W., 'The Disabled and the Law of Welfare', in tenBroek Jacobus (ed.) *The Law of the Poor*, San Francisco: Chandler Publications, 1966.

Thane, Pat, *Foundations of the Welfare State*, 2nd edn, London: Longman, 1996.

——, 'Old People and their Families in the English Past', in Daunton, Martin (ed.) *Charity, Self-Interest and Welfare in the English Past*, London: UCL Press 1996.

——, *Foundations of the Welfare State*, 2nd edn, London: Longman, 1996.

——, 'Histories of the Welfare State', in Lamont, William (ed.) *Historical Controversies and Historians*, London: UCL Press, 1998.

Third Report of the House of Lords Committee on the Poor Laws, printed by and for C. Clement, 26 May 1818.

Thompson, D. (ed.), *The Essential E.P. Thompson*, New York: New Press, 2000.

Thompson, E.P., 'The Moral Economy of the English Crowd in the Eighteenth Century', *Past and Present,* 50, 1971, 76–136.

——, *The Making of the English Working Class*, London: Penguin Books, 1982.

——, *Whigs and Hunters*, London: Penguin Books, 1990.

——, *Customs in Common*, London: Penguin Books, 1991.

Thompson, E.P. and Linebaugh, Peter, *The London Hanged; Crime and Society in the Eighteenth Century*, London: Allen Lane, 1992.

Thompson, R.N., 'The Working of the Poor Law Amendment Act in Cumbria, 1836–71', *Northern History*, XV, 1979, 117–37.

Tierney, Brian, *Medieval Poor Law*, Berkeley and Los Angeles: University of California Press, 1959.

Tomkins, Alannah, 'The Experience of Urban Poverty. A Comparison of Oxford and Shrewsbury 1740–70', 1994, unpublished thesis, University of Oxford.

Trey, Philpott, *A Companion to Little Dorrit*, London: Croom Helm, 2003.

Trotter, Eleanor, *Seventeenth Century Life in the Country Parish*, Cambridge: Cambridge University Press: 1919.

Turner, Michael (ed.), *Malthus and His Time*, London: Palgrave Macmillan, 1986.

Twining, William (ed.), *Legal Theory and Common Law*, Oxford: Basil Blackwell, 1989.

Varley, Douglas, 'The Landscape of Oxton Township 1795–1877', *Cheshire History*, 34, 1994, 13–24.

Vigier, François, *Change and Apathy. Liverpool and Manchester During the Industrial Revolution*, London and Massachusetts: MIT Press, 1970.

Vincent, David, 'The Decline of the Oral Tradition in Popular Culture', in Storch, Robert D. (ed.) *Popular Culture and Custom in Nineteenth Century England*, London: Routledge, 1982.

Vinogradoff, Paul, *The Teaching of Sir Henry Maine*, Oxford: Froude, 1904.

Wales, Tim, 'Poverty, Poor Relief and the Life-Cycle', in Smith, Richard M. (ed.) *Land, Kinship and Life-Cycle*, Cambridge: Cambridge University Press, 1984.

Ward, Ian, *Shakespeare and the Legal Imagination*, London: Butterworths, 1999.

Ward, J.T. and Wilson, R.G. (eds), *Land and Industry, the Landed Estate and the Industrial Revolution*, Newton Abbot: David & Charles, 1971.

Webb, S. and Webb, B., *English Local Government Vol. 1, The Parish and the County*, 1906, London: Frank Cass and Co., 1963.

——, *English Local Government Vol. 2, The Manor and the Borough*, Part 1, 1908, reprint, London: Frank Cass and Co., 1963.

——, *English Local Government Vol. 3, The Manor and the Borough*, Part 2, Vol. 2, reprint, London: Frank Cass and Co., 1963.

——, *English Poor Law History, Part I, The Old Poor Law*, 1929, reprint, London: Frank Cass and Co., 1963.

——, *The English Poor Law History. Part II, the Last Hundred Years*, 1929, reprint, London: Frank Cass and Co., 1963.

——, *The Minority Report of the Poor Law Commission*, London: Longman, 1909.

Wells, Roger, 'The Development of the English Rural Proletariat and Social Protest, 1700–1850', in Reed, Mick and Wells, Roger (eds) *Class, Conflict and Protest in the English Countryside, 1700–1880*, London: Frank Cass, 1990.

——, 'Social Conflict and Protest in the English Countryside in the Early Nineteenth Century: A Rejoinder', Reed, Mick and Wells, Roger (eds) *Class, Conflict and Protest in the English Countryside, 1700–1880*, London: Frank Cass, 1990.

——, 'Migration, the Law and Parochial Policy in Eighteenth and Early Nineteenth Century Southern England', *Southern History, 15, 1993, 87–139*.

Wetherall, C., 'Present State of the Poor Law Question', *Quarterly Review*, 50, 1833, 347–73.

White, Graeme, 'Open Fields and Rural Settlement in Medieval West Cheshire', in Scott, Tom and Starkey, Pat (eds), *The Middle Ages in the North West*, Oxford: Leopard's Head Press Ltd, 1995.

Wikely, Nick, *Child Support Law and Policy*, Oxford: Hart Publishing, 2006.

——, *Wikeley, Ogus, & Barendt's, The Law of Social Security*, Oxford: Oxford University Press, 2002.

Williams, Karel, *From Pauperism to Poverty*, London: Routledge and Kegan Paul, 1981.

Woodham-Smith, Cecil, *The Great Hunger, Ireland 1845–1849*, London: Penguin Books, 1962.

Woolf, Stuart, *The Poor in Western Europe in the Eighteenth and Nineteenth Centuries*, London: Routledge, 1986.

Wordsworth, Dorothy, *Lakeland Journals*, London: HarperCollins Publishers Ltd, 1994.

Wordsworth, William, *Collected Works*, New York: Oxford University Press, 2000.

Wright, D.G., *Popular Radicalism. The Working Class Experience 1780–1880*, London: Longman, 1988.

Wrightson, Keith, 'Two Concepts of Order: Justices, Constables and Jurymen in Seventeenth Century England', in Brewer, John and Styles, John (eds) *An Ungovernable People*, London: Routledge, 1980.

Wrightson, Keith and Levine, Donald, *Poverty and Piety in an English Village, Terling 1525–1700*, Oxford: Clarendon Press, 1995.

Yeoman, Dr J.B., *Some Poor History of the Wirrall Union*, Birkenhead: Birkenhead Libraries, 1965.

Zangerl, C.H.E., 'The Social Composition of the County Magistracy in England and Wales 1831–87', *Journal of British Studies*, 40, 1971, 113–25.

Index

Lightning Source UK Ltd.
Milton Keynes UK
UKOW032213100412

190450UK00001B/47/P